IN THE TRENCHES
1914 - 1918

IN THE TRENCHES
1914 - 1918

Glenn R. Iriam

Order this book online at www.trafford.com
or email orders@trafford.com

Most Trafford titles are also available at major online book retailers.

Printed in the United States of America.

ISBN: 978-1-4669-0048-6 (sc)
ISBN: 978-1-4669-0047-9 (hc)
ISBN: 978-1-4669-0046-2 (e)

Library of Congress Control Number: 2011918506

Trafford rev. 10/11/2011

 www.trafford.com

North America & International
toll-free: 1 888 232 4444 (USA & Canada)
phone: 250 383 6864 ♦ fax: 812 355 4082

Members of the 98th Battalion, Kenora Militia of June 1914

Back Row standing (L-R), D. Parfitt, Brinkman, Woodhouse, Jones, ____, Beatty, Cassell, Mason Button.

Centre Row kneeling, ___,___,___,___, Williams, Vereker, G. Beatty, Frank S, Iriam.

Front Row sitting, Beckwith, G. Peacock, Mathias, Duncan Robertson, Unidentified youth in foreground.

Contents

Frank S. Iriam, 1906

Prologue

Frank Stanley Iriam (Iram) was born October 30, 1886 in Brazil Lake, Yarmouth County, Nova Scotia. He was one of eight children born to Marion Axele Iram (nee Cann) and Henry Rivers Iram.

He left school in the fifth book to go to work at a sawmill where he lost a part of a finger on his left hand.

He served for three years at the British Military Fort known as the Citadel with the 78th Highland Regiment. The British Garrison was ultimately withdrawn in 1906 in response to growing tensions in Europe.

Frank left Nova Scotia in 1905 spending some time in Montreal where the picture was taken of him in his kilts on May 26th, 1906. He later moved on to Kenora where he obtained employment with the Canadian Pacific Railway as a wiper on September 05, 1906. He was promoted to fireman on June 4th, 1907 and then to engineer August 18th, 1911.

Rumours of war started and then on August 4th, 1914 Frank joined the Army along with about 50 others on the role of the old 98th at Kenora.

Frank had developed an angry streak with the German Empire's actions in Europe. The night of August 14th saw them entraining for Valcartier, Quebec where they continued their training.

There was talk of forming a scout section of eight men in the early days at Valcartier, and he jumped at the chance to get in the scouts. These were the Special Forces of that time period. In September they were blended into the Canadian Overseas Expeditionary Service.

The unit sailed from Quebec on the S.S. Franconia on October the 3rd, 1914.

On their arrival in England their training continued. On February 10th, 1915 they sailed from the Port of Bristol to St. Nazaire, a port in France where they were integrated and familiarized by April 15th, 1915 with their duties as they headed into battle.

Frank served as a sniper, scout, and observer in most of the major battles during the Great War. The accommodations were rough on the front lines. Their plush room consisted of a fairly large whole in the side of a trench with what ever they could gather to put under them to keep themselves out of the wet. Curled up here in their great coats they were put to sleep by the melody of artillery shells and machine gun bullets roaring overhead. They slept like this with the hopes a large shell would not land close enough to collapse the roof on them burying them alive. The snipers had their own cook on the front that set up his kitchen wherever this small band of men were working.

There was a bad time in Dad's service where the terrible conditions really dragged him down into a state of depression. I hope the readers of this story sort of get the idea of how rough the living conditions really were over there for these soldiers. He finally decided he went there to do a job and should get on with it. "*So He Pulled Up His Boat Straps*" as he often told me to do when I found some tough going and got on with it.

On August 1st, 1918 his Battalion was used in the battle of Ameins where they changed to open warfare rather than trench warfare. The need for snipers was no longer there. The allied forces brought up enough men and equipment to push the Germans out of their trenches and keep them on the run to their homeland and the end of the war. On the second day of the battle Frank was shot in the left arm by enemy machine gun fire while running forward to the enemy trenches.

The wounded were transferred to the basement of a village church. Surgery was preformed on his left arm there. Then the wounded were taken to a Hospital on the French coast for further treatment. After a period of time they were moved to Folkstone England for another short stay. Once again they were moved to another Hospital called Collition House in Dorchester, Dorsett. After further medical treatment there they shipped off to Canada on the ship Essequibo about May 1st, 1919. While in Halifax he managed to visit his family in Brazil Lake shortly before being discharged.

On September 16th, 1919 he received his discharge from the Army and returned to Kenora as well as his employment with the Canadian Pacific Railway Co.

Frank married Laura S. Reid on January 4th, 1927 and had a home built that year. They had two children Grace Millicent and Glenn Roy.

During his employment years in Kenora Frank enjoyed exploring the many lakes and rivers in the district and also did a little prospecting. He would head out in his inboard boat with the canvas covered canoe trailing behind. Consequently he had an island named after him on the Lake of the Woods, a lake in the Red Lake district and a road in the Red Lake district were also named after him.

Frank passed on in Deer Lodge Hospital, Winnipeg, Manitoba on August the 9th 1957. Both Frank and his wife Laura are buried in a plot in the Lake Of The Woods Cemetery, Kenora, Ontario.

Introduction

Why did I do this book at this time in life? When I was a young lad in the late 30's and 40's I used to sit and listen to my father's stories of The Great War in the kitchen just dad and I with no one else in the house.

I clung to every word, and often wondered how this loving, tender giant of a man had ever been such a violent man dealing out death on a daily basis to any enemy soldier bearing arms and still looked kindly on any enemy soldier who had laid down his arms becoming a non-combatant.

One evening dad said " I would like my story to be told but not until a long time after I am gone". Then he went on to say that some of the things he wrote about some of the people could put him in a libel position. Well from what I have heard on the media dad was very mildly spoken.

Well here I am 74 years old and publishing my Father's Memoirs in order to fulfill his wishes.

Many of our family and some unexpected help from others have made this venture possible. Without those folks this may never have gotten to the publishing point.

The first to dig in was my sister Grace who diligently went through my first production checking out my manuscript for any errors or omissions.

Then my daughter Patricia and her husband Fred wanted some spacing shortened up and definitions for some of the older words.

Our youngest son Roy and his good wife Diane volunteered to have a look at it but found that they were having trouble coming up with the time.

This I can understand with their two young men demanding so much of their time at this most critical time in their young lives.

Then Mr. Reg. Clayton, editor at the local weekly paper, The Kenora Enterprise asked for some material he could use in the paper around the Memorial Day time frame, November 11th. I had a copy run off for Reg. and he volunteered to edit for me while he was reading it. Reg. had his father also read it and the report from the two of them was very encouraging.

In the background of all this is my wonderful Wife Linda who has put up with me working late nights and early morning trying to make this into a printable book. The toughest part was trying to break up some of the long sentences my father was prone to write with to many "ands" without changing the intended meaning in any way what so ever.

Oh! Oh! I must not forget the two Grand Boys Steven and Paul awaiting the publication with baited breath. Paul used information from the Memoirs to create some very informative displays for his class and all who looked at them.

A further Thank You to the National Archives of Canada for maintaining the fantastic collection of Great War Photos and supplying a Description

Record. They supplied the cover photo by direct e-mail to the publisher.

The Publisher has been picked with a recommendation from Reg. So now the fun begins.

Canada

1914 and June. Rumors were on every puff of wind that gusts and ripples among the islands of the Lake of the Woods. Sentries to be posted on all railway bridges at all points near enough to the river to be in danger of a sudden raid by motor boat from the south. Militia officers, quietly making plans of defense and preparing to use all personnel in the old militia units to whip new men into shape in order to fill the ranks of the First Canadian Division in the future. Germany was on the rampage by sea and land and right out to make the rest of the white race take a back seat. The early part of August found about 50 men on the roll of the old 98th at Kenora. Yours truly as sergeant and not enough clothes to go around. Some of the boys out to drill in derbies, straw hats and civvies. Route marches to Keewatin, out to the brewery and open order drill in the vacant lot in the Rideout where the pulp mill now stands. Finally a sifting of the sheep from the goats and off on no. four passenger train to Valcartier to go in training in earnest for the big job ahead. Col. Schnarre in command. The balance of our old militia officers of the 98th turn out to be duds in a pinch and have no stomach for the prospect of the real work looming ahead. My chum Duncan Robertson working at Minaki making lap strake skiffs on contract for Cossey Boat Co. heard that we were going and jumped the job to come in and enlist with us on the last Saturday night. Alick McRea followed us around and decided to go when he found that we really meant to go and leave him on his lonesome. Jack Thrasher showed up too and also Figsby. We are often told now quite seriously (by the ones who stayed home) that we did not realize what was ahead and were suffering from a delusion that we were going on a pleasure jaunt. I don't remember that any of our boys had that idea. Their subsequent conduct and record in the long grind up to 1919 showed that their heart was in the job and though not too talkative they stated clearly on the start that it would be a three or four year job. The ones who advanced that theory now did not have the right spirit and naturally of narrow mind and uneasy consciences, they now try to solve that conscience by an insinuation of lack of intelligence on the part of the boys who stepped up promptly when they were needed. The whole world is now the judge of that point.

The night of August the 14th saw us entraining for the trip east, tears, sneers, cheers, jeers, fears, and some well wishes were strangely mixed for the 42 rank and file and three n. c. o 's for a total of 45. Old ex soldiers, lumberjacks, railway men, pen pushers, young lads in their teens, mechanics, millers. Scottish, Canadian, English, Irish, peasant, French Galician, Russian Jew, Welsh, Yankee, Icelander, Norse, and Indians.

On arrival at Valcartier we were assigned as a draft to the new 8th battalion of infantry then being formed on the skeleton of the old 90th Winnipeg rifles. The old 90th in the final line up for over seas was not very strongly represented and only mustered about one company. The balance was filled from the Rainy River district, Fort William, Port Arthur and Kenora.

There was great rivalry between NICO's and officers for a place in the new unit and patronage got in its work in some cases to the detriment of efficiency. All were put through very stiff physical training starting each morning at sun up, with an across country run without halt for an hour and 20 minutes. Colonel Lipsitt used to run with us and when a man fell by the way or lagged behind Lipsett would say "(you shawnt go to Frawnce with me)". Colonel O'Grady was the peace time (society kind) of c. o. in command of the old 90th and too old to command an Over seas unit. Col. Lipsitt was requested to take command and the battalion was very fortunate. He will always live in the memory of the boys as a real commander and comrade. There was talk of forming a scout section of eight men in the early days at Valcartier. These men were to be given special training in map making, map reading, use of compass and protractor, signaling-Morse and semaphore, night patrol, day patrol, scouting work, and sharp shooting. This course of training took about six months and ended in a final exam at Strazeele (France-Belgian Boundary) early in April 1915 by Capt. Bertram late of (black watch). The bickering and striving for a place as section commanders or platoon sergeants in the four companies did not appeal to me. I never had any use for the (barrack square) form fours, sort of drill at any time. I had jumped at the chance to get in the scouts. I didn't have any more to do with stripes until June 1915, when I was given the job of sergeant in charge of scouts, snipers and observers on the Messines front. There was a trench, three miles long around the base of a hill at Valcartier filled throughout its length with revolving targets for rifle practice. I always had a fondness for rifle shooting and put in some very pleasant days making the old 90th crack riflemen scratch gravel to keep their scores higher than mine. I took a lot of pleasure out of beating the old city sergeants and color sergeants at their own game on the range. There was a big stock of the government's old Mk-2 blunt nosed ammunition on their hands and they used it up in target practice here. It was too slow of a speed for the twist of the Mk-3 Ross and nickeled the rifles badly at the muzzles end on that account. Right there at Valcartier proof was given that the much-abused Ross rifle was not essentially a dangerous arm on account of blowbacks and other defects. There were collected there all the greenhorns and inexperienced from the length and breadth of the continent slamming away all day at rapid fire, section rushes over broken ground, disappearing ring targets, etc. I cannot recall any accidents on account of blowbacks or other defects in the rifle. I wonder could the Springfield or Enfield come through that mess with a cleaner record?

About this time the powers were afflicted with the bug of inoculation and vaccination against typhoid etc. They let loose among us some medical students and some doctors without a practice in their home districts. These gents got hold of some bicycle pumps, several tons of serum and tried experiments on us. For the first dose we got enough for seven men shot into each individual. There were three or four fatalities, the ones that didn't croak had a high fever for 48 hours and were very sick from the overdose. I saw six footers spin around in their tracks as if shot and lose consciousness for some time when the bicycle pump shot its load into their veins. We felt the effects of it for weeks.

Training went on up to the end of September at which point the weak and the unfit were discharged as hopeless, or put into E company to go to Bermuda on garrison duty for further training there. The training in Valcartier ended up in a final grand parade past an inspection point (in line of full companies). This is a hard maneuver to carry out even with seasoned troops especially if the ground is a bit rough under foot. I was grabbed for a pivot man to set the pace and maintain the alignment on the right flank of the leading a company. Any old soldier will know that it is a very ticklish job on rough ground especially when the company in line swings around a corner as a gate swings on it's hinges. I never saw the movie or the still pictures of that parade so never knew how we looked. Sam Hughes did wonders in the short period at Valcartier. I remember there were some U.S military observers present.

It was at one of these early parades that I witnessed an amusing incident. Arthur Currie was at that time in command of what was then called The First British Columbia Rifles. The different units were all formed up and ready to swing into alignment for the march past. Currie was a big man in stature as well as in many other ways. He had a big voice with great carrying power. On this occasion he stepped forward and reeled of a long rigmarole preliminary to the command for his unit to move. This oration ended with (First British Columbia Rifles slope arms). Col. Lessard commanding a Quebec unit at that time. I think it was the old (Vandoos 22nd) cocked his roguish head on one side and listened very attentively to Currie's lengthy command until it was finished. He then stepped up and drawing in all the breath he could manage, he rolled out a command to his own unit the major part of which he invented on the instant in mimic of Currie's effort. Vandoos 22nd Quebec, Ross rifles etc.—etc. slope arms. This was a severe strain on the dignity and sobriety of all ranks present and within hearing of these remarkable vocal efforts. The four companies of the overseas units were getting in shape fast, promising to be a fine outfit and later lived up to the promise at St. Julien. October saw us ready to embark at Quebec City. We had a pretty stiff training during our two months in camp and were in far better condition in October than we were at the close of the year after the shower bath in Salisbury Plains.

Crossing The Atlantic

We were shipped into Quebec City by rail, shown aboard a small steamer that had seen better days and was fresh from the cattle trade. Officers great and small, the rank and file began to size up the prospects of 15 days aboard this craft coming to the decision that the conditions would not be practical or sanitary. Figured out by the strength of troops on board, if we lined up, waited our turn each man would be able to use the latrine etc. about once in four days. Other accommodation a par and very short of practical requirements. Somebody kicked just in time and we were transferred to the (Canarder Franconia) together with div. head quarters staff, nursing staff, hospital staff and on this fine ship we had a pleasant and not too crowded passage.

The river below Quebec City was a fine sight in the bright October weather, with the brilliant coloring of the hardwood bush on the flanking hills making a background of villages with white painted cottages and patches of cultivated lands. There were to be 33 steam ships in the fleet of transports going in addition to an escort of light cruisers something after the style of the Rainbow and Niobe. The meeting point of this fleet was at Gaspe Bay, a landlocked, beautiful sheet of water enclosed by a ring of hills and having a narrow outlet to the sea. The ships come here from all points on the east coast.

Our training was kept up as much as possible while on board ship. The weatherman seemed to be on our side that trip, for the old Atlantic was as calm as a pond during the whole 15 days of the crossing. On the morning we sailed out of the bay it was fun to see some of the boys convincing themselves and one another they had to be seasick. Before we were well out of the harbor some of them had begun to rush to the rail to feed the fish. But strange to say they forgot about it in about an hour when other things claimed their interest and took them away from the idea. The Franconia was one of the latest and biggest ships in the Cunard Fleet at that time. It was like a city afloat. The fleet was formed in three lines of 11 ships each with the escort in front making an imposing sight when all were underway. The speed was tied down to eight or nine knots on account of some of the smaller ships not being able to make more than that speed. The big liners loafed along with banked fires with scarcely a whiff of smoke from their funnels all day except when the fires were cleaned or freshened up. They did not have way enough to enable them to steer properly and some of them rolled badly on this account. This applied especially to the Royal Edward just ahead of us and to the light cruisers. These two rolled so badly in the light swell we thought they would snap off their tall masts with the old fashioned cross spar rigging.

After I began to know the way around a bit, I used to go up to the lookout or crow's nest on the mast, spending a lot of time there taking in the view of the whole fleet. There was no excitement of any kind during the trip with the exception of a day when a deck hand on a scaffold slung over side for painting, fell into the ocean from the ship next ahead. This ship blew her whistle, turned her nose out of line and reversed her engines. Our ship followed suit and a boat was dropped from us manned by a mixed crew including one of our lieut's Shorty Weld or (Pinky Weld). A lifebuoy was thrown that lit up when it hit the water with a white light and a trail of white smoke to guide the swimmer. One of the light cruisers noted the disturbance in the center of the fleet and spinning around came back between the lines at a surprising rate of speed with guns searching low looking for a submarine. The cruiser could turn a nasty wheel and went whisking around us at about 35 knots looking for trouble.

From the crow's nest you could see a smudge of smoke for a few days in mid-Atlantic off to the north in line with us, sometimes we caught a glimpse of top masts. I was told that it was the Battle Cruiser Lion on the flank but she never came nearer.

When nearing the British coast we would occasionally see a smudge of smoke, and a cloud of spray coming our way, and in a couple of minutes the cause of it would be in close and signaling at lightning speed with a set of semaphore arms on the bridge. These were destroyers. Our signalers, who had begun by now to fancy their ability a little tried to read the messages but this navy stuff was too fast for our amateurs as yet.

The night before landing we broke away from the fleet and went at nearly full speed. The next day we dropped anchor in the harbor that the Mayflower sailed out of with the Pilgrim Fathers aboard. It was a strange feeling I had when I looked on this old England that I had heard so much of and studied about in school days. It was a feeling of coming home after a long journey. Some of the old (wooden walls) frigates lay in the inner harbor that had been scrappers in Nelson's day. They were now used as training ships for boys and some as a sort of prison. You may have heard of the (prison hulks).

Our first impression of an English town was the chimney pots. They stick right out at you and the rest of the scenery is subordinate in every way. Rows upon rows of elaborate chimney pots stretching away into mists and smoke with absurdly narrow streets between leading up steep inclines away from the water front. Inland through the mist we could hear shrill piping whistles frequently, and inquiry brought the information that these were locomotive whistles on the railway. Shrill thin notes.

We of the scout section were not as yet a unit in the real sense. We were kept on the strength of our respective sections, platoons and companies and under their officers, drawing our rations etc. from them. I was on the strength of a co. under the command of Capt. Watson who was a good sport, efficient in most things and well liked. He was later to go through some remarkable experiences, of which you will hear more later.

England

That evening we disembarked with all our worldly goods on our poor backs. We didn't know how to spare them yet and loaded ourselves with tons of unnecessary junk till we were staggering under a pile like a coolie with the sweat trickling down in our eyes. A feeling of bursting with heat and the pressure of the leather straps in the old Oliver equipment. In this shape we started to climb the steep hills on wet slippery cobblestones. We wanted to make friends with the English folk that crowded in on either flank to express their hearty welcome but, we were too short in the puff and too busy keeping our feet and pawing the sweat out of our eyes, but not too busy to take note of the red-cheeked lassies that rushed in to steal the first Canadian kiss.

We entrained in the queer little English railway (wagons) with their two seat compartments and here our excess of baggage very nearly did us out of a seat, and were off to Salisbury Plains. No boxcars here or freight trains. They are goods wagons, goods trains and they shunt instead of switching. Instead of hand or lamp signals they toot a little tinhorn. I guess that is the origin of the term (Tin Horn) meaning one horse or haywire.

We were assigned to tents in a part of the plains called west downs and west downs south a few miles from stone-henge or Stonehenge, of the old druid temple. Mud was here, rain was here, and the roadway was of chalk. The traffic had made its surface about ankle deep with a sort of wet mortar that splashed up your shins and put your legs in a plaster cast in jig time.

Here in the wet we went to it, hammer and tongs, for the balance of the year. Drill all day rain or shine and no shine. The platoon system of drill was comparatively new to us and had to be mastered. Then there was an open order skirmish drill. I always liked this kind of drill for it seemed to me it might be of practical use in warfare. I never did think that so much time ought to be used in close order drills when there is so much to learn of real practical value. Useful training is neglected in favor of drill that does not make for efficiency in the field but has its sole object in appearances and smartness during parades. Five years in the army has only served to strengthen that belief. Three years and seven months of that was in the front lines. There is patrol work, outpost duty, bombing with all its branches, machine guns, rifle grenades, trench mortars, stokes guns, sharp shooting, map reading, map making, use of compass and protractor, director boards, signaling and all its branches, including cooperation with aero planes in attack by infantry. Observation, construction of communications, front line trenches, telegraph and telephone lines, wireless a form of radio, working in conjunction with tanks, sapping and mining operations and open or moving warfare training. Close order drill takes up a lot of the time that should be spent on the things named above.

One day while out on open warfare practice, which culminated in an attack on Yarnbury Castle, we came to a small stone bridge across the Avon River. According to the umpire's orders this bridge was supposed to have been destroyed by the enemy. Our captain looked around and seeing no umpires in sight sent some of his men across the bridge. In no time at all there showed up a couple of imperial staff officers who inquired how he could use a bridge that had been blown up. Our captain thought quickly and replied that the stone falling from the bridge into the stream had left enough footing to be used as a ford in crossing. The staff grinned. It was Sir H. Robertson or Sir H. Wilson. I am not really sure which one it was.

We dug into scout work with both feet on the plains. Road reports, patrol reports, map making, map enlarging, panoramic sketching, observation, night marches across country by compass and by stars, distance judging, concealment and utilization of cover, semaphore signaling, etc. Our field training was given to a lieutenant ex school teacher, ex surveyor from Emo in the Rainy River district, a conscientious soul with his heart in the work all right but seeming to us to be addicted to traveling in grooves and lacking the spirit of initiative and broadness necessary to work ahead, and inclined to be fussy in a school marm sort of way that would not be so bad with boy scouts at home. Over and senior to him was (Capt.—later to become) Major Andrews of Winnipeg a grand old man. Too bad he was so old. He was really too old to be soldiering at all but too game to be left at home. He was supposed to oversee our training and did so to the limit of his physical ability. He went on a night march across country in wet weather with us. Became over heated, caught pneumonia and near died with it. He did not recover in time to go to France with the battalion but followed when recovered. To him as to a true pal we have put our fears about the lieutenant. The upshot was a decision (at an Indian Council) to put in what is known as a round robin asking for his removal and the installation of one of our number, a private named Knobel as our instructor with the rank of sergeant. This was done in a few days.

Knobel was a mining engineer of good education and world wide experience including being with Dr. Jamieson on his famous raid on the Boers in s. a., mining in the Yukon, Alaska, Northern Ontario, etc., and four years at school in Germany speaking German and French fluently. He was an expert surveyor, map man, artist and photographer etc. We now felt more confidant and looked forward to seeing things when we progressed where we could try out our system of scout work in actual practice in the field.

Putting troops in tents on the plains in the winter is not usual practice but was thought feasible in our case as we colonials were supposed to be a tough lot and physically able to survive it. Quite a few of us did live through it and quite a few did not. Spinal meningitis due to exposure and wet also pneumonia due to the same cause carried away quite a number.

A few weeks before going overseas we were transferred to wooden huts at Stonehenge. The huts were better in that it gave us some chance to keep blankets and clothing semi-dry. I know that the after affects of that exposure was the death of a lot of men during the winter and spring of 1915 by cutting down on their vitality, making them easy prey when they were again exposed to tough conditions in the front line.

The collection of huge stone slabs at Stonehenge is an interesting monument attributed to the old druid priesthood. As far as I know we have no definite history of its origin though the nearest stone of the kind is at or near the coast and the ancients must have done some engineering to get them there to the present site. We used to form a hollow square in front of it every Sunday morning for church services. The drums were piled in the centre and served as a sort of pulpit from which the padre held services. The rolling land must have looked on some strange gatherings at this spot, ancient Britons, Romans, Normans, Norse, Angles, Saxons, Danes, old English, modern British and lastly Canadian troops under arms. I am afraid I used to stand and conjure up mind pictures of these old time savage battalions against the background of the grassland instead of listening to the services. The whispering wind in the grasses seemed to tell weird tales of the doings at this historic spot and ones eyes seemed to wander back to the alter stone or sacrificial stone in the centre with each whisper of the south wind.

I caught a heavy cold and a touch of pneumonia early in December. We were put on cross country foot races, a run of six miles with whole companies and battalions in the run, up hill and down dale in the winter rain through wet grass and pools of water. We would finish the run steaming hot, soaking wet with sweat and rain water, ending up in a tent where you waded in soup ankle-deep to the door. No fires here, no change of clothes, no rub down, not even dry blankets. We would squat in the slithery mud smooched floor and get busy with a knife scraping the mud from our clothing to make it presentable on the next parade. Marksmanship tests were on now and we were sent to the ranges from 100 to 800 yards. I was subject to ague-chills and a heavy cough with eyes running water badly. The targets were a blur as far as the bulls' eye was concerned though I could make out the square outline of the white sheet alright. I used that as a guide to centre. Maj. Andrews was an old Bisely rifleman, and had been over some years before with the Canadian Team. My shooting up to now had been a little better than the average so he challenged me to a shoot off in the finals. I was leery about the ague-chills and the watery eyes but took him on. We shot the course and I was on top by two points only.

On account of something like 52 percent of the division being of British birth or having relatives in the old country, it was decided to allow all ranks a furlough–leave or vacation to the address they specified in the period at or about Christmas or New Years. Alick McRea invited me to go with him to his home at Brora in Sutherland–Scotland. We went via London and while strolling up the Strand we had a rather amusing encounter with a military body of shining aspect. Busy with plans and jabbering like two kids we failed to notice an artillery officer in (full dress peace time parade uniform) with broad red strips on his trousers, cap, oodles of gold braid and trimmings. Failing to notice and duly salute the trimmings we were jacked up very short, questioned as to the intelligence, training, origin of our ancestors and future hopes on this earth. Quandary was here as well as some embarrassment. I stole a shy maidenly look at the broad red strips stating that I had mistook him for a Salvation Army Officer. There was a snort something like a bear makes when disturbed in a blueberry patch and the man of many colors was on his way without any ceremony at all. Oh! You Lassies of London.

I began to be sorry of my plan to go to the top end of Scotland but Alick rushed to the depot and we were off. Great Eastern and Caledonian through train to Edinburgh. Here were coaches like the ones at home with compartments and general layout similar. Traffic was very heavy just then and standing room only was about all that was available on that train. I remember a sailor on leave to London from the fleet in the Cromartry Firth and on his way back to his ship. He was several sheets in the wind and had the big black neckerchief (a relic of Nelson's Time) filled full of winkles or periwinkles and was seated in the centre of the coach isle hailing all comers (Hi! Mitey, Have a winkle Mitey)? It was interesting to see him fish the meat out of the shells with a bent pin. I tried one but lost interest at that.

Scotland

We had a glimpse of old Edinburgh Castle and some of the city and went on to Inverness. This town was more like a town in eastern Canada than any place I saw in Europe. Alick went out during the evening and being lonely I tried to pick up conversation with some folk at the hostelry where we put up. That must have been an ungodly thing to do, for I can still remember the icy stare that rewarded my efforts at sociability. (Unheardof- you-know). Really I can see through it now but was puzzled at the time. I know of one G. R. Gibson of Hollinger Mines who went on leave from the trenches to Edinburgh in a private's uniform. His own sisters would not be seen in public with him because of his low degradation and visible proof of same in his raiment. Class!! The Caledonian Railway and away north again to the mists and the Heathered hills awa "away". Firth of Forth and its bridge Cromartry Firth, and the Fleetmore Hills "seven hills" and old castles and mist and Brora a (*wee bit*) fishing village at the mouth of a burn. Greetings from Alick's ain folk and real folk too. A drive in a wee pony cart, two wheeled, with one seat facing front and one back, for 8 miles up the glen following the north side of the brawling burn. What kind of a factory is that Alick? What? Yon? It's a distillery. This question was asked and answered a couple of times in route. But there was white birch and pine in the gullies and I spotted deer tracks across the road ahead. I could see the real heilands "highlands" with their blue purple heads lost in drifting sheets of cloud mist. McRea senior was Gardner and general caretaker at a hunting lodge. Alick's brother helped the old man and also ran a power plant on the burn that supplied electric light for the lodge and the village.

Hospitality is here and the guest is put to bed at night with a bowl of hot punch, his buttons are polished, ditto his shoes, and his socks are washed and warmed for his use in the morning. He is awakened in the morning by the daughter of the house bearing a tray with 1st grade Scotch and glasses for a (*wee bit*) eye opener.

I happened to be about the first Canuck to arrive in those parts and become quite an object of interest to the local folk. Most of the neighbors are gamekeepers and old friends of Alick. We had to make the rounds and visit them all and drink with them. It is a deadly insult to refuse a drink in a Heilanman's Hoose "Scotchman's House" in the holiday season. I had not been accustomed to much liquor and it did tax my ability to go the full rounds, but I made it with honors and firm on the two pins at the finish.

Alick's brother was a piper and we were treated to a concert in the little stone cottage with its low ceilings. The piper marched up and down the length of the hoose "house" and the old man kept time with his walking stick and criticized when a note was dropped or a false one played. The noise in that small place was terrific and I had to plead guilty to not knowing much about piping.

The Wee-Hoose " Wee-House" had an open fireplace with all the old time fixings, irons and suspended hooks for the cooking pots. There was a big brick and stone bake over built into the side of the kitchen entrance and in it the bread was baked. Oval shaped loaves similar to the ones in the rural districts of France.

A dance was put on for our benefit and a number of the Lads and Lassies of the Glen gave a sample of their dancing ability. They can dance too and it was worth the trip to Scotland to see it. I was grabbed and taken into the whirl, and being well fortified I did not mind though it must have interfered badly with the dance. Lassies were plenty here but the lads, sad to say, were beginning to be very scarce there about and war has yet only begun. War has always taken a brave sad toll in Scotland and you will always find them to be among the first in any field.

The first dead I saw between the front lines at Ploegstreert were Kilties fallen in the autumn of 1915 still lying as they fell.

The game keepers told us of four barren does that were to be killed on the hills for venison. The meat of two was to go to the master and two to the keepers. The first two had all ready been shot and Alick and I were taken out with the keeper to look for the others. We went up among the Heather Broom and Gorse to where there were no trees. Here we put up some big dark-colored mountain grouse that roared off in fine style making a clucking noise. They are similar to our prairie chicken except that they were larger and very dark in color. The keeper carried a telescope and presently we began to crawl on our stomachs through a small depression or fold in the ground and came out at last at a point on the west side over looking a basin or saucer-shaped depression in the hills about 600 yards. in diameter. On the skyline eastward was a small gully or depression filled with stunted spruce. On the far slope immediately in front of this gully lay the band of deer with a stag up on sentry. These are real wild deer and good strategists for the wind was straight out of the stunted spruce. They could hear or smell any approach from there and could see clear around the rest of the circle. We got to within about 450 yards, but not without being seen for another stag rose to his feet and stood facing directly our way. One or two does also rose and stamped impatiently. We froze and studied them with the glass. They have the habits and actions of our woodland caribou and remind me of them very much. We drew beads on them with the rifles and the range was known by the keeper nearly to a yard. There was little wind and a good light and I think we could have made a couple of kills with little difficulty. The keeper was undecided about the two particular does wanted, or gave that impression. I for one did not relish the idea of slinging deadly lead into that brave looking band, and was more interested in studying them for comparison with our deer at home. The sweep of their antlers is a little different from our deer and the beams are dark, almost black, with white tips on the tines. The body looks darker in color and this I found later by close inspection of a dead one, is caused by the inner hair being of a bluish-slate color instead of white as in the case of our red deer. I don't think they will average any larger than our deer and are about the build of what we know as the Virginia deer in Canada. The hair is the same stiff stuff and loses all its gloss after death. We met a real old highland sheepherder in the hills about six foot three in height, raw-boned and spare of flesh over a mighty frame. He gave me a hearty greeting and extended a hand about the size of a ham. His voice was a treat and the burrrr-r was 13 Karat. I had to get Alick to act as interpreter as I could not master the combination of burr and dialect.

The time had come to go back to our unit, the Wee Pony Cart was brought out again and adieus were said all around but there is one scene that still sticks hard in my throat. It was Alick's mother as she stood alone outside the wee-hoose clasping her hands and watching him go out of sight around the bend in the road. I can't help but think there was premonition in that look. How many highland mothers have had to stand thus and watch their lads out of sight and out of their lives.

The brave hearts are not all in kilts behind the pipes and drums. Some of them stay in the wee stone hooses. Half way to the village we passed a cottager in front of his home dancing reels in the roadway all by himself. The holiday spirit of the New Year was strong in that old "Heilanman". Maybe he had no sons left to help him celebrate, but there he was spinning with no mean ability and doubtless with no mean load under his belt. Back to Inverness. We waited there overnight to make train connections south again. I met a tall dark Lassie who taught school in a kindergarten on the outskirts of Edinburgh. She also was going south and eventually inquired if I was traveling light. On account of the crush of traffic I had to travel light but it was not from choice alas.

England

Alick fresh from home had no stomach for looking over the city of the big smoke so we did not linger long in London and went directly back to the battalion. We found the River Avon in flood with bridges submerged and some whole villages under water. We had to make some detours and cross some submerged bridges on our way back to the plains.

About this time there started to be a lot of agitation in the First Division about discarding Canadian manufactured equipment. Where this was started and how it was carried through to fruition is probably only known to a few. The O. C. of the division at this time was General Alderson an English officer of the old school or South African war vintage. The rank and file being over 50 percent of old country birth were very strongly prejudiced in favor of things of English make. A contract to supply all the equipment to the Canadian government for the balance of the campaign meant millions of good money to someone. It was easy to get complaints enough from the rank and file to make a strong showing. The native Canadian of an observing turn of mind has his own ideas about how the thing was engineered. The taxpayer at home today is still paying the bill. Poor old Sam Hughes protested at the time in no uncertain voice but he was drowned out and swamped out as thoroughly as our equipment that was stored in a basement warehouse at Salisbury in readiness for the annual flooding of the Avon. That is as regular as the tides and well known to the Imperial authorities. Motor lorries, dray wagons, Indian motorcycles, clothing, boots and rifles, were condemned for active service use. We were re equipped for overseas almost wholly with English made goods. I would like to know the personal history of the committee of inspectors who went the rounds with Alderson and clinched the deal at Salisbury Plains. Canada paid dearly for her ignorance about things in the military. We had no one in a position to say to them "nay".

The division was beginning to look and act like troops and it was decided to have an inspection by Earl Kitchener. We were all pleased at the prospect of seeing this old warrior. We had read so much, heard so much of that old lion that I think he had found a place in the corner of all of our hearts and we looked forward to seeing him in person. Our interest in him was different from the interest taken in Royalty and other celebrities. A thing distinct. I was not disappointed in him on first sight and he looked every inch the part he played in the drama of the Empire on its outer and rougher edges. There was the stamp of the deserts and raw wild lands in him. I still believe in him in spite of the carping, place seeking politicians who besmirched him before and after his death. He had an eye that seemed to look through and through you and a face like the face of the Rocky Mountains. His name will stand after his critics are mostly forgotten.

The raw lands know it and fierce suns glare
The Dervish breathes it at his evening Prayer
As well to sneer at the old Union Jack itself as at him
The poor little (street bred) people
That sputter, and fume and brag
And lift their voice in the stillness
To yelp at the British flag

We must have made a fairly favorable impression as to fitness for service for we soon heard rumors of something doing about our going overseas. We were taken on route marches with full equipment occasionally. One day we did not return to camp but were entrained and found ourselves in Avonmouth, the Port of Bristol, went aboard ship there and left Old England on the lee "sheltered".

Crossing The Channel

We were off down the Bristol Channel, destination unknown aboard a freight tramp Ahoy! The freighter that carried us was of an all-steel construction shell with decks from top to bottom of all-steel plates. Ribs and deck girders were of all-steel I beams or T beams. Each man had his spot on the lower deck to spread his bed and equipment on the steel riveted deck floor, and there was little room to spare. All the ships were loaded to capacity. Bristol Channel, St. George's Channel, then away south and still south until the breeze began to smell balmy and warm. I began to sniff and have visions of the Straits of Gibraltar, and hopes of seeing the Mediterranean, or perhaps Egypt, the Dardanelles or at least Marseilles. We got in the neighborhood of the Bay of Biscay and fully expected to meet a storm as that quarter has an unenviable reputation for dirty weather.

It stayed fine and sunny, and in mid afternoon our old R. S. M. brought a crock out on deck to issue our first ration of rum on active service. I sat on top of a hatch cover and watched the proceeding, which were quite interesting. Some of the boys were teetotalers, some were the opposite, some were merely curious about the old Jamaica, trying it as an experiment and gagged on it with wry faces. I took mine finding it strong enough to make me blink and swallow a few times before getting a free breath. I figure it must be 35 or 40 O. P.

We passed several queer-looking craft and met one Nova Scotia Man loping along and nearly becalmed. The "herring chokers" hurried to the rail waving greetings. It was a brig and what they were doing in these waters I don't know. Maybe hunting subs with their old seal guns.

When I turned in at a late hour we were still pounding away to the south and it was getting to be quite warm. Awaking in the morning I had a suspicion that things had changed. I was shivering in a damp cold foggy draft and the steel plate mattress felt like an ice floe. There was a fresh breeze with a choppy sea on, a drift of scud, fog, and we were drumming away full speed to the north getting colder every minute.

In the course of the day we saw a couple of queer bunchy awkwardlooking naval craft through the fog on the port bow. These turned out to be French cruisers lying outside the entrance to the Port of St.Nazaire. We soon picked up a pilot and worked our way into the roadstead and in due time swung at anchor in the inner harbor. Here was a long straggling water front of mixed shipping and a mixed looking town stretching back from it into fog and smoke.

I heard a French bugle some place on shore playing reveille. This call has the same notes as used by the U. S. Army, was no doubt introduced here by Lafayette. We sized up the grimy looking shoreline.

Here it was at last
It was the land of France
The chosen home of Chivalry
The garden of Romance

It turned out that we had slipped across the Bay of Biscay, pretty luckily, just ahead of a nasty storm that caught some of the transports close behind us nearly swamping a couple of them that were loaded with horses and forage. I believe there was a loss of some of the horses.

St. Nazaire

A Co. or No. 1 Co. was left here a couple of days on account of the battalion being over strength. For this reason they could not ship us all on the regular number of cattle cars assigned to a French battalion. 42 hommes or 10 chaveaux to a car. We had to wait and follow at earliest convenience. We eventually landed in our turn and were marched through the town to a camp of tents in the suburbs.

Now St. Nazaire is an old time seaport infested with all kinds of drifting and sea going people of many nationalities and colors. Turcos, Lasgars, Maltese, Indian, Coolies, Negroes as well as the white scum of a hundred water fronts.

There is on sale at the numerous estaminets wines of all kinds, cognac, bismuth, cride, minth beers and other drinks with a kick from Algiers, Italy and other foreign parts.

There is also plentitude of women on sale to the first bidder regardless of color, cleanliness or origin of the buyer.

We had about 300 young devils in the prime of life with coin in their pockets in a new and strange land raring to go. It was some responsibility on the hands of our O. C's to hold them for the time of our stay here and keep them out of trouble. Some of us were detailed off to act as sentries at some of the more unsavory joints to steer the boys away. I was nailed for this, my first job in La Belle France. I only had to turn away a couple of them during the night.

The last one was a lance jack or one strip corporal out of my own platoon. He had gone into some place where the inmates were all busy, or sleeping, or out. At any rate he gravitated to the kitchen part of the house and ran up against a big sideboard or chest of drawers or shelves loaded with a variety of bottles with all kinds and all degrees of kick. Being primed to a jovial and devil may care stage he proceeded to load up all the pockets of his great coat, the inner clothing with the best that the house afforded before leaving. When he passed me he had a heavy cargo and was rolling some in a light ground swell but with all sails set. He promised to go directly to his tent and did so. I helped him a little with his cargo when off duty.

On the third day we took the train and were off on the long detour by rail, three days and three nights. We were very crowded in those stock cars and found difficulty in having enough room to stretch out for a nap at night. Most of the time we were hunched up with our knees under our chins, but occasionally found a place at the side door of our Pullman where we could get a glimpse of the country. We passed through some very beautiful valleys in what I was told was Normandy. Of course all troop movements were under a very heavy and strict censorship, and we had to guess at our route and destination at all times. We were often able to pick off information en route and take note of names. While passing through the towns and while stopped in rail yards we had a chance to view the people and donate bully beef and biscuits to the swarms of pinched looking children that crowded along side with their perpetual whine of Bulee—Bif—Biskee—Pennie-Anglais-Soldat-Plees. There must have been a lot of poverty and hardship even at that early stage of the war to judge by these Waifs. We must have passed over a height of land some where in mid-trip for we climbed for several hours on steep grades. After passing through a long tunnel we came out on a different sort of country, level and flat almost like our prairie. I suppose that was our entrance to the Flanders Plains.

Hazebrouck

We eventually arrived at Hazebrouck, France, and this was an important railway point from which troops were distributed to all parts of the Ypres Salient and points south.

Here I got my first taste of scout work. I was notified before our arrival here to report to the O. C. in full marching order. On reporting to him I was given a map and told to go to Strazeele, find the balance of the battalion, then report to the O. C. of transport, and have wagons sent to Hazebrouck to fetch the company's baggage. During the absence of the wagons I was to hunt out our billets in the countryside by their numbers and map locations, and having located them come back on the road and guide the different platoons to their respective quarters. Another scout named Closett of Belgian Nationality was sent with me to act as an interpreter in case of need. We found our way there alright fulfilling the rest of the contract and the platoons were quartered in their billets ok. These billets were barns or stables with straw on the floors to sleep on. I was tired and hungry when that day's work was done for it represented quite a number of miles of travel with many inquiries, and hustling to and fro to complete it.

When I hit the straw I found a large cotton sack of coffee beans under my pillow that some soldier had pinched. On arrival at Hazebrouck we noticed the tracks torn up in a couple of places by shells. Fritz had been shelling the railway junction at long range with naval guns.

Plug Street Wood

Immediately on detraining we could hear the rumble of guns away to the north and east. All night as we lay in our first field billets we could hear the dull thunder and grumble in the north. We continued our training for a short time at Strazeele. Then one day we were moved up near Armentieres, and were then sent into the front line in the Pleogstreete Wood sector to learn trench duties, routine and to get accustomed to the work. We were attached for this purpose to the Imperial units holding the sector at the time.

Writing of our stay in billets near Armentieres recalls to mind recent controversy re: the soldier's song or ditty entitled (Mademoiselle from Armentieres). At that time, middle of February 1915, we were billeted in barns out in the country and used to walk into Armentieres in the evenings just to see what we might see. The song was apparently sprouting at that time or in the formative stage. I remember we invented several lines to fit the air while walking back to our billets at night after visiting the town. When I say (WE) I mean the old original eighth battalion scouts who were trained in Valcartier and on the Salisbury Plains. The fact that these particular lines are still in common use seems to indicate we may have been the originators of the main body of that soldier's ditty. I have read several very misleading articles in current papers and periodicals in regards to this song. An Australian lieutenant laying claim in one instance to its having originated with his unit during 1916-1917. He even went so far as to name a particular lady of his acquaintance as being the original Mademoiselle of the song. Truth is stranger than fiction and there happens to be a slight error in his data of about two years in respect to this famous song. I do not claim that we were the originators of this song and I do not remember just how it came to us. I do know that quite a few of those lines were invented by us at that time while walking back to the billets at night, and those lines are still in common use by ex-soldiers who sing it at times when they obtain sufficient lubrication to cause them to bust loose.

Night winds across the great Flanders Plain moaning in the high elms, and Lombardy poplars, and with a drizzle of rain on wet cobble stones. Kitchener boots slosh sloshing through the mud. Intermittent flashes like summer thunder and lightning with it too.

Our detachment was assigned to the Somerset Light Infantry, and a fine body of men they were. They used us first rate, doing all they could to help us out and show us around. We had two days and nights in the line with them. Their breastworks and dugout shelters were in good repair, and their communication lines also, and every thing else was as clean as a new pin. There seemed to be a community feeling in that outfit and no wrangling among the rank and file with no excess show of authority and abuse of same by their officers.

We had a man badly wounded here. He went out on day light patrol in front of the line with some others and came under rifle fire. The first night on the line I was sent along with one of the Somersets on listening post. Ploegstreert Wood in winter time is a swamp. Standing in pools of water with a thick growth of good-sized hardwood timber, oak, elm, beech, willow and several other kinds of hardwoods. A glimpse here and there was all we got of the German trench owing to the density of the timber at that time. As soon as dusk thickened towards dark in the swamp we crept over the parapet and along a footpath crossing pools on a plank laid in the mud. You took a ground sheet with you to lie on. The listening post turned out to be a semi-circle of filled sand bags laid down to make a spot high enough to be just above water level. Here the two of you spread your ground sheets and lay quietly to listen and watch for two hours. There is a sort of cuckoo bird in that swamp that keeps up an incessant and never varying monotone Co-o, Co-o, and another swamp bird with a one-note whistle of a dreary mournful kind.

A few yards to the right front I could see two dead Scottish Kilties lying on their faces in the swamp. I got chilly after a bit and not being where I could have a smoke I took a chew of MacDonald Plug as a substitute. My mate requested a chew and bit off a generous hunk. In a few minutes he started to roll around groaning and grunting appearing to be in pain or feeling very sick. I asked what was the trouble" (Mon) he says that is an awful twist ye have. I gathered that twist meant tobacco and apparently he had swallowed some of it. He was a sick Somerset.

One of their sergeants showed me how to challenge and halt any person or persons unknown moving about at night. I still think this is the most sensible and effective method I have heard. The sentry called Halt! If the command was not obeyed it was repeated, if still disregarded the sentry shot without further parley. If the command was obeyed and the party halted, then the sentry commanded, "Advance one", then one man of the party advanced close enough to be recognized or identified by the sentry. "Pass friend". The sentry carried this out from cover or concealment when possible. I tried it out the next night and they certainly did not wait for a second command when challenged.

After two nights here we were sent in again with some of the London Rifle Brigade. Here was a contrast. Their breastworks were poorly built, there were no board walks in the bottom of their trench, and they slopped along through the water and stood ankle deep in it. Their shelters from the weather were very poor, leaky and wet. The men stood humped up shivering with wool scarf's wound around their necks on sentry, snapping and snarling like husky dogs. The officers and sergeants prowled up and down steadily, every time they passed you could hear some poor private being browbeaten, lectured savagely always ending up with the old refrain. "Take that mans name sergeant, and the poor devil was put on the crime list ending up in the orderly room next morning for more browbeating or worse. They sure did love one another in that outfit. Holy Mackerel! It was all discipline and no brains there, with a vengeance.

Col. Lipsett had some of the boys build a log cabin in Canadian style about a quarter mile back of the line before we left the Plug Street Wood. We had lots of lumberjacks in our outfit and that was a treat for them.

Labutillere

After finishing our term of schooling in trench routine we were shipped to Fleur Baix and took over a section of front line trench on our own at a place by the name of Labutillere just to the left of Neuve Chapelle.

Here the scouts got busy in real earnest, and we worked day and night during the eight-day terms that the battalion was in the front trench. When our battalion was out of the line in supports, we rode up on bicycles working day and night behind and in front of the other units of the 2nd Brigade.

I was put on sniping as soon as we went in, varying this with some observation work, panoramic sketching from points of vantage during daylight, and at night going out on patrols with the scouts between the opposing front lines in what was known as no mans land.

We were the only battalion scouts in the brigade at that time that is the reason we were used on the time and frontage of the other units. Some of the other battalions had what they called company scouts but they were under their respective company commanders and not in a position to get trained or organized in any effective way.

The ground here was low and wet making it impossible to dig trenches, so the front and support lines were built up with sand bags to about shoulder high. This breastwork or parapet had loop holes in it near the top for shooting through. We used to stuff an empty sack into the hole when it was not in use. This kept the light from showing movement behind.

We used crude methods in those early days. Some of the men who came out in 1917 and 1918 will no doubt laugh at some of them, but we did the best we knew how, making use of what was available for offense and defense, and that was not much, I can tell you.

We had a couple of batteries of thirteen pounders (horse artillery) in the hedge rows and willow clumps a few hundred yards behind the front. Further back there were just two sixty pounders that we had brought from Valcartier and one of them blew up quite early in the game. That was the sum total of our artillery support. For machine guns we had three colts guns to a battalion, and we later got hold of an old Vickers maxim and nursed it into service. Brigade M G Cox's, Div, and M. G. Corps along with various other able supports were unheard of. For hand grenades, we had milk and jam tins filled with any kind of small scrap, loaded with a bursting charge, and with a fuse attachment that had to be lit with a match.

There was another elaborate sort of rig called the hair brush bomb, so called because it had a flat handle and a wee wooden box built on one side were the brush part would be in a long handled hair brush. This was lit the same way. There were generally some men behind in a dugout or shelter on fine days busy at the manufacture of these weapons.

The trenches were anywhere from 200 to 500 yards apart along this sector and the first few days I certainly took a very keen interest in bombarding anything that looked as though it would do for a target. I had a long Mk 3 Ross with an aperture sight on the receiver bridge and hooded front blade sight. It had a perfect barrel making for some wonderful shots and I enjoyed myself immensely.

As yet we took it all in good spirits and more in fun than otherwise. I remember how we used to laugh about it when Fritz occasionally spread a salvo of whiz bangs or 16 lb shells along our trench and made the sand bags fly.

I got a lesson quite early in the game that set me to thinking, leading me to temper my enthusiasm with the use of a little caution and better judgment. I had been doing a lot of target practice from one particular loophole. There was a stove pipe sticking up over the German parapet a foot or two, ordinary stove pipe. When Fritz fogged up the stove good to boil his kettle at meal time I used to slam a bullet through the pipe and Fritz would choke of the smoke right away. These sort of games went on for a couple of days until one day I had just fired two or three rounds from aforesaid favorite loop hole, got down to one side, a shade lower and was busy with the pull through cleaning my rifle-when-Crack-Snap-Crack-Snap-just like that. Two bullets came through the loophole and two came through the top of the breastwork right where my head would have been a minute before.

This was real shooting (by gum) and carried out by two real snipers working as a team. I began to watch for any well-aimed shots that came over and tried to dope out the spot they came from with the view to making a comeback that would count. We found out some months later that these snipers had all along been equipped with telescopic sights and powerful glasses for spotting us, and furthermore were organized into companies and relieved by sections in the line at regular periods. The relief coming in took over posts, information gathered and range cards of the ground on their front. The wonder is that we held our own so well and even at times got them cowed down so that some days there was scarcely a German bullet came over our lines.

Sniping was a deadly business the first two years of the war and the toll taken that way was heavy. There were a number of reasons for this. Communication trenches at that time were non-existent or at best in very poor repair and shallow. The men were comparatively new at the war game and took more foolish chances than necessary. They were often taking short cuts across open ground in daylight and in other ways exposing themselves. Three seconds exposure in daylight is time enough for a trained sniper to get in his shot. Then the new men were unnecessarily noisy when reliefs were on, careless about making smoke, showing movement and lights. All these things drew hostile fire and the sum total of loss from these causes over given periods was heavy.

This applied to both sides for there were few days that we did not have something to write into the sniping report that had to be sent in nightly. All shots were checked by an observer with a telescope that worked along side the sniper and verified hits and helped to locate targets.

Sergeant Knobel got busy as soon as we arrived on this front putting out night patrols between the opposing lines to gather information about the lay of the land, the enemy's wire entanglements, position of their listening posts and activity of their moving patrols if any.

One night while up close to the German trench in a muddy flat piece of ground covered with Indian corn stumps or stubble our patrol must have been heard or dimly seen. Perhaps the sentries fancied they heard or saw something for they began to shoot up flare lights one after another and then started to sweep the ground with machine guns. We felt we could crawl into a rat hole if one was handy. The tearing ripping sweep of these guns would come roaring and snapping over us sometimes covering us with showers of wet mud, other times passing just over our backs to rip up the mud behind. There was a lad with us by the name of Johnston of fair complexion and medium height. He served on the Fire Department Team, at the Twin Cities at the head of the lakes before the war. A German flare light shot up in a high arc and came hissing down directly on top of him and they burn with a fierce white blinding light. Any movement on our part, even the slightest move while the light burned would have betrayed our position and sealed the fate of the whole patrol. He watched it come down coolly until it appeared certain to hit him on the legs. He spread-eagled his legs without another move until the light burned out and died between his feet. I suppose we were under this fire and shower of flares for upwards of five minutes though it seemed more like 45. Our teeth were loose in their sockets from setting them together and our nails nearly cut through the palms of our hands from gripping them. Not succeeding in their efforts to find us or failing to detect any signs of movement the Germans must have concluded there was nothing there for the flares and the m. g. fire ceased and we were able to make a safe get-away.

The lines were about 500 yards apart at this point and we had to cross a swamp creek fringed with polled willows before getting back to the vicinity of our own lines. Soon after crossing the creek we saw something moving back and forth in the vicinity of our own wire. Catching a glitter of light reflecting from something. We studied this and it turned out to be a lad from our battalion who had been sent out on listening post in front. Here he was with rifle at slope, bayonet fixed pacing up and down an improvised (tow path) as large as life. We sure had a good laugh at this exhibit. It was rare.

A. Currie was in command of the 2nd Brigade at that time and asked for a detailed map of the ground on our frontage. Sergeant

Knobel ran a base line in daylight with a prismatic compass and tape among the old ruined houses and enclosures close behind our front. From this we worked forward and on into no-mans land traversing with luminous compass and tape at night. We had fixed the locations and got dimensions of all landmarks and physical features on the ground to be covered. What we could not get in this way was sketched in or located by intersection from three known points of observation in ruined houses. The position of these again was established by resection onto the original base line. We eventually turned in a map on a scale of 1 over 5000 (1/5000) and Currie got complimented for being well informed as to the ground on his part of the front line sector. This was supplemented by a series of panoramic sketches made by setting a telescope in a rest and sketching in all detail showing in its field of view. By swinging the scope the width of its field and repeating over a wide arc you could connect up with another arc sketched from the next O. P. to your flank. In this way we got a lot of detail of the German front lines that would not have otherwise been noted.

There was a patch of broad beans with high green stalks stretching from the German parapet outward toward our lines for some 75 yards. It looked like a place that might conceal a post for a m. g. a bombing post, or listening post at night. At any rate we needed it placed on our map, and I was sent out with compass and tape to locate and measure it. We worked across a creek with an old ladder used as a foot bridge, thence along a ditch marked by polled willows at intervals, till we came to the end of the last survey. A lad named Fred Barker was with me. It was too dark to see much, and there was a rise or roll in the ground in front that hid the German lines. Barker struck out on his own hook from here to try to locate the bean patch but came back unsuccessful in a short time.

The scout at this time was not equipped with a pistol, bomb or other convenient means of offence or defense in order to enable him to crawl easily and quietly through the mud, grass and pools of water. His sole companion was a long Ross with bayonet fixed. The breach and trigger mechanism soon became a solid ball of mud when worming along like an alligator through the soup. We used to squeeze a plaster of wet mud onto the bayonet in order to prevent its glitter from betraying us while in the enemy wire or in the vicinity of their flare lights. I now started off over the top of the rising ground in front, and was crawling down its far slope when a German flare showed me the outline of the bean patch across my path. I was now in dry stiff grass that seemed to make a very loud noise whenever I moved forward. Was there a post at the out end of it? I decided to listen for awhile and not hearing anything suspicious I went on to the edge of the patch lying in under the edge to listen again. I could hear someone crawling quite close. I flattened to the ground to catch the light filtering through from the far side of the patch. About 30 feet from me a German crawled past on his way to his own lines. I was uncertain as to how many more were at the point he crawled from, so I did mighty little moving and a lot of listening for a few minutes then went on to its end, took its width, and later its bearing with compass from the top of the rise in the ground I had passed on the outward trip. I often wondered if this was the first close contact of Canuck and German in the field. I know it was for the 1st Division but probably some of the Princess Pats had an earlier contact.

Fritz used to use search lights in those days to sweep our lines at night and the ground in front. These lights were mounted on an affair like an extension ladder used by city fire departments. This in turn was mounted on a small truck that ran on a narrow-gauge rail track following the course of his communication trenches. If a shell landed close to this outfit he could telescope the extension ladder affair and hurry the whole works by rail to a safer spot.

The night following my trip to the bean patch was wet with a fine drizzle of cold rain. Knobel planned to make a long patrol led by himself. Two nights before we had placed a ladder across the creek about 100 yards from our front. This had been used as a bridge for two nights. Some of us had suggested that it be removed each night after using it so that it, and the path across, would not show up to the aero planes in daytime and give away our line of travel, but this had not been done. Now on the third night we had just got nicely over and started along the old ditch when we heard a noise ahead. A large stone or lump of mud fell into the ditch with a splash and following this we could hear the clump, clump, and swish, swish in the grass as someone hurried away from there. Somebody was evidently watching our bridge for a purpose. We carefully crept forward a bit to where we could get the light showing over higher ground on each side and in front. On this work you hug the low places and any movement can be detected in the light at the skyline around you. We began to size things up. On either flank as far as you could see there was the usual amount of night rifle fire by the sentries and the usual amount of flare lights rising and falling. But in the section occupied by the cabbage patch or bean patch there was neither night firing or flares. Only silence, darkness and a thickening drizzle of rain. Then the search light started to sweep back and forth, away to the north back on the south, but it always paused for a space when it came to our sally port in the wire and our ladder bridge over the creek. We put two and two together deciding that the big German patrol that was in ambush for us that night could have the rain all to themselves and we went elsewhere that night.

Later on we lost one of our scouts by rifle fire while out on the left flank of our battalion on night patrol. Our left flank was in what they call a re-entrant or a deep concavity in our line and the unit next on our left had somewhat of an enfilade view of our left sector. I believe it was the 7th Battalion in there at that time. We had notified platoon commanders and sentry groups of the patrol but through some mistake the post of the 7th opened fire on us and W. Naylor one of our number, was hit in the groin by a rifle ball and due to the severity of the wound died a few hours later.

I got a taste of shellfire here one day at the time of the battle of Neuve Chapelle or the (Blunder of Neuve Chapelle). The Imperial troops at that point were to make a frontal attack on the German line and if successful in getting forward, we were also to follow it up and roll up the part of the line to the left of them on our front. During their attack we were busy putting over rapid rifle fire thickened up by our colt m. g. along with the 13 pounders and the lone 60 pounder. The attack at Neuve Chapelle fizzled out against great odds in artillery and other arms and we came in for reprisals from Fritz in the shape of shellfire from his field batteries. I was in the south end of a trench bay next to a traverse and in the opposite end of the bay was a man named Peacock. Both of us were plugging away at rapid fire as per instructions. Peacock was taking aim through a loop hole with his finger on the trigger when a shell took away the whole of the breastwork between us. I got a wallop on the back of the neck with a sandbag half full of hard-baked clay that could give points to Jack Dempsey. When I got the mud out of my eyes and things started to clear so I could see, there was Peacock's rifle still in its place in the loophole but with the bolt full back open, only half of the loophole was there and none of the breastwork to the right of it. Peacock presently came running around the traverse on hands and knees at a good speed in a very dazed and shaken-up condition from concussion. There was a man about 15 feet behind us who had been stooped down to go into a small dugout entrance.

A sandbag full of hard clay hit him in the stern and drove him in head-first nearly breaking his neck. We were beginning to get a light taste of what was in store for us over the next three years as a steady and daily diet. We had several casualties. I think the total was about 18 in this unit.

We will leave the night prowling now for a bit, and follow the doings of observers and snipers in the daylight hours. Our first eight days on the line completed we went back in billets in reserve for a few days at the town of Estaires, roughly about eight miles to the rear.

From here, we of the scouts took our lunch with us in the morning and mounting bicycles, rode back to our old sector in the front line to snipe and do observation work during the daylight hours. There was an old pinnacle, a fragment of a convent tower that had stood just behind where our front line now was and near the right flank. Into the chinks and mortar on the west side of this we drove spikes and to these attached ropes and hung a ladder up which one could climb to the top of the slab of wall. The part left standing was perhaps 10 or 12 feet wide and 35 to 40 feet high. On the top of this there lay some loose brick and these we arranged as a head cover to screen us from the enemy and form a rest for a telescope while taking observations. A long and lanky sandy-complexioned kind of guy by the name of Carson was detailed along with me to climb up and continue the work started on the telescopic panorama. There was a raw March wind, blowing quite hard, and the top of the old unsupported slab of wall wavered and trembled so that the quiver of the telescope lens made it hard to distinguish detail at all. My eyes ran water with the cold and ones hands got so numb in a few minutes it was impossible to control a pencil. We had no assurance that we could not be seen from distant points on the flanks due to the curvature in the front lines. We spent part of two days sketching from there and were not troubled by rifle or shell fire though we did a lot of moving up or down to relieve one another on account of the cold. Knobel went up there the next day and he was fired on so he decided not to use that o. p. for a little while at least. We had several other observation posts in ruined houses along our front. We used to snipe from the same places too. In one of these the upstairs floor had been blown out by shell explosions all accept a small section in the n-e corner up under the eaves. In this corner we had our o. p. and sniping post. The sills or girders of the top floor were still there and to one of these we attached a rope, which hung down to the entrance of the wine cellar in the basement. These old French and Belgian wine cellars were built strong, and deep, with arched or vaulted roofs, and were very seldom smashed in by shellfire from the lighter class of guns. At our roost under the eaves we would hold forth and snipe etc. Fritz got suspicious then whizz-bang!! Over he would send a couple or three shells. We would run across the floor girders, slide down the rope and into the cellar. Of course the first shells had done their worst long before we got to the cellar but we took pot luck on them out of necessity. From this point we located a couple of enemy m. g. emplacements, also a (strong point) or sort of redoubt that was being incorporated, and built into their front trench at a salient in their line and from this fortified emplacement they could bring enfilade fire to bear both right and left along no-mans-land.

These we located on the map by intersection of compass bearings and they were shelled by our artillery.

From the o. p. described on the last page we got some long range rifle shooting one morning. It was one of those still spring days without a breath of air stirring, no bright sunlight, an overcast sky but air very clear. An artillery observer would describe it as a high visibility day. A couple of observers had been studying the country behind the German line. About 1100 hundred yards from us we could see a house standing broadside with a road stretching away to the east beyond. This road passed by the south end or gable end of the house. In the side facing us were a door and two windows. They had noted some Germans going in or out of the door and standing around outside quite unconcerned. It was quite evident that this place had not been subject to either rifle fire or m. g. fire and Fritz was quite at home there. I think it must have been a quarter masters stores or its equivalent in German.

The observers sent for me and we decided to try a shot at Fritz. I picked out a spot in the middle of the tile roof that faced us for a target. We wanted to register and make sure we had the range perfectly before trying to snipe at that distance. My first shot broke a tile and with the telescope the observers saw the pieces slide down to the eaves dropping to the earth. We had the range to a hair and the lateral was perfect. If the Fritzes noted the shot at all, they probably took it for a stray bullet.

At the right corner of the house wall and about shoulder high there was a white patch as though somebody had cleaned a paint brush on the corner of the wall. I used this as an aiming mark, got the rifle bedded down comfortably in a sandbag rest and waited. Presently the observers said there was a man coming around the house from the back. He came toward us along the south gable. I waited until he was in line with the house corner and the white spot and fired. He staggered out to the right about 15 feet, fell and lay there. Another man came out and I shot him also. This one appeared to be dead but the first one still moved. In a little while a wagon came down the road at a gallop and swung in behind the house. Two men with a stretcher removed the first man shot. We did not fire any more shots then but after a while we decided to put some rapid fire through the door and windows, and along the roof about two feet above the eaves. We did this, but on after-thought, it was a foolish move for it told them that the shots were not strays or accidental and put them on their guard. Also it betrayed our sniping post badly. A cold-blooded recital of a typical incident exactly as it occurred (Confirming Sherman in his name for war).

We had another post off to the right flank and one day there were three of the boys aloft in it when Fritz put 12 shells into it, but the boys escaped with only scratches.

Estaires was a pretty little town, but it was destroyed by the Germans during their big drive in the spring of 1918. During the time we were billeted there he bombed it with an aero plane. There was a fat old cook who did the honors for the officer's mess. He had his cook house in a shed or outbuilding. When the plane came over there was a transport wagon standing in the cook house. A bomb dropped there and the roof fell down on top of the transport wagon. The wagon being there saved the cook's life.

We were not getting enough exercise so while we were here Knobel took us out through the country on forced marches to keep us in trim. We had to make a road report of each trip giving details of everything en route. That Knobel was a wonder. He could march at a fast clip through a town, and then sit down drawing a perfect map with the names of all the streets, principal buildings, squares etc. together with a hundred and one other details that we did not notice at all.

At La Saillee we met a troop of Bengal Lancers and I never expect to see finer looking mounted troops. They were a treat to see and a thing of beauty. These Bengalis were a part of the Army of India, some portion of which had been in the line to our right.

The Gurkhas or Gurcas a hill tribe, looking like Japanese only heavier built, had been next to us in the line for a short time. Their patrols were out next to us at night, and it was a creepy sensation when alone and expecting to encounter some of them. They were like tiger cats at that kind of work, and as, silent, swift and deadly. They went armed with a kuri (big knife) of different sizes and weights. The heaviest knife weighed seven lbs, and was close to two feet long with most of the weight well out toward the point.

They could flatten themselves blending into the ground or shrubbery and snip off a man's head so quick he wouldn't know it unless he happened to shake his head. There were some tall stories going the rounds about doings at night along the front. In their case however truth was stranger than fiction. I know of an authentic case that occurred just to our right.

The Gurkha scout had noted the head of a German sentry over the parapet at night. Like a jungle cat he slipped through, and under the wire and flattened himself against the sandbags of the enemy breastwork directly in front of that sentry. At intervals he would reach up with one hand and make a tap-tapping noise on the baked clay. After awhile the sentry got curious no doubt thinking of a rat or stoat and stretched forward to see what was making that peculiar noise–Zip. Away went his head and it was brought back as a trophy or souvenir. These were great troops in an attack.

As long as they could see the enemy and had something definite to fight they were fearless fighters. The difficulty was to control them. They forgot all about schedules and time limits. They would keep on and on and then get all cut to pieces with their own barrage fire. At close quarters they would ditch their Enfield and bayonet and wade in with the big knife. They would seize the enemy's bayonet with their left hand and slash off his head with the right. It became necessary to equip them with a heavy gauntlet glove for the left hand, as the dressing stations were full of them after a fight all wounded in that way.

On one of our route marches and road patrols we had an experience with a German spy. We, of the scout section in charge of Knobel were out on our own, marching south on a road running parallel to the front line system and about a mile to the rear of it. Here we met a tall man walking north. He was dressed up as though he had just stepped off one of the main boulevards of Paris. A spotless black suit and tall tile hat, gloves and walking stick, a regular fashion model. This looked a little peculiar to say the least for you never saw anyone dressed to that degree in country that close to the front lines. He walked with the stiff necked straightness of a military officer, and in his case, the clothes were a very thin disguise of the soldier underneath.

He had his mustache twisted out to two needle points as affected by some French gentry. He eyed us as we went by. Two of us sized him up then as worthy of investigation, but the sergeant said he did not want to make a foolish mistake and passed him up. He only got a short way down the road when some artillery men held him up and sure enough, he was an enemy officer spy. He had overdone the dressing part. I suppose he was going by pre-war standards and did not realize he was so conspicuous in his elaborate toilette and high tile.

There was another spy case while we were on this part of the front that seemed like a fairy tale so strange it was. At Labutillerie, as before stated, we had a couple of batteries of horse artillery concealed in the hedge rows a few hundred yards behind our front lines. Immediately in their vicinity there still lived an old farmer of Flemish or ex-German nationality. He still tilled his little fields enclosed by their thorn hedges.

He was the owner of an old white horse, a white cow and also an aged wife. The batteries were concealed on the margins of his estate in willow clumps and hedgerows.

Some of the gunners complained that the old man would take his white cow on fine days when the visibility was good and, leading it on a long rope would get directly in front of the gun position running his cow around in circles.

This they claimed was done in front of different gun positions and soon after that the guns were shelled by the enemy. He also pulled off something of the sort with the old white horse for variation I suppose. Not much attention was paid to these tales however. It was also reported that smoke signals or smoke puffs were sent up from his chimney after the manner used by the Red Indians and some of the Zulu tribes in Rhodesia. These they claimed were unmistakably signals and worked out in a code.

On account of all these rumors Sgt. Knobel was sent one day to interview the old couple. They told him they were terrified by the shell fire, and that they had been burning incense, offering up prayers for their safety and this accounted for the smoke. They succeeded in convincing Knobel that they were quite innocent and a harmless old couple he so stated.

There had been some men of our unit sniped and shot at behind our front lines. An officer of one of our units took it on himself to watch the old man one day as he was working up and down the east side of a thorn hedge with the old horse and a harrow. From concealment he saw the old man snatch a rifle from under a coat or blanket on top of the harrow and shot at somebody on the road winding away westward between the hedges. The officer shot the old man without further parley.

Then there was hustling around to find more evidence of the sniping business. I was one of the search party and climbed up to the garret loft of a barn that stood length wise of the road and had a round ventilator hole in the peak of the west gable. Standing on the attic floor behind this ventilator hole was a tall round topped stool such as you see in a restaurant at home at the quick lunch counters. On the floor at the bottom of this stool was a heap of empty rifle cartridge cases, some dozens in all. This sniping business must have been going on intermittently over quite a long period.

The very unlikelihood of the thing was its screen that had enabled it to go on so long. I suppose the casualties were put down to stray bullets.

Death Valley

In the early part of April we were moved from this sector, heading north eventually arriving at Poperinge, about eight miles south-west of the City of Ypres. From here we were sent north again marching through Ypres when it was still full of civilians carrying on the life of a city. Men, women and children crowded out to cheer us on as we marched through. Some of the finer buildings were still standing including the Cloth Hall. Part of it had been shelled badly however, I can remember a large roofless room with elaborate frescoes or wall decorations.

Fritz had been dropping some heavy howitzer shells into the town in the neighborhood of the square. Here I saw a shell hole that included in its diameter the whole width of a main street and a row of houses. I was told that this hole was made by one of the big berthas or 17 inch skoda howitzers. While we were passing through he was shelling the city with 11 inch howitzers. These shells made a terrific roar during their high arc through the sky sounding like death itself made vocal when they started on their downward plunge toward you from out of the skies. Something like a heavy express train passing at speed through a tunnel. The ground literally rocked from the force of their bursting.

When we came next through this town it was a crumpled ruin, void of all civilian life, and a charnel house of riddled corpses, and heaped up brick and stone. We still tramped away to the north getting out in the dismal flat swampy country to the east of Passchendaele. Here we were to take over a section of line from the French. We began to meet the Frenchmen coming out long before we got near our objective. I had a trip into the front line sector on some message and immediately on returning I was nailed to act as guide to two companies back over the same ground. I must have been exhausted from all the hiking to and fro under full equipment, for that trip seems very hazy in my memory and more like a nightmare than a reality.

I had not gathered much knowledge of the lay of the land the first trip up and was really hazy as to my location now, for the night had shut down as black as ink and there was a deadly monotony or sameness about all the crossroads with a total absence of anything in the way of landmarks. In addition to this I was being heckled by some upstart of a junior officer. You're a scout aren't you? Why don't you know this and why don't you know that, Blankety, Blank-Blank etc–and so on. It came to a clash of opinions at last. He wanting to go his way and I determined to go mine. Another officer by the name of Lieut. Durant struck his spoon into the soup and agreed to follow me. Eventually we got into country with no roads, and only slippery foot paths meandering over flat low grass land. I was staking all on a sort of Indian instinct of direction and location by this time for all other guidance was useless. As far as the map and compass were concerned I was going from no—place to no—where and had nothing to start from. I landed eventually among some dilapidated trenches filled with water. The earth thrown out of these formed a zigzag slippery ridge which we used in the pitch dark as a foot path. I eventually recognized a trench junction I had seen earlier in the evening and heaved a great sigh of relief for I had been right from the start. This French outfit was supposed to have guides posted to meet and guide us into our proper sections of the line. They did not furnish any and we had to locate ourselves as best we could, straightening things out the next morning.

This was a hard looking piece of front line when we were able to see around a bit in the morning. The trench was in a very filthy and unsanitary condition. There were no provisions what ever for sanitation and in addition to this the dead had been left all over the place. Their legs sticking through the parapet. Dead were in the bottom of the trench with only a very thin sprinkling of earth over them. Out in front you could see them lying all over the place, both French and German. Phil McDonald was put on sentry duty in the front trench as soon as we got in. All night at his post he smelled a powerful smell. Daylight showed that he was leaning against the soles of a big pair of German boots built into the parapet. The owner of the boots was built in too. Paddy Reill crawled into a small dugout shelter to snatch a bit of sleep during the night and woke up to find he was using a corpse for a bedmate and pillow.

Lieut. Durand, a fine big fellow, in command of one of our platoons had a little sawed-off batman of cockney vintage. Durand was big and strong but several times on the long and hard march up here he had hitched and shifted his pack finding it heavy. Lo! and behold the Wee Batman had stuffed it full of his own belongings, including some choice souvenirs such as shell noses etc. Durand had lugged it all the way.

These Frenchmen must have been a lazy lot for the breastwork along here was very low, only one bag thick and patched up in the most slipshod manner imaginable. A 22 caliber rifle could have put a ball through it any place. The ground was too wet to dig down lower, and at any rate it was so full of filth digging it would have been almost impossible. There were no support trenches in the rear and God knows what would have happened in case of an attack. This place was known as Death Valley, it appeared to be well-named judging by the number of dead lying in it. It was a big wide depression in the plain with higher ground all around gently sloping into the bottom.

Directly on our front and stretching away for a couple of miles to the west was a long bare treeless ridge with its highest point about two and one half miles away and half mile on the left quarter. We were to get a closer acquaintance with the bare ridge off to the left a couple of years later. It was the Hill of Passchendaele. Our front line was at the bottom and following the base of some slightly rising ground along the south side of the valley. The bottom of the valley was flat, quite low, and wet in places. Opposite our right flank and at the far side of the flat was a straggling wood lot or bush. The German front line showed along the front of this, but was not occupied in full strength on account of it being too low and wet. Their main line followed the base of the hill further back and somewhat behind the woods. There was a re-entrant in their line about opposite to our centre, and here the lines must have been upward of 600 yards apart for some distance.

There were flares shot up from the German trench at night where it passed along the front of the wood lot, but studying it through the day we were of the opinion that these flares were only a bluff to give the impression that it was held in strength. To make sure of this we made a patrol at night, went over to this trench traveling along it for about eight bays without encountering any Germans. It was evidently only occupied at night in spots by patrols that shot up the flares we had seen. In the course of this patrol we came upon what had been a French outpost of eight men placed out in front of our right flank and facing the woods. This patrol or outpost had gone to sleep on duty one night. A German patrol came along and heard them snoring, crept up and bayoneted the lot. We had heard a rumor of this from the French and sure enough there they were, just as they had been left. Further to the left and in an open piece of ground we came on three Frenchmen in three separate shallow holes that they had tried to scoop out. They were about 15 feet apart and all facing the German lines. They looked so life like when we came upon them that we were startled and thought for a moment that it was an enemy patrol playing possum. They had evidently been caught in the open and tried to dig in but were killed before they could accomplish this. The whole valley was like this, and the night winds whispered over the dead in gusts and sighs , plucking away at their sleeves and moaning away among the willows along the water courses.

There was a ruined farm well out in the valley about 150 yards from the German line and approximately 400 yards from our lines. There had been several buildings in that location now mostly in ruins. What had been the dwelling house was still partly standing. The gable end toward our lines was still intact, but the opposite one had been blown down with the slate and tile roof sagging down on the upstairs floor. You could get in below, climb the rickety stair, getting in between the sagged tile roof and the standing gable, have a clear view of the enemy lines over a wide front. You had no real protection from rifle or machine gun fire but had good concealment and could look out between the slats and tiles of the sagged roof. Our O. C. wanted us to make frequent patrols to this place for fear Fritz might occupy it or fortify it with earth works making a strong point of it or a machine gun post to be later connected with his front line trench by saps constructed at night.

I wanted to study the enemy lines here, doing a bit of sketching, also trying to locate his machine gun and trench mortar positions, and try to get compass bearings and intersections on them where possible.

Another scout by the name of Closett went with me one morning before day break and we reconnoitered the place eventually getting up under the sagged roof staying there all day as the valley was exposed, so any movement during daytime was sure to draw enemy fire. We took a bit of lunch and a bottle of water each. There had been a lot of live stock killed here laying all over in the enclosure around the buildings. Cows, pigs, horses , even dogs and cats and they also were all swollen up like balloons. The early April sun came out very hot and sultry beating down in that valley like a July day. Occasionally there would come a slight puff or breeze bringing the smells that we had to survive that day.

It was strong point alright. Directly in front at about150 yards was the enemy front trench. They had evidently tried to take the farm from the French sometime earlier. There in the hay field out front lay about 40 dead, lying in even rows on their faces like nine pins that had been knocked down in a bowling alley. They had full packs on their backs and were dressed in all the glory of the Prussian Army of 1914. Field grey from the tips of their toes to the top of the spikes on their helmets. They had dug a sap out some distance from the main trench using this as a jumping off point for the attack on the farm. Evidently the French had a concealed machine gun at the farm. There was about a dozen dead French out there also but somewhat closer to the farm house. How they met their fate I could not figure out, but there they lay in their spotless horizon blue uniforms. In the course of the afternoon one of our co. commanders got an idea in his bonnet to make a patrol working his way out there by following ditches shrubbery etc. taking about six men with him. I heard footsteps below on the gravel and broken tiles, and for a minute I did not know who it was. Closett took a sort of panic attack wanting to rush down and out with a lot of clatter which may have betrayed our presence. I had a job to hold him quit. A moment later I heard voices and I knew it was some of our men. I sat tight and let them away for I was not pleased with their stunt of exposing themselves and drawing the German's attention to the farm.

They were spotted alright and Fritz opened up with a splatter of rifle fire on them. They made off the way they had come and back to our lines.

When they got in they reported us two scouts as missing, believed captured, or killed. A lad from Kenora went down to hospital that day with a wound in his hand and while there wrote home about me going missing etc. My obituary came out in the home paper. I met the man that wrote it some months later up at Bulford Camp on the Messines Front. It was Billy Mitchell or (Slim Mitchell) and he still thought I was among the Angels.

We got down out of the loft about an hour after that patrol went back as it was sort of a trap up there with only one way of exiting and I was expecting a visit from Fritz for sure, now that the over-ambitious Capt. had advertised the farm. We had arranged for Corp. Gray and six men to come out that night after dark and relieve us acting as a listening post at the farm. Ten o'clock came and no patrol yet. I was just going to send Closett into our lines to see why, when I heard a noise in the orchard enclosure in front toward the enemy line. We had taken up a position in the rubbish at the centre of the farm court or enclosure flanked on three sides by the ruins. The whole place was enclosed by a thorn hedge with an orchard on the German side. Straight behind us was a gateway in the hedge. I could hear quite a large number of men moving about. They were whispering among themselves and finally started to encircle the hedge. I could hear them crawling outside the hedge in front and on both sides of us. I thought we had stayed long enough so poked Closett in the ribs and said go! We ran for the open gate behind, which was probably 50 yards away. There were broken tiles, brick, glass, and other rubbish under foot. We made quit a clatter as we broke cover. Before we got through the gateway fritz shot up a flare light from the orchard. We heard the putt and hiss of the flare going up and flopped flat, laying still until it burned out, when we were up running again. From the gate we ran about 80 yards to the left where there was a sort of embankment or terrace under a thorn hedge. We flopped behind this and peering through the hedge listened for awhile.

Then I happened to think about Corp. Gray and his six men. They might walk, unsuspecting right into the big German patrol, which I knew, must be at least 20 or 30 strong. I sent Closett back on the run and he was in time to intercept them just as they were coming out to look for us.

They came out quietly to where I distributed them along the low side of the terrace. Orders were to start nothing rough but to make sure that the enemy did not attempt to fortify the farm. I went back to the lines soon for I had been out for over 18 hours and was tired, hungry, thirsty etc. The enemy patrol prowled about examining the place quietly and then made off without disturbing anything. I had often thought that if our officers had hurried a big patrol out, there working in from a flank quickly, they might have captured the lot.

In addition to all the dead cattle and pigs in that valley there were two or three live hogs roving about. We saw a huge white one mooching along at the front of the enemy trench at the edge of the woods one morning. Fred Barker shot it. We had found evidence while we were out on patrol, that these hogs were living off the bodies of the dead.

One morning after being on night patrol and feeling the need of a sleep we crawled out a few feet back of the breastworks and lay in the sun for a nap on a smooth patch of the hard baked clay. I think it was Corp. Gray and myself along with a couple of others. This spot must have been visible to an observer on the higher ridge back of the German lines for we were rudely awakened by a couple of small shells bursting right alongside us. I could reach over and touch the edge of the nearest hole. The shells were too small and slow traveling to be whiz bangs, nor they did not seem like trench mortars.

The little Cockney Batman before mentioned developed a sort of ghoulish tendency while we were in this part of the front. He started to pry teeth from the skulls of the enemy dead and collect other beautiful trinkets which he kept for souvenirs. I suppose his officer had to carry them too when they marched.

Things remained quiet here during are stay in Death Valley, and there were no outstanding events that I can recall now. I don't know what unit held this part of the line when the big German drive started for Calais a week later. They must have had an unpleasant time unless there were new trenches dug further back during the intervening week before the big smash. The warm spring weather was rapidly ripening things on that valley. From that place we were moved to the left marching up the line again through St. Jean and St. Julien, then finally on down a long gentle slope to the bottom of another valley. Here again the ground was too wet for trenches and breastworks had been built instead.

St. Julien

The breastwork on our battalion frontage was not continuous but was built in sections with spaces in between that were innocent of any defense. In going from one section to another you hurried across the open. On our right there was a gap in the line 500 yards wide very low, and wet with a small stream in the centre. This stream had a fringe of polled willow stumps and small scrub along its course. On our left the line swung back a bit and formed a sort of re-entrant. There was a battalion of Canadian Kilties holding this sector. I think it was the 5th Battalion on our right at the far side of the 500 yard gap. The breastworks here were in better shape and there were some support trenches of a sort close behind. There was a low almost imperceptible ridge on our front, and from our centre to the right, the ground also rose ever so slightly for about 400 yards ahead. There you could see the enemy's earthworks that appeared to be on slightly drier ground as usual. There was a slight salient there in the German line along this swelling of the ground. This part of their line appeared to be strongly trenched and it was from here that they let loose their first great gas attack on us. It was discharged from reservoirs or cylinders and wafted across on a slow sluggish breeze.

Col. Lipsett was a very energetic sort of commander wanting to be very thoroughly informed about every thing on his part of the front. Sgt. Knobel was a twin brother of his as far as energy went. They certainly kept us scouts on the jump day and night. Every foot of a new frontage had to be gone over, right up and into the enemy's wire and in some cases into his trench.

We were out practically all night every night here and then on sniping and observation work during the daylight. There was a small cottage still standing on the crest of the low ridge opposite our right flank, close up against the enemy parapet and well inside his wire. Lipsett ordered that we investigate this building. We made a preliminary patrol or two to size things up getting the lay of the land. The nights had turned still and rather cold with a white blanket of mist verging on frost lying in a shroud in all the low sags and along the water courses. About the first night in we stripped off all unnecessary clothing to make crawling easier. We went up a long drainage ditch that angled off straight as an arrow from the close vicinity of the cottage mentioned above. This was touchy work for an enemy could look down the whole length of that ditch and shoot down it very nicely with a machine gun. It had been dug through the wet clay and the sides sloped up at about 45 degrees on both sides. There was a stream in the bottom about three feet wide. We went up this bit by bit flattening into the mud when a flare rose or when a chunk of mud or a rock dislodged and went splashing into the water. Getting up within a few yards of the cottage we saw and heard a great deal of activity going on. There appeared to be scores of men working at something. They were sawing, hammering pounding and digging all the time talking like 300 Quebec Frenchmen.

We gathered one bit of information from watching and listening to the forward part of the gang. They were making movable sally ports to put through their wire entanglements. They were making an arrangement something like a saw horse in form, only much higher and longer, to be strung with a network of barbed wire. Then a zigzag road is cut through the main mass of wire entanglements, and these horses are set in these opening to let their troops pass out through the wire to the attack. They were installed in a zigzag fashion so they would not be readily detected.

On returning from the drainage ditch I was detailed to go on a listening post with another victim for the balance of the night. The post was at the creek at the centre of the 500 yard gap on our right flank. I was unable to go to get any heavier clothing, so I spent a very cold, and exceedingly miserable time trying to shiver myself warm till daylight, watching and listening in the blanket of mist along the water course. It is a penetrating sort of cold in that country on an early spring morning before dawn which gets into the very marrow of your bones in a very different way than the dry crisp cold of Canada.

I could hear railway trains pulling in from the north and east behind the enemy lines all that night. Bands were playing with their drums beating as the troops detrained and marched away. We heard this same thing every night right up to the day of the big attack and reported same to our officers. We were supposed to be in this sector four days and then be relieved by some other unit. The four days came and went with no sign of the relief troops. The enemy shell fire gradually got heavier as the days went on. We who had seen the sally-ports being made, heard the troop trains pouring in day and night for a week or so knew that we were in for it hot and heavy. Every thing pointed that way. Our battalion transport had been shelled and broken up on the St. Julien road. For the last four days of that battle we had very little, if any, food or water. We got a dose of combined teargas and chlorine gas on very empty stomachs which no doubt contributed to the number of deaths from gas. With food in our stomachs it would not have gotten such a quick and deadly hold and we would have vomited some of it out. The enemy artillery fire got very heavy during the last two days and we were well tied down to hugging what little shelter was left us. This was mostly the sections of breastwork that were braced or supported at a traverse. Most of the unsupported parts were all gone or nearly so. Shrapnel and high explosive shells were well mixed with mustard or tear gas shells especially through the night proceeding the attack by chlorine gas. This tear gas inflamed the lungs, throat, nostrils, and eyes until we were nearly blind even before the chlorine came over at all. Towards midday of the day before the assault I began to see by evidence all around me that I would have to strengthen the shelter at that place if I hoped to live much longer in the storm of shells. I worked all that afternoon and by piling up bags etc. made an embankment that was still more or less intact when we left that place later on. I know I would not have survived in that spot without the extra bit of shelter that instinct told me to build at that time. The Germans started to enfilade our section of the trench with a gun battery somewhere to the north and were doing great damage with this fire.

Knobel, our scout sergeant, had established an observation post in an old building close behind our front lines. He had us scouts hunting the country-side the night before for a ladder to put up behind the wall of this old building so he could get up to a shell hole he wanted to look from. We could not find a ladder but ripped a set of stairs out of a house about half a mile back carrying it bodily down there and putting it up for his O. P. He knew what he was driving at too. He was after the observer that was directing that enfilading enemy battery and he located him, watching him in the act of using a field telephone to the battery. After having gauged the map location correctly, our lone 18 pounder put a shell directly on him and then the enfilading stopped for awhile.

Just before daylight on the night we carried the stair-case we went to another old farm close behind our supports and lit a bonfire that would smoke, and smudge, and smolder for hours. The Germans took it for a cooking fire of troops in support plunking shells into that spot all day, and that was so many shells that never killed anyone.

The morning that we did all this I got very hungry from doing much hustling around the country, and seeing a fairly good looking tin of bullybeef sticking out of the mud, I nailed it, opened it, and ate part of it getting poisoned and was so sick I rolled on the ground with the pain. I don't know if ptomaine poisoning is an antidote for chlorine or not but I had my full share of both and am still able to tell about it.

There was a corporal by the name of Harris who was armourer in our company and did any small repairs on rifles etc. He was a fine fellow and the afternoon before the gas attack he and I lay together behind the strengthened spot in the breastwork while a hundred kinds of scientific death smashed down, shrieking, roaring, crashing and rattling about our ears. He had a premonition that his hour was at hand and talked quietly about it. He showed me a picture of his wife and their two little children, a sweet looking trio they were too. It must have been a hard thing for him looking at them there and then. I saw him dying of gas poisoning the next day.

There was a peculiar thing happened to us as we sheltered behind that pile of heaped sand bags. A string of enemy shells pumped one after another into the front and base of that double traverse, until we counted 12 that drove in, repeatedly we could feel the heave and bulge of the earth in front of us and below, without a live shell in the whole lot. The fuse setter must have been a casualty on that gun for awhile, or our Guardian Angel was on the job, and we were not to be blown up that day. Every little while fritz would sweep the breaches and torn spots in our defense with savage bursts of machine gun fire. We of course on our side were not able to make much comeback to all this for we had practically no artillery at all and we were trying to save as many men and scanty machine guns as we could for the hour of assault that we knew was not far away. The day wore on with the night shell fire never ceasing although there were more mustard gas shells and less H. E. during the night. I remember we got so exhausted mentally and physically that we felt as though we were suspended with some sort of wire. There were pauses two or three times in the tornado of fire, that came suddenly, with every gun pausing at once. In those moments of sudden stillness we would drop and slump down into sleep in a second of time, and our heads would fall on our breasts as one man. It was as though we were strung on a taut wire and somebody had cut that wire. Gray light of another morning with the shell fire dribbling off gradually to a desultory fire lessening as though they had exhausted themselves with a long drawn out excess of hate and fury. We must have stolen a few odd winks of sleep during this gray hour just before dawn, for we were awake now and peering toward the enemy line through the misty light for this is the favorite hour for an assault when the light is too poor for the defense to shoot accurately, but not too dark for the attackers to make their way over the ground fairly well. We strained our eyes through the swollen up puffed slits that served us for eye lids. The tear gas had not left us with much in the way of clear vision by now.

We saw what looked like a whitish wall of smoke about 15 feet high all across the enemy front. The word snapped along the line. We thought they were going to come over behind a smoke screen. We watched it coming slowly across, and when it was about half way we opened rifle fire into it for we figured the enemy would be forming for the attack behind the smoke screen. We wanted to get the lead flying into them as soon as they were out of their trenches. That smoky wall moved nearer and when it got close you could see it was not white at all but a dirty yellow toward the top, shading from that to green down next to the ground. It seemed to hug the earth running and flowing thickly into every low place and follow depressions in the ground. It was thick near the earth and progressively thinner towards its crest. We manned what was left of our defenses pouring lead into that smoky wall, then it was over our trench, and among us, and we knew it was no smoke screen. We began to choke and strangle with it, asking one another what in Hell this could be, when a tornado of machine gun, rifle, and shell fire swept down on us again to hold us close to the ground so we would get the full benefit of the gas treatment. The poison did not take immediate effect except in a couple of cases and these two men had been old dope addicts. During their travels in France, they had secured some more of the cocaine or (snow) or what ever it was that they used to light up on and had started playing with it again. When the chlorine hit them they only lasted a very short time, then snuffed out like candles. I am rather hazy about some of the details but it must have been nearly an hour before some of the men started to show yellowish foam from the mouth and nostrils, then beginning to double up in the throws of strangulation exactly as one drowning. All through that day and on into the next they kept dropping off. It was not so bad if one could keep still and quiet and not go in for any exertion, or movement or deep breathing. As soon as one moved about the foam, boiled up through your throat and nostrils choking you off. We would lie flat on our faces holding onto grass or anything to steady us till the spasms passed and we could get our breath again. Excitement under these kind of conditions accounted for a lot of deaths by strangulation.

When fritz thought that his medical treatment had sufficient time to work he made one final shower of machine gun fire and shrapnel, then they started to come over to what he evidently thought was a place of the dead. I could see them popping up over their trench in hundreds and then down into a slight sag close in front. The old Mark 3 Ross had a sight on the bridge that folded down, and when down a course notch in the top of it giving a point blank range of 600 yards. The adjustable peep sight was useless to us now owing to the condition of our eyes as a result of mustard or tear gas. We used the old open battle-sight aiming a bit low and there were a good many Germans that fell back into the trench instead of jumping down in front for the start across. The first attack got most of the way across. You could see the officers pointing directions to this and that and machine gun crews trying to set up tripod guns so they could return our fire. In that first advance some stragglers got within about 30 yards of us, and there, were drilled full of holes.

Our rifles were coated with a thick furry coat of red rust from the action of the gas. All metal parts first turned a sort of pink or lavender, then changed from that to green, then black, and finally to red rust in a thick coat over all the working parts. They become stiff and hard to work and no small wonder. We would drop the butt to the ground and kick the bolt open with a foot. The straight pull action made this possible. As long as the bolt handle held out you could still do business at the old stand and did. I had four rifles I had collected. There were plenty of spares now. I used these four alternately all that day and some times they were all pretty warm. In addition to the three advances that fritz made against our battalion front there was a long unbroken string of enemy troops passing through the valley to our left at about 600 yards distance. From the apex of A Company's position I could bring fire on that procession and did not waste any time, but kept at it with all the cartridges I could rustle. There were a lot of discarded cloth bandoliers full of shells lying about in the mud and in odd corners. These we dug out cleaning them off enough to get them through the rifle. They were perfectly good shells too, not a misfire in the lot.

Lieutenant Durand was in command of the position on the left. Wounded in four places he kept at it keeping his platoon right up to scratch. I could tell by the volume of their fire that they were making hay on that endless line of Bavarians that trailed past through the valley to our left like a caribou herd around the east end of Lake Athabaska. Some of those heinies walked as though they were drunk or doped with something. If you ever saw a drunk they too break into a run, and noted the hard bumpy way that his heels strike the ground, as though they could not gauge the distance to earth. That is the way they ran, and at the same time they kept up a sort of monotonous chant while blowing intermittently on some sort of hoarse sounding horn that reminded me of the old conch shells they used in Nova Scotia to call the workmen for dinner. I was told that this horn was a national relic of Bavaria handed down through generations of warriors way back to the time of Attila The Hun and had sounded over many a field of slaughter.

Durand began to worry about his supply of ammunition and sent corp. Pozer a native of Quebec over to our section of trench to see if there was anybody with lungs still working good enough to pack ammunition across to his platoon. Pozer came to me and asked if I would go. I went along with somebody else, I don't remember who, and being too weak to handle a case we ripped the cases open taking as many bandoliers as we could drag, crossing the open stretch three or four times. Between strangling periodically and flopping in the mud to dodge sweeps of machine gun fire, I was all in at the end of the second trip and sat down to rest and get some breath at the right of Durand's breastwork. Here I had my last view of Duncan Robertson, my chum who had enlisted with me at Kenora. He was in charge of one of the colt machine guns attached to Durand's sector. His gun had broken down and he was returning from a trip over to the right of the battalion with some spare parts under his arm. We exchanged grins and he hurried on his way. I heard his gun start to chatter about 10 minutes later but it did not last long. There was a German aero plane swooping up and down, up and down over our lines, spotting for machine guns. As soon as Duncan got well started again, there came over a salvo of shells from the enemy batteries that buried Duncan's gun in a volcano of death. He was killed instantly, his head and shoulders blown off. He came from Fernlea, Pern Hill, and Isle of Aran. It must be a good place.

After the session of carrying ammunition I was nearly all in and beginning to get sort of dopey, and groggy with a hazy sort of feeling that seemed to be creeping, creeping right into my vitals. I had just survived a spasm of choking and lay on the ground. A man came along with a jug or crock of rum, hailed me, telling me that some of the boys had taken a shot of it and it had helped them. I laid on one elbow and took a drink of that stuff that would have jolted a horse. It was a case of kill or cure, and I was at the stage just then where I didn't worry much about which way it went. When that slug of (fire water) hit the bottom of my tortured stomach it rebounded and came back as though it had hit a set of coil springs. I threw out about a pint or more of a bright green sort of jelly, having a rough passage for a few minutes, with the yellow foam and froth from my mouth and nostrils shutting off my wind for so long. I thought my heart and brain would burst before I got a gasp and gurgle of breath again. I lay still for awhile after this but soon started to take interest in things again, upon hearing Big Dave Halcrow raving and cursing like a berserker at the breastwork. I woke again to the fact that there was something doing and crawled to the parapet and to the rifles for they were coming over again. There were still some men left to man the rifles and say "no" to them. To the right they swept back the 5th Battalion pouring past us taking our right-hand platoon in their drive. Sergeant Aldritt, who was a sort of athletic instructor around the Y. M' S. swimming baths etc. in Winnipeg, was manning the machine gun in that platoon that was swamped and over run in that drive by the square heads. Aldritt worked his gun right up to the time the enemy swarmed over the breastworks having done some good execution. The remainder of that platoon was captured, officers and all, spending three years in Germany.

Good old A Company was sticking out into the swamp like the bow of a ship in a hurricane with Durand's platoon still doing business on our left flank. Lipsett figured that we were in danger of being cut off and grabbed cooks, batmen, clerks, transport men, and anyone else on two legs, sending them in to form a connecting link from our left flank back to where there were some more of our troops.

The Kilties on our left had fallen back too and were out on the point of a salient. This rabble pushed forward and got to grips in one place with the Germans with their bayonets. A lad by the name of Eddie Platt got up against a big German about twice his size and had to stick him or be stuck. Now it is a very revolting thing to some people to have to use the cold steel and Platt had to summon all his nerve to do it. He stuck fritz alright fainting with revulsion immediately after. Now there had been some troops sent up to try and relieve or to support us.. They were the 8th Durham's and green troops of the Territorial Army who had come to someplace in France to finish their training before being sent into the line. They were grabbed and rushed in to stem the tide of the German drive. A remnant of them survived the advance that they made down that two miles of slope over exposed ground to our position. They must have been exposed to terrific fire during that advance and all credit is due them as green troops for ever getting there at all. I think some of our own men also made that advance. Part of company, or No. 3 company who had been in reserve were sent forward to join us on the spear point of the defense. Most of the officers and N. Co's of the Durhams were killed before they got to us with the remnants of the rank and file being a bit bewildered and shaken by this sudden drop right into Hell itself without any warning or preliminaries. Finding friends that still had a stiff spine and could still curse while facing the right way they were alright and took hold with a good heart. Right here I noticed a sort of queer comedy right in the midst of all the horrors.

There was at least one officer of the Durhams that got to the front line. He was a treat to see. He must have been spawn of the Creme De La Crème for he had the airs, the monocle, spotless cream-colored pipe clay faced breeches and all the rest of it. His servant carried an air cushion which he blew up and placed on the parodos to keep the cream colored breeches spotless. Here was the meeting of the extremes if ever it was. He adjusted the monocle and chatted in the best afternoon tea manner for 15 or 20 minutes without ever saying anything that had any bearing on the doings around us. The wildest imagination could not picture any object more utterly out of place on earth or yet in Heaven. He lasted about 20 minutes when a shell swept him away into the void along with large chunks of our ragged parapet. If he wakes in some drawing room in his special Heaven, he will no doubt still have the monocle uncracked and will enquire as to what those rude fellows were doing.

Conan Doyle said St. Julien was the greatest unsupported infantry defense in military history and he had an uncanny way of getting at the truth of things. The proper relation of all these events one to the other and their proper sequence is a bit blurred to me now. I cannot place them in their exact time and place, for a person in the thick of a mess like that is not always able to see it as a whole or remember dates and statistics.

The Northumberland Fusiliers worked their way into our line. I think it must have been the night after the gas attack and now our boys who still represented what was left of the L. B. Ds. were outnumbered by the newcomers.

Relieved From The Front Line

Sometime during the day corporal Gray came down from what had been our battalion headquarters. He said that orders were that any of A company who were able could work their way back to headquarters as best they could and consider themselves relieved from the front line.

About 10 of us started back across country to the rear and we were not taking any hurdles in our stride either. We crawled for a while till the froth boiled up choking us off. Then we would lie flat on our faces hanging onto the grass until we got our wind back again. We proceeded in this way for short distances. Some of the bunch overdid themselves strangling to death on the way. I think there were about four out of that particular party of 10 that followed me that finally got through to headquarters. We had to cross some low rough ground close behind our lines and then started to follow up an old shallow trench with a green slime of mud in the bottom. This gave us some cover for awhile but it angled of too much to the north and I figured it was liable to take us into the German lines where they had broken through on our left. I could see a clear open field to the right with thorn hedges on the far side, and decided that was the direction I wanted to go. Away I went straight across. I had not gone far when a German sniper picked me up and fired two or three shots. I came to a shallow shell hole and laid there for awhile to get my breath back again as usual. Fritz merrily sniped away at me and I swore when I could get breath enough to do so. I lay perfectly still for awhile to settle my lungs, and probably fritz may have counted me out, for he quit his sniping at me perhaps having found a better target. After awhile I crawled on to the edge of the thorn hedge. There was no opening in it so I worked

63

along to the right for a few yards to where there was a hole to crawl through. While I was following to the right fritz took a few more shots at me but I got through the hedge, and there I was looking at some Imperial troops in a concealed trench. I passed through them moving on back in the direction of our old headquarters. I was getting pretty weak by this time and decided that the rifle I was dragging was more of an encumbrance than use, and that I best conserve my energy if I hoped to make it at all. I discarded my rifle and was now in the invalid or non-combatant class. I remember that ran through my mind while I plodded on and on, then finally coming to the place that was originally our battalion headquarters, passing through a doorway that was screened by a hanging blanket.

There was a room maybe 15 feet square with plain brick walls all around. The walls were lined and the floor covered with wounded and gassed cases in all stages of misery. Some had died since arriving and some were on the way. I recognized three or four of our boys among the lot. There was Murdoch, Nicholson, Simon Gourevitch and an artist Claude Gray who used to sketch for us. There were a couple of others that I knew but I cannot now recall their names. One of them was a young lad not more than 17 who stayed with us on the road all the way back to Ypres. We laid around in that room propped up against the walls during the balance of that day. Fritz dropped a few shells there too. We were sitting with our backs to the wall that was toward the enemy lines. A salvo of shells came over with one landing in a heap of bricks and rubbish that was behind where Nicholson was sitting. The wall bulged opening a long crack in the brickwork above his head with the dust and mortar showering down on our heads. One shell a couple of feet higher would have come right in cleaning up the whole parcel of us in that place.

I began to get the hunch it was a good place to be away from, and with the coming of darkness we left there and hobbled along in what we decided was the main road from Ypres. We struck a path along a row of willows that seemed to have the right direction and in time came to a large barn that was close to the road. We were all in by now and were ready to crawl in any place. There was a part of this building where they had evidently kept cows, sort of a manager divided off in small sections by slabs of slate with the floor well covered with clean straw. I crawled in between a couple of the stone slabs and was dead to the world in less than no time. I didn't chew my cud.

Sometime in the wee small hours I was awakened by a shout. A young Imperial soldier was there in full equipment and was telling me I had best be on my way if I didn't want to get taken prisoner. I sat up and listened. There was a rain of machine gun bullets across the barn wall out behind and I could hear a melee going on. Men were shouting and yelling, and bombs were popping. Rifle fire, and machine gun fire came in fitful bursts and squalls. I called Nicholson and Gourevitch, along with one other, and we passed out of the barn into the ditch along the main road and started to hike and hobble away. We were feeling stronger after our rest walking along fairly well in stages without choking up too much. The froth did not boil up on us nearly as bad as the day before so we made fairly good progress. In front of a big barn I could see some Red Cross ambulances that had been shelled on the road, along with the wreckage of some transport wagons. We passed a couple of young English soldiers hobbling along the ditch together. One of them, with a foot gone, leaning on his mate and hobbling along. A pitiful sight. We were physically unable to render help to anyone being just able to navigate dizzily along by ourselves. Soon after leaving the barn we got a shower of brush, twigs, and leaves. Looking up at one spot we saw the thorn hedge above on the embankment of the ditch being cut with what appeared to be an invisible scythe. It was an enemy machine gun sweeping. We were still a bit too close for invalids and noncombatants and kept plodding along with short rests until we got out of the immediate zone of the fighting. That was a grisly, ghastly stretch of road and we saw a lot of misery and suffering along that eight miles of cobblestones. There had been heavy shelling all along this piece of road by the looks of the wreckage and the numerous dead.

On coming to a cross road there was an English soldier left there as a sentry with orders to stay. God only knows why he was left there and I guess He alone could tell. The soldier didn't know and there he was tied to that spot by order of someone who may have gone over the River Jordan. Shells came roaring in frequently and burst with a wicked crash on the hard pavement and scrap iron whirled and shrieked and spun in all directions. I often wondered how long he would last there for it was no health resort. A lot of lives were thrown away like that to no apparent purpose, and there was a tiresome case (in point duty). At every cross road there was a shambles where the shells had caught the traffic, and looking down on it the inevitable crucifix or life size figure of the Christ on his cross. We got into some odd ways of thinking in those days and I remember remarking, that if Christ died to save the world he must have made a poor job of it, for in the last week we had seen more crucifixion, suffering, and agony than it was possible to represent by the figure at the cross roads that gazed down with a face of clay. We felt sometimes as though the whole Christian Faith must be made of senseless clay a thing impotent. We had seen self—sacrifice to the last utter able limit with souls and bodies flung into the teeth of hell itself to support a cause and backing up an earthly faith, and an earthly belief in it.

We saw a rather humorous thing along the road. A man by the name of Carson from our battalion went into a wayside dressing station to get a small wound dressed. There was a patient there with a head wound and these kind of wounds are liable to turn the patient sick or cause him to become faint or unconscious at any time. The surgeon requested Carson to accompany the patient, a colored man of the French Foreign Legion along the road. They walked along quietly for awhile until a couple of shells lit on the road close behind. The Algerian man began to speed up and Carson, being gassed and quite weak, could not keep up. Another shell hit the road and the patient stepped on the throttle a little more breaking into a run. The last view Carson had of him he was rounding a curve in high with a with a long streamer of bandage trailing in the breeze behind.

At one place along the way I saw a direct hit on a man and a horse by a high explosive shell. The rider came loping across a field and jumped a hedge landing on the road. About the time the horse's feet hit the road a shell hit them. There was practically nothing visible to show that a horse and rider had passed.

We began to meet troops of the Indian Army marching up to the front. They had come all the way from near Labassie and were marching in a new issue of army boots. Their feet must have been cut up badly on this account for they were hobbling along as though walking on hot bricks.

We met a battalion of Gurkhas and at the tail end of the procession was an elderly man of very husky build, chesty, with a Vandyke beard, loaded down with what appeared to be a medical kit and first aid outfit. He stepped briskly along close up to the rear file looking around in all directions, turning his head with bright beady eyes that missed nothing. They were a husky-looking lot giving a good account of themselves later when they got up the line.

We got to St. Jean at last and here Gen. Currie newly in command of the 1st. Division had his headquarters. We stopped and rested there for awhile. We were told that Currie had been quite upset over the cutting up of the division and had been pacing up and down the road in tears at one time. It was quite a strain for a new and inexperienced commander alright.

We were getting into quieter country now with less shell fire. We passed more troops and were questioned by one English officer as to who we were and where bound. They must have got a few guns forward from some place for we began to meet a string of ammunition limbers going and coming at a fast clip. At last we happened to come past a Belgian gun team when the driver was waiting in the traffic. He made signs for us to climb on and have a ride. We did climb on and away he went at a gallop over the rough cobble and shell-torn road. A gun limber is about the most rough riding thing in the world. Our stomachs were not in any condition to stand that kind of treatment. We were whisked around the edge of Ypres City to where the Canal Du Nord enters and we were not sorry to get through there quickly for it was still being shelled. Then Ypres was behind and we were at the limit of our endurance. We caught the eye of the driver at last and he let us off. We rolled into the ditch in bad shape for the shaking had stirred up the gas again in our innards and we knew all about it for awhile. I thought Simon Gourevitch was going to pass in his chips right there and then. We were a sore and sick bunch of boys.

We had been so long without food or nourishment that we were in a sort of waking dream, and were like automatons that moved but had no feeling. If someone had set a good meal in front of us we could not have eaten it. We were beyond that stage. I remember in the latter stages of that march my fingers stiffened out like rigid hooks with the outer or end joints drawn up in a queer way. Every once in awhile we would get a sort of asthmatic gasping wheezing fit and stand there for a minute on the road gulping and goggle eyed. People peered at us queerly along the road and no doubt we were beginning to look sort of queer. I am sure we felt queer enough and no mistake. Our faces were pinched, wan, and a deep yellow jaundiced color from the gas and that complexion stayed with us for a long time. Even now I can pick out the men who were really seriously gassed from among the returned men. They are still dying from the effects of it 16 years later. There was a Hanson buried in Kenora about three years ago.

After passing through Ypres we began to inquire for the 1st division transport lines eventually getting directions from someone. The refugees from Ypres City were still to be seen in some of the small villages close behind and we stopped at one cottage, or a relic of an estaminet where a group of them were sitting comparing notes and sipping coffee. I don't remember how long we were on that march. There are parts of it that are lost in a sort of haze and never will be quite clear. I remember going in through a gateway, and being greeted by familiar faces, and seeing transport and cook wagons about. Somebody came up handing each of us a big beef sandwich. We rolled over on the grass and slept with the sandwiches in our hands.

We were awakened by the R. S. M. who wanted us to go back up the line. Mind you, "he said" we should volunteer as we were needed up there badly and so on. He even insinuated that we were shirking our duty by not jumping up and starting out. It was too laughable, I don't believe we could have staggered as far as Ypres, and as to buckling on full fighting equipment somebody would have had to prop us up after we got it on. That gives you an idea how little people who have not been brought into hard-ship realize the meaning of it. He was so near and yet so far from the realities of the war. After the heroic R. S. M. left us I think we rolled over and had another sleep. We had a lot of sleep to catch up with believe me, especially we who had been in the scout section through the past two weeks. The rest of the front line boys began to dribble in one way or another through out that day and night.

We were taken to a field of growing green oats and told to dig in. We each dug out a hole in the ground like a shallow grave, just big enough to lie in and deep enough to bring us level with the sod when lying in it. That was our home and bed. Enemy aero planes were active looking for targets for the German artillery. That was the idea of getting low and staying low in daylight. The following dawn we held a roll call to try and get a record of as many of the dead, wounded, and missing as possible, so as to pass the information on to the proper authorities. They in turn could pass it on to the friends and relatives at home. As each name was called in the regular alphabetical order the man if present answered "Here Sir". If there was no answer the men were questioned as to where and when the person was last seen, what had happened to him or in what way he had met his end. In this way the record was pieced together and made ready to send away to many anxious friends and relatives. Our old A. company mustered 21 men at that roll call. The other companies were in not much better case, and the toll of officers and n. c. o,'s had been heavy too. It was Lieut. Morley who called that roll.

Col. Lipsett came along and gave us a few words of greeting but he was too full for words and did not attempt to say much. He made it clear however that we had more than lived up to his hopes, he could not find words to express his pride in the way his battalion had stood up under its first great trial and ordeal. It had made a name that would be spoken of with respect by all real soldiers.

A number of our men who from one cause or another had not been seriously gassed, principally men who had not been in the bottom of the valley in the thick of the gas attack, or had been in reserve or with transport etc., were sent back up the line again. They stayed up there and fought with other units for upwards of another four days. Some of these men had some experiences to relate of the doings up there after we left our line in the hands of the Imperials. The Germans drove in the line quite a long way after we pulled out of there but did not make any sort of an advance compared to their plans, having thrown a million and a half men into that attack that was supposed to take them right through to Calais before it stopped, and here they were only a measly couple of miles from where they started. They had all the artillery they could wish for and we had practically none. They were well equipped with aero planes and we had practically none in that sector.

The stubborn defense by the First Canadian Division had been the means of throwing a monkey wrench into the machinery of the advance and held things back long enough for the British staff to make hasty plans, and stiffen the defense and dragging the big drive to a stand still completely in eight days from its start.

The feeble remnant of the old 8th stayed in the green oats for a day or two and then went into some wooden huts shaped like wedge tents that were in a field near by. We were supposed to be reserve for the 5th and 7th battalions who were in support trenches and dugouts in the bank of the Canal Du Nord to the north or north west of Ypres city. The 5th and the 7th were supporting French troops. Everybody was one the quivive for we could not believe that fritz would abandon his great drive with so little gain of ground and besides he still continued to hammer the whole Ypres Salient with thousands of rounds from massed artillery. During the two weeks of that battle the German expenditure of shell must have been enormous. They put creeping barrages right across the whole width of the salient from the bluff, the ravine, and Dickebush on the east to the Canal Du Nord, St. Julien, and Langemarch on the west. There aircraft had complete control in the area. Our few scattered pieces of field artillery had to be dug in until the tips of the gun barrels were flush with the sod leveling everything off, using good camouflage too, great caution, to prevent being blown right off the map by the enemy's superior weight of metal and observation facilities. I nearly walked on top of one of our batteries one day in a level open field before noticing anything. All of a sudden I noticed a sort of dark slot in front of me in the green sward and there, looking me in the eye, was the muzzle of a 18 pounder. I sidled off a bit right then for I felt as though it might accidentally go off.

In case of another attack we were to go forward to the canal embankment joining forces with the 5th and 7th. I was out on a regular night patrol across country from our battalion lines to the head quarters of the two units on the canal. There was of course a complete system of field telephones with a central or (report centre) about half way. Fritz was sweeping the roads and every thing else with shell and shrapnel all night long. The cuts and breaks in the field telephone line were frequent. My patrol was to go back and forth every two hours all night avoiding all roads and cutting a path with clippers through hedges etc. across country as an additional precaution in case of telephone failure. If there was a sudden attack I could guide the battalion across country to join the troops at the canal. I had to report at the headquarters' dug outs of the 5th and 7th and at the report centre every two hours. They gave me a side-kick to go along with me for company and to carry on through in case I got plinked or plugged. He was a small dark guy with a very long tongue and the first night I arrived at the O. C's. dugout in the 7th lines I decided he would not do. He nearly talked a leg off the O. C. of the 7th and that worthy eyed him up and looked at me with a very large question mark across his countenance. Next morning I requested that Carson, my comrade on the sketching stunt on the old convent wall at Labutillerie, be sent along as my mate on the patrol job.

We made this patrol regularly for about a week and one night while making my report to the O. C. of the 7th in his dugout at the canal an officer of the 5th came in and said there was an 8th battalion man just killed outside by shell fire. Carson had not followed me in and I could not imagine any other 8th battalion man that would be in that locality at that hour, about two a.m. I hurried outside and called Carson's name. "Hi" came from under the edge of the embankment just outside the dugout door. That "Hi" was a musical sound to me. I could have hugged him. I was so glad to know the casualty was someone else. It turned out that the man killed had been on a visit to some friend and had got strayed in the darkness getting caught by a sweep of bursting shrapnel on the road.

In our cross country night patrols we came across the lines of some of the famous French Foreign Legion and called in at a building that apparently housed their transport outfit. They seemed a more or less a sociable outfit and we called there several times in our cross country patrols. They had real Algerian wine in a large canvas bucket or pail in the middle of the room with a long handled tin dipper in it to drink it with. Somebody tipped us it was a custom to trade gifts among these people otherwise you would not be likely to get any wine. We accordingly donated some cigarettes etc. on each visit and were quite welcome to dig into the wine. It seemed to us to be really fine wine and certainly never missed an opportunity to sample it.

The nights were dark and windy and the roads in the locality were all lined with rows of lofty elms. You would be hurrying along in a drizzle, splashing through pools of water, when there would come a blinding flash and splitting crash right overhead mingled with the peculiar whirring and swish of shrapnel balls. Some times the upper section of a tall elm would come crashing down onto the right of way. On one of these nights I noticed myself springing straight up and sideways at the burst of a shell. This would happen before I had time to think. I was beginning to feel the effects of shell shock and the long continued nerve strains. Being sick enough to be in bed on account of the gas treatment may also have had something to do with it at the time. A number of the boys began to go into quick or galloping consumption or TB from the gas and the O. C's. were sending them off down the line. Carson and I were going around leaning up against every wall or post we came to, feeling queer with periods of high temperature. We did not seem to be picking up or getting any better.

One day we held a conference and decided we had better report sick and go down the line for a few days for we didn't have any ambition to become tubercular and pass out that way. We knew there was something radically wrong with us and wanted to find out about it.

During the time we were here we got a new draft to fill up the gaps in the battalion. This draft came from the 32nd battalion. They had no sooner got into their huts then a shell came over resulting in some casualties. This old 32nd draft was a fine bunch of men. You would not see that long bread line of them every morning on sick parade to the doctor's tent as we did in 17 and 18 when the mama's darlings and college fry were sent out. It runs in my mind that we got a small draft from the 79th Cameron's too, at or about this time of only a few men.

Hospitalized

On the 5th of May we reported to the M. O. as not fit and were sent along with about 20 others on our way to the railway at Hasebroucke. We slept one night in a barn out in the country and the following day we were loaded on some double Decker London buses landing in an old theatre that was being used as a hospital. I guess it was the queerest show that had yet been put on in that house. There were a lot of deaths from gas poison at this place. Across the street there had once been a racing stable, and there was a long low shed. Here the dead were placed in a row sewed up in blankets. The long shed was well filled from end to end when I saw it. The surgeons here removed the lungs from a young man about 20 yrs of age who had died from gas. They found that all the cells of the lungs were expanded or stretched and without elasticity, something like the lungs of a very elderly man. They were four times the natural weight and filled up part way from the bottom with a fluid or sort of condensation of a watery nature. The men who survived the dose had peculiar voices for a long time. The voice would break or vibrate as an aged man's voice does frequently, and their complexion was as yellow as a china man for a long time. Our turn came to entrain and we were formed in a long line two deep. They split this line while entraining and Carson and I were separated. He landed in hospital in England and I landed in Le Treport on the French coast.

At Le Treport there was a large hotel on the cliffs that had been the property of Kaiser Bill before the war and now was used as a hospital. On the flat behind the hospital there was a line up of big tents or marquees also used as a hospital. I landed on a cot in one of the tents. We were kept in bed from time of arrival and given some sort of fluid of a lemon color every 30 minutes day and night. I never heard what that stuff was. We were also told to smoke and smoke a lot, as this was supposed to act as an antidote. We were furnished with cigarettes and tobacco.

I believe I was the only Canuck in that tent, all the rest of them were old countrymen and some were from the Indian Army. There was a man aged about 45 yrs next to me who had served in India. Rheumatism was his trouble and he had it badly. One night he told me that I sat straight up in bed looking over either side as though searching for something and yelled out loud, "Where in Hell Am I Anyway?" I then laid down and slept again. I had been dreaming about that night guiding a party into Death Valley up north, thinking I was again following that slippery zigzag of mud along the old trenches full of water in the dark.

During the time I was hospitalized here a peculiar thing happened in our marquees. Everything was kept scrupulously clean of course but the nurses and patients began to sniff and sniff. We could smell a smell, a strong smell. Every patient was allowed a small box or locker of two shelves and usually a haversack or small bag. Here he was allowed to keep his personal belongings or any small things he valued. There was a wounded Gurkha a few cots down from us and the smelly smell was finally traced to there. On opening his haversack they found he had a nice collection of German ears and fingers that he was preserving for souvenirs.

We went through the stages of standing up and then walking, finally going on short marches. At last we had the option of volunteering to go with a draft of convalescents up the line back to our unit. There was a shortage of men those days and as soon as one was able to stagger along under kit and equipment he was hustled back to the trenches. On the march out of there I was swaying like a weaving horse, with periods of very high temperature, and dizziness with it.

Before we left we had somewhat of a mix up with a bunch of Imperials who were stationed in the vicinity. There was a regimental "Sawjent Majaw" of excessive importance who delegated himself as a committee of one to show those "Blawsted Canadians" a thing or two or three. He belonged to the guard's brigade, "Daunt You Know", a browbeating man, driving had been his breathe of life for a long time.

He was great at it (among his own troops). I guess that is how he kept his bomb-proof job miles and miles way from the rude "fello-ows" who went to war with their rude and unheard of ways. Why ? It was really "too utter for anything".

All the Canucks were collected together from the nearby branches of the hospitals, formed into a platoon and turned over to the gentle mercies of this gent. He was raring to go and started to walk rough shod over the top of a bunch of native Canadians. Some were ex-bush-whackers, some were ex-railroaders and some were ex-something else. Of course this was all Greek to him. A private was something to roar at, curse at, revile, and insult. In his outfit a thing to be bodily jostled pushed about and even struck with a stick if his state of mind happened to turn that way. He started in to teach us bayonet work. The old style was out of date, and the British troops in one action (Battle Of Loos) had a lot of casualties from their own bayonets due to the bum system they were using. There was a great hurry to get the men trained in the new drill. We did not perform to suit him. He swore he would show us and brought a platoon or two of English guardsmen of the six foot kind to do bayonet practice with us. They took their cue from the R. S. M's attitude and very foolishly adapted a superior attitude also. They lasted quick. The whole caboodle of them left there with broken heads and bent noses, with a few of them needing hospital treatment I believe. However the R. S. M. had not yet learned his lesson or taken a hint. The next day he produced a couple of platoons of Irish guards. I'll show these colonial blighters. The Irish guards suffered a worse mauling than their English cousins because they showed more fight. Of course these victims got past the R. S. M. Someone higher up had sense enough to interfere, making arrangements to have Canadian drill instructors for us. Our days were quiet, peaceful, full of profit, of recuperation and rest. That is what we needed more than drill just then. We were not so bad in a bayonet mix up anyway. After leaving Le Treport and a camp a few miles from there I was shipped back to the battalion.

"AWSK THE GODS"

The Duck's Bill

During the time I was in hospital they had been through the battle of Festubert and, had been cut up some more. Some of the gassed cases went into that fight dying on their feet and never came out of it. Some of them landed in hospital where I had been before I started back to the battalion. I remember one case of a lumberjack camp-foreman who hailed from the Dog River country north of Fort William. He had been a very hardy and able man all his life. It was pitiful to see the wreck and poor shadow that represented him now. He had foolishly gone with his battalion through Festubert when he should have been some place recuperating. Only his unusual vitality kept him on his feet where others failed and died.

When I got back the boys were in Cuienchy and Givenchy at the left of the Labassie Canal in another low swampy place. They must have thought we were some relative of the muskrat or the beaver for they assigned us to all the swamp holes in the length of the line. Here it was breastworks again. We were at what was known as the Duck's Bill. It was a tiny salient jutting out into the swamp. Why it was held I don't know. It did not seem to serve any useful purpose. It was very costly in human lives, (on our side only). At some points the opposing breastworks were only 30 yards apart, and you could start something anytime you felt like by throwing a hand grenade across. At one place a sort of high dyke had been gradually built up until it must have been 12 or 15 feet high and about that wide at the base. Here you could lob a bomb into Fritz too if you wanted to start a rough house. It was often done. At one point of our sector toward the left there was an old field gun in the front line trench. It had a look like dirty work and corpses but what they were doing with it, or intended to do, I don't know. The R. A. M. C. might.

While we were in this place someone got the idea of straightening the line to the left of the Duck's Bill so as to do away with the deep inward curve or re-entrant in that part of our front, and make the Bill itself a little less of death trap for our men. The idea was alright I guess if there had been enough artillery to prepare the way, making a feasible and practical thing of it. To try to do it with infantry, with practically no support in other arms was murder. They got as far as trying it however, and we pulled the old stuff we had pulled before at Neuve Chapelle. Manned the breastworks, and put over spasms of rapid rifle fire. Stuck up our hats on bayonets above the parapet, cheered and in other ways carried out instructions in what was known as a demonstration. The idea, we were told, was to keep the enemy from transferring troops off our part of the front to strengthen the point where the real attack was to be made. I don't suppose we fooled fritz any to speak of. I figure that he was as well posted about that part of the line as we were and, demonstrations or no, he had a good idea what we were driving at all right and there was a lot of good strong unbroken wire entanglement all along that part of his lines. I know because I spent a night or two or three investigating it. There used to be some awful fool stunts pulled off in these early days of the war.

One night an officer went out on patrol in command over a couple of survivors of the old scout section. He had an idea of finding a hole or weak place in the enemy wire. It started to get nasty while we were out there, for fritz knew we were planning to pull off something and was putting over a lot of fire of several kinds. This officer decided he had urgent business back in our trench and not being much on location he left a light out there to make sure he could find the place again. Fritz was supposed to have poor eye sight or something. In addition to this he gave us orders to remain there until he returned, which he never did. Neither did he send anybody to tell us to come in. We had natural sense enough to keep well away from the light. During the night fritz moved the light to another spot but did not extinguish it. The ground was a bit broken and rough out there giving us some cover. We survived the rough house on that account alone. We came in before daylight on our own initiative, for we knew then the officer was well—What—What Ever!

Another night at the same place our wiring party put out a string of nice new entanglements or hurdles all fixed together, well made and very nice. Dawn showed that Fritz had come and pinched the whole works incorporating it into in his own wire defenses.

The time came when the straightening of the line was to take place. I think it was the 1st and 2nd battalions who were then on our left who were the intended victims that were to be hung on the wire for exhibition purpose or a sort of variation of the roman holiday idea. I never heard just what really did happen but I gathered that it was a fizzle. At the zero hour we went up on the breastworks to demonstrate some more. I happened to be where that high dyke was situated and we went up to the top of it opening rapid fire etc. We found that while we were up there we were exposed to an enfilade of rifle fire from some place to the left of us and the bullets were plunking into the sand bags on the same side as we were. Immediately behind us there was what was known as the (KEEP). This consisted of a network of support trenches and shallow dugouts clustered together in rather close formation. This (KEEP) was full of men at the time, stationed there as support to the platoons manning the breastworks. Fritz evidently knew all about this place for the zero hour was the signal for him to drop 27 coal boxes or eight inch howitzer shells into it. A piece of cast iron about three inches square from the base of one of these shells flew across to where I was perched on the upper part of the high dyke shooting through a loophole. It hit me over the right kidney on a line with my waist belt. I had on full web equipment and it hit right where the straps and buckles of the shoulder braces cross the waist belt. It cut through about four thicknesses of web and two brass buckles making a tear in the tunic beneath but did not penetrate further. Talk about your kidney punches, Dempsey would have envied that coal box. I could not straighten up at all but backed down cautiously to the trench below and seeing Simon Gourevitch there I asked him to take look and see if I was punctured. Simon became quite excited when he saw I could not straighten or stand up and set up a yell for a stretcher bearer right away. I had a blue and black bruise about six inches in diameter and a soreness around that kidney for a long time, but no further hurt until later years.

One of those coal boxes there in the (KEEP) smashed up poor Alick McRea. I did not know of it at the time. He sustained 34 wounds to his head and body. He was a very healthy, clean living boy and had always had good health and strength. They shipped him to the Royal Infirmary at Edinburgh. There he survived all those wounds and the removal of one of his eyes. He was well on his way to recovery when a bit of hard luck took him off. He was convalescent and soon would have started on a trip home to Brora. Some of the hospital staff took him out for a drive in a car one day. Now it appears there was a small fragment of shrapnel imbedded in the base of his skull at the back. They said he caught cold in it or something like that. Inflammation set in and killed him. I had just written him a long letter, we were making plans on what we could do canoeing on The Lake of The Woods. The letter was returned together with one from his sister telling me of the manner of his passing. Duncan and Alick were both gone now and I don't believe they can ever be replaced. I have never ceased to miss those two comrades and I miss them now after many years. There are places on the lake and river where we used to play in the old days that seem to still hold their ghosts and I cannot remain long in those spots for it hurts yet. While on this part of the front we used to swim in the Labassie Canal.

One day an enemy shell hit in the water and the force of the burst being transmitted through the water knocked some of the men unconscious. I don't remember if there were any fatalities from this cause. The French had a long tom gun mounted on a floating barge further back along the canal on our part of the front. I think it was about eight inch caliber. I watched it firing on the enemy earth works on the north side of the canal one day. They were making direct hits on a trench and I remember seeing a German soaring into the air about 30 feet spinning endwise like a wheel. There was an old wooden pump with a lever handle at a well behind our lines among a group of buildings. We used to go there for water at night. Fritz had a set rifle on this spot and the old pump was riddled with bullet holes. When some bullets come over you would quit pumping for awhile until the shooting stopped, then return and get your water. The approaches to this spot were also swept by fire at night. I believe this may have been the original pump in the cartoon by Bairnsfather. The general layout was similar.

The Messines Front

We were moved from this sector up to the Ypres Salient and finally landed at the Messines Front remaining there for the balance of the summer and following winter. The old original scout section was pretty well broken up by now due to casualties, sickness, and on account of some of the men taking commissions and going to other work. Knobel left us for a promotion and also Platt. On my return from hospital finally, I was the sole available and active member left in the line. Col. Lipsett and Lieut. Knobel came to see me with a proposal that I organize a new section of scouts, snipers, and observers, eight men in each section or 24 in all. Undertaking the training and discipline of same. I figured I could perhaps train them alright as to their different lines of work in the front line, but I did not feel so confident about the barrack-square kind of drill when out of the line and the discipline part of it. I never tried to master close order drill and to this day would not be able to drill a platoon if I was to be shot for it at dawn. This was on account of a strong dislike of that sort of work which I was never able to overcome. That is really the reason I did not at any time try to take out a commission. The taking out of one meant a whole lot of Barrack-Square work and I had certainly no stomach for concentrating on that. The idea of bossing a bunch of men and being arbiter and controller of all their behavior, comings and goings was certainly out of my line. It did not form one of my ambitions in the slightest degree. However I was the only trained one left in the unit with Lipsett and Knobel insisting that it was up to me to go ahead with trying to see what I could do.

I was given the rank of sergeant and told to "hop to it". I also was given the privilege of going to any company commander and demanding a man out of his company for my work if I thought he would fill the bill. I was given a cook with a cooking outfit and we drew rations separate from the companies. We were billeted as a unit by ourselves. We were equipped with signalers telescopes for the observation work, and special rifles for sharp-shooting. Maps were furnished but we had to buy or rustle all other equipment such as prismatic compasses, protractors, drawing material etc. For patrol work we needed pistols etc. as a rifle was too clumsy for that work. We had to rustle our own pistols. We were not as yet on the books as a separate distinct unit. The work of the old original scout section had come under the notice of the higher staffs and there was talk of a scout organization in all the battalions in the division. This was all in the future and was not realized until mid-summer of 1916. We were on a sort of probation and if the unit was found to be really useful or indispensable they would become a recognized unit. An officer would be detailed to take charge, and allowances made for their needs in the way of tools etc. In the mean time we were a sort of "Bastardies Unit", and had no special allowance for equipment and had to rustle what was needed as best we could producing the work and results with or without tools. We were in the pioneer stage of our particular line of work.

Lipsett said he would not press me for smartness of parade drills if I would deliver the goods in the other lines of work while up the line. I picked out men from the various platoons accordingly as they seemed suited to the work ahead. In a few days I had the section nearly filled up and was a very busy guy, both day and night and Sundays during the following 14 months which was the period I was in charge of the triple unit. At the end of that time the scout unit was indispensable, not alone in our own division but throughout the whole Canadian Corps.

The scouts had even come to the notice of the British and French staffs who sent officers during the winter of 15-16 to study our methods and accompany us on patrol, observation, and sniping work. Through incurring the (enmity) of a Col. I was done out of any credit for this pioneer work with the unit and pushed out of the job just when it was brought to fruition with the unit being made universal throughout the corps. The sole and only credit I ever got from him was on one occasion when a lengthy dispatch came from General Hedt's headquarters complimenting us on the work done by my unit. He was compelled by regulations to read this to the battalion while assembled on parade. He did it with a poor grace and a wry face. I was (blackballed) effectually later among other officers through his efforts, and did not attempt any further active work.

Some sportsmen's association in B. C. donated us three rifles equipped with Winchester telescopic sights. The rifles were too light in the barrel and to short to give accuracy at any long ranges. They were fine for work from one to three hundred yards. We then got some long MK 3 Ross Rifles equipped with a sort of prismatic sight of a magnification of six diameters. This was a beautiful sight as far as the visual requirements go. The mounting of it on the rifles was rotten and always gave us much trouble and difficulty. The recoil threw it out of alignment with every shot, and it had to be readjusted and re-sighted by a test shot. It was the Warner Swayzey. We had one long Le-Enfield of S. A. war vintage, a beautiful rifle, good at all ranges, equipped with what was called optical sights. This arrangement consists of a sort of aperture sight near the eye with a tiny lens in the peep hole. There is another much larger lens mounted at the muzzle of the rifle with a dot in the centre or thin crosshair markings. The front and back sights are entirely separate not being connected by a tube or other arrangement to exclude the light. They are only useful in certain stages of light and visibility. We had two short Le-Enfield equipped with the same as above. Later on we discarded all these mixtures and adopted the Ross Mk 3 with a Winchester A5 telescope as standard equipment. We never found anything to equal this combination on the range or in the front lines. The sights would stand a remarkable amount of rough usage giving very little trouble once mounted and adjusted to zero. If we could have had marking scales of yards on these sights they could have been almost ideal for all round work. All sights of whatever make should have a plain scale of yards adapted to the cartridge to be used. All other arrangements of degree markings etc. are pure humbug for practical or active service use.

The same thing applies to sporting rifles, or should, by all means.

At Messines we were in another low valley but the ground started to rise immediately behind our front lines and continued for a mile back to a low hill. At the back or west side of this hill was a wood. The road from Bailleul to Messines wound around the south edge of the hill and then struck eastward across the valley, crossing our front lines and the German lines and continuing on up a slope to the town itself, that stood on the crest of a ridge at about 1600 yards from our front. In the German front line opposite our left flank there was a group of buildings known as Petit Douve Farm 100 yards south of the Messines Road. Our line swung back to the south west facing toward another group of buildings in the enemy lines known as Avenue Farm, named from a tall avenue of elm trees extending in line with the enemy front trench. The opposing lines on our left were about 200 yards apart. This widened to 500 yards at one point between the road and Avenue Farm. On our right there was a salient in the enemy line, distant 300 yards from our trench. Here again a north and south road crossed the two lines of trenches. The ground between the lines was low and swampy except on our right flank and opposite the enemy salient above mentioned. There was a small creek flowing from n-w through our trench, and along the front of the enemy trench. It swung away south eastward through the enemy line just to the left of Avenue Farm at the widest spot in no-mans land.

In front of Messines and southward for a mile we had a good view of the enemy country and his support trenches giving us a great opportunity for observation and sniping work. The ground between the lines gave us some interesting night work on numerous patrols. Looking south east beyond Avenue Farm we could see nothing, for the land fell away sharply toward the River Lys and was not visible, or was what is known as dead ground. Close behind our lines there were several ruined houses. These, along with a number of old grass-grown trenches and hedge-rows, gave us fine locations for op,s and sniping posts. We developed quite a system on this front and, on account of our locating numerous targets, there was one of the supporting field batteries that was available to me for sniping at ranges too distant for rifle fire. I had the privilege afforded of calling them by phone and giving the map location of any target.

Among the men I took on as snipers at this time were (Paddy Riell) descendant of the famous Louis Riell of n w fame, Phil McDonald, W. Scarrow, Fred Minty, J. Ballendene along with his brother Jim from Battleford, Saskatchewan, one Smith whose initials I forgot along with a couple of others. Among the scouts proper who worked alternately on patrols and observation were Taylor, Mitchell, Bole, Maitkin, Powell, Carson, St. Louis, Nicholson, Gunne, Green, Millan , Risebrow, Jones along with several others. Four of the snipers were partly of Indian blood One half or one quarter breeds of Scottish or French fore bearers and they took naturally to that work appearing to enjoy it very much following it keenly. Among that gang of mine were surveyors, architects, lumberjacks, cowboy, preacher, school teacher, college students, railroad men, farmers, graduate of the Royal Engineering College, artist, bank absconder, pugilist, a couple of young school boys, trapper, Alberta forest ranger, wireless expert, bush camp cook, and several other trades. It was a fine bunch and we had great times together working on our various lines of work. This work gave the boys more freedom where they were able to use initiative and were far better off than with the strict and rather monotonous duties that fell to the lot of a man as a plain Pte in a platoon of the regular companies.

We established regular o. ps. of known and measured locations. We were able to get accurate intersections by compass on any new work by the enemy. If he dug a new support trench during the night or strung out a new line of wire entanglements, we would get busy at daylight taking a series of intersections along its whole length. These were worked out by protractor and marked them on the map by dots. Then the dots were connected up by a pencil line and there you had the new work laid down on a chart exactly as it was on the ground. This chart went by runner to Brig' Hq. and then to the artillery, machine gun emplacements, trench junctions, strong points or redoubts etc. All came in for the same sort of attention from us.

We discovered that Avenue Farm was being strengthened with a lot of concrete filling, and indications were that it was being made into a strong point or redoubt. We got a line on this work by climbing the tall elms that still stood to the right of the Messines Road. This was touchy work in daylight and only about 350 yards from the enemy's observers who could see our observation point from three angles. Detection while up one of those trees meant certain death from m. g. or shrapnel fire, not to mention the enemy snipers. Archie St. Louis did the bigger part of that job. He was the smallest man in our outfit and less likely to be spotted while up a tree. We succeeded in getting this spot shelled by a six inch Naval Gun and a couple of nine. two howitzers that were stationed back near the Bailleul Road. I was amused by a couple of artillery observers who were in our support trench to watch this shelling. They had been told that all this dirty work was due to a mere Sgt. of infantry scouts. As I passed one remarked to the other. Oh! Is that the guy? He isn't much to look at. I checked the variation of my compass by theirs and out of a group of about six compasses, mine gave the closest to a true reading. One of them tried to make a deal or trade right there but I wasn't having any. A true reading compass is a jewel saving a lot of allowances and calculation.

After awhile the ground in front of the line sectors became so seeded with iron of all kinds, it affected compasses badly. Eventually the artillery refused to take map locations obtained by this method. We were not stuck, for a lad in my outfit was somewhat of an inventor and built three rigs of wood and brass, with a straight edge rule swinging from a fulcrum point over an arc of 90 degrees. The arc was marked with a scale of degrees and minutes on a smooth board similar to a drawing board or plane table. The whole works was set and embedded so as to be immovable in the observation post and a known point (visible and fixed) was taken as a reference point. The relation of the reference point to a meridian taken and all bearings for intersections taken with a set of sights mounted on the swinging straight edge. A sheet of foolscap could be pinned on the board under the swinging rule and all rays penciled on it directly, together with all particulars re-location of o p, ref. point etc. on the map. This did away with the trouble from local magnetic attraction. Out of this crude arrangement there grew some elaborate contraptions later on that were equipped with powerful prismatic magnifying lenses and cross-hair sights with sliding scales of degrees and minutes. We never got hold of any of the later models. They were all used by the artillery (Great Trees from Little Acorns Grow). We never got any credit for this machine that was later known as a Director or Director Board. The o. c. of the 2nd army workshop took all the credit to himself after pumping all the details out of the man I sent there to get working models made. There was nothing really new about the arrangement but it enabled you to make practical and effective use of old principals. The man that worked this out was one of my scouts by the name of Young.

He also invented a system of locating enemy batteries by sound waves. This was adopted also by the army workshops and used to good purpose later. He also invented a machine for locating guns from their flash at night. This was worked by a moving picture machine that exposed a belt of film in the usual way. Two fixed lights similar to battery spot lights were set on the ground so as to show on the corners of each section of film. When the enemy gun started firing you turned the crank exposing the films, and the enemy gun-flash on the horizon was registered on the film in fixed relation to the spotlights. The film could be enlarged to make the working out of the angles easier, or they could be worked out from the original with instruments fine enough to match the size of the film section.

The sound locator was worked out with diaphragm vibrators set in receivers something like phone receivers. These in turn were set in arcs or groups equidistant along a larger arc. The strongest vibration came from the particular receiver directly on a bearing toward the enemy gun. The vibrations graduated off either way from this point and registered sound waves in lesser degrees of intensity as you got further from this point. The same thing is used now to steer steamships into our harbors in fog or storms. Newton was the man in charge of 2nd army workshops and working (hand in glove) with Major Bertram late of our battalion. The two of them succeeded in pumping Young dry as to all details of these appliances. Then they kicked him out with insults sending him back to the trenches again. Young worried over this dirty deal until he took brain-fever and was sent away to England as an invalid. He left us when we were on the city of St. Pierre front in the Lens sector late in 1917. I met him at Epsom November 1918 convalescent.

South east of the Messines on the banks of the River Lys their lay a railway junction and distribution point for the Messines area. Wolveringhem I think was the name on the maps. From here the enemy supplies were distributed by motor and horse transport at night. On still moonlight nights I could hear the roar and rattles of their transport even hearing the shouts of their teamsters. By taking a bearing on the centre of disturbance I could accurately place the position of their train of transport on any one of several roads that led up from the Wolveringhem area to points north. In this way I would get their location and wire it to the sniping battery and they would put over salvoes of shrapnel on any sector of road specified. In this way I got well into them on several occasions which was evidenced by the great commotion and shouting and the clatter of runaway teams on the cobblestone paved roads. A couple of miles south east of Messines there was a junction with the main road to the north. One night we could hear the roar and rumble of heavy motor or caterpillar tractors moving north at the vicinity of this junction. It was out of range of the 18 pounders but could be fired on by four point seven and six inch howitzer batteries. We succeeded in bringing fire to bear on this transport also.

At night we got plenty of exercise crawling on patrols along the enemy front. We examined their wire defenses making detailed reports of it on all parts of our front. We located their listening posts which were withdrawn within their wire soon after we came on this front. This was due to our trying to capture a couple of them at Petite Douve Farm on a patrol one night. We crawled under the enemy trip wires and found ourselves looking into the bed of the stream that ran along the front of their trench but outside their main wire defense. Close examination showed a zigzag trench or sap leading out through the main mass of wire and down to the water. I suppose they had been using this path to draw water for some purpose. We saw here a possible entrance for a raiding party. If the trip wiring on the outer bank of the creek could be cut without detection, mats or portable foot bridges could be thrown across the creek and a raiding party would be able to penetrate the enemy trench in a surprise attack. We reported this layout and were relieved or moved back to supports the next day. The 7th Battalion relieved us and were given the information about the above. They took advantage of it and made a successful raid on the place the same week securing several prisoners and inflicting several casualties on the enemy in the course of the raid. This was the start of a regular craze for raids. Every O. C. along the line from that time on either made raids on the enemy line or tried to make them. The disease spread to the imperials and to the French becoming epidemic along the whole length of the line. Our officers became infected with the germ immediately after the successful raid by the 7th Battalion.

I had spent several months examining the enemy wiring along our part of the front in the sector from the Messines road to the salient beyond Avenue Farm. Along here the enemy worked feverishly every night to strengthen their massed wire. Until now it presented a solid mass of angleiron hurdles, wooden hurdles, etc. all lashed together and reinforced by a lot of heavy wire thrown loosely on top of the whole. In front of the main mass of the hurdles was a line of what were known as goose-berry bushes.

These were tighter coils of wire somewhat in the shape of a barrel. A row of them were placed end to end and the whole works lashed together with more barb wire. In front of this was a line of what was known as accordion wire in a cylinder shaped coil that could be stretched out or telescoped. In front of this again was a system of apron wire and in front of that was the trip wiring. Behind the main mass of hurdles and close against the enemy parapet there was a solid mass of woven wire on upright wooden posts from four to six ft high. On the actual top of the parapet there was a sort of variety of apron wiring on iron screw stakes. In places the whole mass must have measured 80 yards in depth from the trench outward to the open ground in front.

I was asked by Col. Lipsett as to what I thought about the chances of making a raid on this part of the front. I gave him a complete report of the enemy wire that was the product of months of hard and dangerous patrols. I stated that I did not think that a raid here was practical and would no doubt result in heavy loss to the raiders. Lipsett evidently agreed with me.

Later another colonel decided to try to make a raid regardless of this, and rehearsed it on special trenches dug for the purpose of the rehearsal at Bulford Camp. Upwards of 80 men were to be used and the scouts were expected to find an entrance to the enemy trench for the raiding party. They did not leave it to the scouts to select the place but specified the enemy salient to the west of Avenue Farm and opposite our right flank. This colonel then started to supervise the scout patrols and specified when they would go out and where they would go out. He insisted on continuous patrols at the same points and over the same ground night after night at fixed times. This lead to there being beaten paths worn down and plainly visible to enemy aircraft and observers in daylight.

The enemy got to know just where and at what hour to expect us. This was contrary to all my experience and the methods Knobel and I had been using. It was also contrary to the dictates of common sense. I naturally protested against this supervision of the scout work by one who by nature and inclination was so unsuited to over-rule all our work and plans, turning it into a sort of humdrum, rule of thumb, barrack square, bone-headed ritual. I could see the plain white streaks on the aero-plane photos marking the paths taken by my patrols in this senseless performance, and knew that the enemy photos of that same ground would show up these routes equally well. I was nightly expecting an ambush and a loss of some of the Scouts It was not long coming. One night we were in the enemy wire in front of Av. Farm. I think there was about four men in the patrol all crawling in line, with each man close enough to touch the foot of the man ahead. In this formation we could pass a message or signal without noise or movement and always had the whole unit under control. What was most vital (in case of a mix up), you knew where all your men were and did not need to fatally hesitate about throwing a bomb or shooting, when a strange head or heads loomed up suddenly in the darkness with seconds meaning life or death. We had crawled in through the enemy trip wiring this night and were on a wire patrol. The front of the patrol is supposed to watch and listen to the front. The men in the middle watch to the right and left, with the last tail end man watching to the rear. As we passed through the outer line of enemy wire posts there was a rifle shot and I heard a slight noise behind. There was a short dark Scottish lad in the middle of the patrol named either (Richardson or Ferguson) and he lay dead. Shot clean through the head. On looking back I could see that some of the wire posts on the side toward the enemy line had been treated to a coat of luminous paint or sort of phosphorescent coating that would show when any object passed in behind it at night. They must have had a set rifle on the spot and had noticed the blanking of the spot of phosphorous. We were in a ticklish spot and any noise or movement would have sealed the fate of the whole party. I don't know why there were no flares sent up then or why the spot was not raked with a machine gun or smothered under a shower of bombs. The man on that set rifle must have been deceived by the absolute stillness and lack of movement out there. It speaks well for our skills as Indians that we got out of there unscathed and without so much as jangling a strand of wire in our passage.

I could only be present on one patrol at a time and the colonel insisted that there be three patrols out at all times from dark to daylight. Why? I do not know. Eight men can only do so much and the darker, colder, and more rainy the night the more patrols. We all began to get badly crippled up with rheumatism and heavy colds from the constant soaking rain, and from crawling on our faces through the mud and lying in mud and water the major part of every night. The men got colds in their lungs and it was more like a procession of barking dogs than a patrol. Silence soon got to be out of the question and you can guess how nice it was when a fit of coughing break out in its infectious way while in the enemy wire. This, combined with the lack of sleep, had the men in bad shape with them beginning to fall asleep right in the enemy wire. Several times while we stopped crawling to listen, I was jolted to hear audible snores coming from the patrol. The men knew as well as I did that this senseless routine was not serving any useful purpose and consequently grew lax and disinterested. At our right flank there was a road with ditches on either side that went right across to the enemy line. Along the west ditch of this road and something over a hundred yards from our front there was an old shell hole or crater in the bank on the west edge of the ditch. We were out on a patrol to the right of this in an open grass field, when we noticed movement at the old shell hole and could see forms looming there in the darkness.

There was a sort of furrow or very shallow grass-grown ditch extending past our patrol with this furrow leading east to the road ditch and making a junction with it very close to the old shell hole. We decided to chance a crawl up the furrow to see who had occupied the shell hole. It gave us very little cover but we were beginning to be experts on the panther or crocodile stuff. There were three of us and two were armed with .45 caliber colt automatics that we had rustled off dead officers. I had three rounds in mine and the other man had about the same amount of ammunition.

We were totally without other weapons or bombs etc. We could count five heads in the old shell hole and they were (square heads) too. We snaked it right in front of their noses in that shallow furrow till we were not more than 25 ft from them, when Alick Gunne who carried the other pistol fired two shots. I followed with a couple of mine at another fritz who appeared to be trying to untangle some potato-masher bombs that they had with them. Alick's victim was hit in the forehead by both his shots and it lifted the top of his skull off. My victim was hit through the lungs and we could distinctly hear the noise a man makes when froth chokes him. We were now out of ammunition and if we wanted to tackle the remaining three we would have to do it bare handed. I decided to back out, and we got away under the fire of this patrol and also that of another enemy patrol that showed up on our right in the field. A man in this patrol was shooting our way with a mauser pistol. I hurried to our trench and met one of our Lieut's. who was aroused by the noise.

I got the loan of his pistol and returned. We took up the trail of the enemy patrol trying to cut them off before they got through their own wire. We could not make it however for we had to keep in mind the other patrol that had fired on us from over to the right. We got close enough to see them dragging the man that was shot through the lungs and could hear the noise he was making. We sent a shot or two at them but they were under cover now and were lost to us. They were dragging the casualties along by their armpits with their heels trailing on the ground. You could trace the marks for some time after. We got a couple of rifles, some bombs and a haversack of rations along with the cap of the man Alick shot. The cap had two bullet holes in the front rim and was full of brains etc. Had we been properly armed and equipped with bombs etc. we would have made short work of the whole five or perhaps have secured a prisoner or two. In the haversack mentioned we found a tin of potted meat that seemed to be of fair quality, some smoked or roughly smoke-cured pork, dark and poorly cured, some small white biscuits about the size and shape of dominoes. Some of the potato masher bombs had the string with the butt on the end pulled partly out but had not exploded afterward. It must have been a case of faulty fuse arrangement or perhaps our Guardian Angel on the job again. I have some marks yet on my left leg from some of those old potato mashers that they used to throw. The Co. showed his love of me by questioning the veracity of myself and the other members of the patrol when we made a report of the occurrence. Our collection of fresh souvenirs didn't seem to affect his attitude. He was unmistakably was out to queer yours truly by fair means or foul. I was on his bad books and no mistake. My crime was that I was too plain spoken and was given to taking short cuts to expose subterfuge, and given to calling a spade a spade.

I had come near getting one of my patrol reports past his office on to brigade without his adjutant culling it over first. This particular report might have done some good if it had gotten through. The adjutant was on the job incidentally and the report never got past battalion headquarters. There was certainly some contrast from the treatment we had received from Lipsett. He had always treated us white and could talk intelligently about our line of work and helping us with plans to improve it. Anything like that was now a thing of the past and we did not look into the future very hopefully. Those days were gone forever.

The plans for the raid went forward. I did not intend to be the cat's paw or the tool that would be used by the O. C. and two or three junior officers to hang about 80 of our boys on the German wire. I knew the raid could not be made on the sector that they had selected as a suitable field for getting military medals for the (two junior one pips) or (second lieutenants). I had to brave the insinuations and worse that came my way along with the veiled remarks by some of the officers who got posted by the o. c. and adjutant and were not in a position to have opinions of their own. Any officer that showed symptoms of having his own ideas about things, soon was transferred to other fields and was not further known in his old unit. Capt. Smith, Durand, Weld, Knobel, Denis Toun, and several others were practically cold-shouldered out of their own unit for the same sort of crimes that put me in bad with the o. c. I stuck to my resolve about the proposed raid and at the finish they took a poor devil of a sergeant out of no. 4 co. and filled him up to the gills with rum, and then detailed one of my scouts to guide him out to the enemy wire. The two of them were equipped with pliers or clippers to cut a path through the enemy wire. They were out laying there clipping wire until the rum worked off when they returned. The (military medal prospects) were out in a shell hole part way across doing a lot of phoning back and forth to our front trench. Fritz must have had fun listening to this dialogue on his ground circuit or amplifiers that had a radius of 1,100 ft. If they had gone out at daylight and fritz had agreed not to interfere, I don't believe they could have cut a path in that line of wire by sunset. That was the end of the raid but not the end of my troubles with the o. c. and the adjutant.

I would have considered trying to get in the enemy trench at a spot a little way south of the Messines Road, but I was not in any position to make suggestions or get support for any feasible plan. Scouting had been put down under towpath sentry rules and initiative, or skill, or experience no longer counted for anything in our young life. I had been over to the enemy lines in daylight with one other man just to the right of Messines Road. I went into the enemy sap that led directly out to their listening post and brought back evidence of the trip which I showed to Capt. Smith. Fritz had looted all the huge stores of fine cloth that were in the warehouses in Belgium and taken it to make sandbags for his parapets. Expensive and heavy cloths of all kinds with vivid colors were built into his breastworks giving an odd appearance to the front. I brought back some samples of this cloth and some freshly fired mauser cartridges as mementoes of my visit to of his extension of a trench to a point beneath the enemy's fortifications by daylight. We could have doubtless have made a raid there, for one place.

Only to show that the heart of the scouts was in the right place they pulled off a daylight raid all on their own hook. Just to the right of the place where the o. c. had tried to stage the (roman holiday) there was an enemy listening post well out in his field of wire and protected by a thick halfcircle of wire with a covered sap or trench leading back to his main trench. There was an old grass-grown trench (relic of the autumn of 1914) that zigzagged across no mans land from this listening post almost to our front trench. It was very shallow and caved-in in many places but would screen you while crawling in daylight. We planned to cross over by means of this old trench and clip our way along the old sap right up to the listening post. Then conceal ourselves there and pounce on the two fritzes that would come out at about eight p.m. to man the post. We had previously noted the layout along with the usual time the outpost came on duty, figuring that our chances of getting a prisoner for identification purposes was at least as good as that of the big raiding party planned before hand. Three men went out on the final trip to put the plan into action. The weak link in the scheme was the fact that their path to the listening post for the last 20 yards under the wire, or nearly that distance must pass along a shallow trench 101 with water and mud in it. Also it was so low you had to crawl on hands and knees and even on your stomach in spots. Getting the prisoners out through this hole without noise or detection presented a problem to solve. Warner Bole, Bill Maitkin, and Jones delegated themselves a committee of three to carry out the interview. I was up to the eyes in a job of tracing maps that the brigade had asked for and wanted delivered the next day. I might have put the proposed visit off a couple of days and gone with them too, but figured they could do it if anybody could for they were a splendid trio. (3 Aces)

Bole went off ahead with Maitkin close at his elbow and Jones watching on all sides for interference while they worked. There was only room for one man to work clippers in the narrow way. They got to a spot within a few feet of the actual enemy post where they could look up the enemy sap to as far as the first bend or traverse. Bole was stooped down busily clipping away. Maitkin was looking over his shoulder. Jones was at a fork in the trench behind, to watch against being cut off that way. Suddenly there were sounds of feet in the sap and around the traverse came a fritz officer in full war paint, followed closely by a non-commissioned officer with a great coat on and carrying his rifle slung. They were evidently making a round of inspection before dark. It was still broad daylight. They threw an awful queer into our plans by this uncalled for appearance on the scene. There was no place to hide in time to miss their scrutiny and let them pass. Maitkin looked straight at them and they at him, then he plunked three bullets into the officer from his old .455 Webely revolver and the fun was on. The n. c. o. ducked back around the traverse and opened fire from there with his rifle. A big fritz climbed to the top of the parapet hurling a huge bomb of the hair-brush variety. The boys (stood not upon the order of their going but went at once) as they say in Macbeth. They dove along that old sap like seals or walrus and the spray flew high. Fritz brought a machine gun to bear and raked the old shallow trench across no mans land pretty bad. They had some close squeaks from this cause but got home.

I was out one morning in a thick fog at this place with the o. c.of a new cavalry r. c. m. r's. or c. m. r's unit who wanted to get local color or something. He was new over from the training camps and I guess they intended to make infantry out of his unit. He wanted to get posted a bit about frontline doings. There were three patrols of mine out at the time, one near the Messines road and one in the centre of our frontage. On our particular patrol we had no mix up though we were close enough to one to hear it going on but could not make it out at the time on account of fog. There was an imperial battalion next to us on the right. One of their lieutenants had gone on patrol the previous night and happened to pass just to the right of the corner of the enemy salient that jutted out opposite our right flank. He had traveled on for some 500 yards and come back with the report that there was no enemy trench over there at all. He had traveled straight ahead for five or six hundred yards and even then could not even see a trench or anything ahead. He had of course been traveling along no mans land parallel to the enemy trench. From the salient onward to the right the enemy line was invisible from our trenches on account of a rise in the ground between. This fact led to his tale being taken seriously. What they couldn't see they didn't worry about. Another English hoffiser started out in the fog on the same morning while I was out with the gent after local color. He hesitated not but marched boldly forward counting his paces and not taking any precaution what-so-ever. He was accompanied by a couple of victims of the n. c. o. and pte variety. They proceeded like this for perhaps 300 yards. when they were challenged by the enemy sentry on the corner of the salient. They had walked almost on top of him. Following his challenge the sentry opened fire and shot the officer and one of the men. The remaining man though wounded succeeded in dragging his officer away far enough in the fog to enable them to make a getaway. The officer was severely wounded. I don't know whether fatally or not. We could hear this all going on from where we lay in the grass a short distance to the left. With the sentry's challenge sounded so close that I thought it was us he detected. Haltd-ta! Is the way it sounds and is accompanied by the hollow clatter and the rasp of mauser rifle bolt shot back and forth followed by the peculiar double-crack of the mauser-slappbang- slapp-bang. There was no lead that came our way, and we could hear talk in the German trench. We laid still for a bit then edged quietly off to a little safer distance to listen again. We did not hear the details of the mix up until the following day. Soon after getting in off this patrol I was met in the trench by Carson, St. Louis, and Nicholson who held out a riddled rag to me and said ,"Here is all that is left of Sid Green". Sid had been a member of the centre patrol that had been out in the fog during the same time I was out. On account of being on familiar ground and the density of the fog they had abandoned caution for speed walking smartly along in single file on a foot path that had become worn by the o.c's new system of patrols. They had gone close to 200 yards like this with Green leading. St. Louis next, Nicholson, and then Carson. They remember seeing Green stumble as though he had stubbed his toe or stepped into a hole and then there was a roar and the flash of a heavy explosion. St. Louis was blown clean over the next man (Nicholson) behind. When the dust cleared and they picked themselves up to take stock, there was a crater in front about seven feet wide and two feet deep with no sign of Green anywhere. They circled in search of him but found nothing at the time, except the cap that they had showed to me, in the trench. We searched the ground later and found his body a long distance from the scene of the explosion. The back of him was intact but practically all the front of his person was blown away and death had been instantaneous. The tow path system had begun to work out as expected. We investigated this spot and at a distance of 70 yards and behind some shrubbery, we found a mound of fresh earth with a trail showing that it had been taken from the path carefully on a blanket or ground sheet and dumped here so as to leave no sign at the place where the land mine or trip mine was placed. They must have covered the hole with grass and smoothed it to match the rest of the path. The patrol next to Messines road did not have any adventures but said they heard somebody shout something from the German trench immediately after the explosion of the ground mine.

I wanted to see what the creek and its banks where like were it flowed along in the German wire just to the right of the Messines Road. I also wanted to locate a listening post that I knew he had in the vicinity but had not located definitely as yet. At about 150 yards south of the road there was an old drainage ditch extending down a slope at right angles to our trench and so on down a gentle slope to within about 40 yards of the bank of the creek. This old ditch was fringed thickly with willow shrubbery, tall grass and weeds etc. It was dry in the bottom being filled thickly with a rank growth of nettles, thistles, and other nice things and was the home of several stoats, and an army of big rats. We burrowed a rabbit path through this layout right down to the far end from which we could get quite a view of the Fritz trench and wire from a range of about 50 yards in front. I determined to use this point for a jumping off place on a night patrol of the creek bed. The night turned out to be moonlit and still and not very well suited to the job. We had about 70 yards to go in a half-left direction from the end of the old ditch. This was down hill toward the enemy line, and covered with a coat of dry loud-rustling grass that was bleached out to a near white color and would be in contrast to any dark objects moving through or across it. We knew we could expect the enemy listening post to be close to the bank of the creek. The layout did not look good on account of the clearness and stillness of the night that made detection quite possible. We sized it up for awhile, heard a man sneeze and cough to clear his throat and figured it was in the Fritz listening post. After awhile we started a very slow and cautious crawl toward the creek with frequent stops to listen. We had made it about half way when a couple of shots were fired and we could hear the moving back and forth of the bolts as they pushed home a new shell in the Mausers. We heard the thud of the bullets in the field not far above. This did not jibe with the usual night firing that went on at odd times all night and had no particular significance. These shots were directed low and it looked as though somebody in front had heard something or imagined they had seen something. I decided we were in a bad place in case a flare went up. We were not in a position to go forward to the cover of the creek bed on account of the enemy being suspicious and on the watch now. I could imagine those sour-crout square heads with the round ears, sour-crout trimmings, listening under the inverted kettles for our next move. I whispered that we must go back to the end of the old ditch and go quieter and more cautious than we had come out if possible.

I was expecting a flare to go up at any second. We turned with as little rustle in the dry grass as possible and started to crawl steadily back. We had barely started when phut-s-s-ss-up went something that landed about 20 feet from us in the mud with a thud. We thought it might be a bomb at first but there was no explosion so we decided it had been a flare that had turned out to be a dud one and had not lit up when it was shot. After this we heard voices in the Fritz trench and a man run off at the double on the duck-mats of the trench towards Messines Road. I figured he had gone for some flares. There were two or three more rifle shots that all went over us into the field where you could hear them plunk in the mud. We crept on and got to the old ditch with the shrubbery just as they shot a flare up that was not a dud. My two feet were still trailing at the top of the bank when the flare went up. I remember thinking that they might see the steel plates on the soles of my boots shining in the flare light. It is a wonder that they didn't take the odd shot at the end of the old ditch on spec, but they evidently thought they had been hearing things or seeing visions and beyond a few mutterings we did not hear any more from them. We would need a darker and windy night for that particular job.

During the summer we got some new drafts from the 52nd and among the new men was one R. E. Brash, Alias Steamboat Brash, late of Kenora who insisted he must be put on the strength of the Scouts without further delay. Eventually we took him on and it so happened that he got initiated into the mysteries of patrol work on his very first time out in front. We were out on a patrol some distance to the right of the old ditch mentioned in the last patrol account. We had been across the widest part on our front and just to the right of where Petit Douve River turned East and went through the enemy lines. We had been out some time and were on our way back to the vicinity of our own lines. Somebody in our trench had thrown out a flare light setting fire to the dry grass and it flared up over quite a wide area. We were crossing an open piece of field at the time between the fire and the enemy lines. We must have shown up plainly for Fritz opened up rapid fire on us in grand style. I planned to keep my patrol flat down in the lowest ground in reach and keep crawling till we got out of the line of fire (meaning two kinds of fire). One of my Scouts took panic getting on his feet and ran for our lines. He got there too but it was more fool's luck than anything else for there was quite a squall blowing across there and it wasn't wind either. I struck a shallow ditch leading off to the south and though it was full of stinging nettles as thick as they could grow, I burrowed through them at the best crawling speed I could muster and told the rest to follow. We were soon out of the line of fire and the grass fire and the rifle fire, both died down. Then we began to consider ways and means of getting into our own lines. Previous experiences told me that the Commanders of the sentry groups had forgotten all about our patrol. They had changed shifts of sentry groups and listening posts during the time we had been out and this new outfit now on duty clearly did not know of any patrol on their front for they had shot up a bunch of flares. They were sending back a lot of rifle fire in reply to Fritz's strafe. I had a method of my own in these cases that generally worked in a pinch. I would crawl cautiously to speaking distance to the listening post and hail them. This was usually the signal for them to cock their rifles and it wasn't a pleasant sound. Then I used to start in to curse them in good Canadian curse language that they could not mistake for anything else. This familiar sound coming out of the swamp usually had the desired effect of soothing their savage breasts so to speak. If it was an old hand in the listening post he would carefully put the pin back into the lever of his mills-bomb. If it was some of the new drafts it was still risky to bring the patrol ahead for they were subject to sudden fits of panic and might yet cut loose on us. It was new draft stuff alright this night, and the rapid fire burst out from our trench directly in front of where we were. A bullet slammed into the mud right under my hips as I was crawling flat. The force of the impact lifted me from the ground at the time. I dug into the shallow ditch and away off to the South again till we got out of line once more. We compared notes finding that nobody was hurt so far but Steamboat B. had a bullet hole punched through the shoulder strap of his tunic. I succeeded in getting in by going to the point furthest removed from two listening posts on my flanks and knowing my way through the wire I crawled directly to the parapet, sprang over notifying the nearest man that it was only a patrol coming in and not to call up the heavies.

I hunted up the Trench Officer on duty that night and it was directly through carelessness on his part that we had the rough passage. He had known about the patrol but forgotten it or something to that effect. I don't remember what remarks I made to him but they were not complimentary. I fully expected to be fetched to Orderly Room but he never had any more to say to me. Nor did he speak to me at any time after. I was riled and didn't care at the time how I spoke, and on second thought I was right.

I had suggested to Lipsett that the snipers be equipped with .280 caliber Ross Rifles for sniping. They gave a velocity of over 3000 ft per second, and a flat trajectory over a range of nearly 500 yards. Lipsett was impressed with the idea and approached the British War Office with a view of getting their consent to use this rifle. The .280 rifle, of course, was of Canadian make and must be barred of them. Lipsett made a mistake in consulting them at all. He could have wired to Canada and the rifles would have been shipped together with the ammunition for them. We could have been getting the benefit of them while The War Office was still hemming and hawing about it and figuring out a lot of red tape forms or endless correspondence to give employment to their over crowded bombproof staff. They did send a man to enquire into it one day. Word came from Brigade Headquarters that a Sniper was to come down there with his rifle. I thought it was another of the Bomb-Proof Officers that often came across the channel on a sort of Cook's Tour, that wanted to see a real front line Sniper and paw over his rifle asking a lot of foolish questions. We had a number of visits from this type. Quite innocently I sent down Buck Shepperdson, ex cowboy and windjammer from away back. Buck had a great line but it had a habit of soaring off to the heights of fancy with him stretching a very long bow at times when he got well wound up. The visiting Officer at this time was none other than the one sent by the War Office to get first hand information about the .280 Ross and its possibilities for sniping, He accompanied Buck up the line to a Sniping Post. He had him fire a shot or two, and asked a whole lot of questions of a technical nature about the .280 etc. Buck said he told him it had a velocity of, I don't remember how many thousands of feet per second and a lot of other fool ideas that happened to occur in his peanut-sized bean. He had stretched the long bow with a will and the Officer had put this (bunk) all down in his note book for the benefit of the War Office. Ye Gods. I groaned and writhed in spirit when I gathered the gist of what had taken place. Our hopes of a real rifle for sniping were now shot higher than a Kite. I could have sniped Buck with his own gun I felt so sore at the silly trick he had played on me. The officer had returned to the W. O. with that note book full of rubbish.

Major Andrews was later on leave in London and met Sir Charles Ross himself. He mentioned the 280 to him along with the fact that I wanted some of those rifles. Ross had two equipped with telescopes and told Andrews he could bring them out to me. Andrews went to a banquet 107 and got pickled and just thought of it as he reached the boat at Folkstone on his way back to us. He wired to London but Ross was out of town and could not be reached. I never got the two rifles.

There was method in the madness of some of these patrols at least, though not in some of them that took us out repeatedly on the same frontage night after night with no clear task in view, but just because the O. C. said so. It meant a lot of foot slogging before you got out at all. I had to notify all Trench Officers, Platoon Commanders, Heads of Sentry Groups, Machine Gun Crews and the Bombing Officer and his men. Some of them would swig too much (rum) and forget about you, some of them didn't give a damn about us anyway and would just as soon shoot at us for diversion. Others were just plain careless, absent minded and forgot about it. I think the case above mentioned came under the first two headings. In addition to the night and day work with the observers, snipers, and patrols I had some map work to do, enlargements, tracings, transfer of detail from aerial photos onto maps adjusting the scale. In the morning I had a full detailed report to make on all the previous night patrols. Every night I had a detailed report to make of all the Observation work and Sniping that had been during the day. This included the working out of intersections on enemy work and exact details of it in all respects. I reduced this mixture of reports to a regular form with headings for each separate subject e.g.: Enemy front line trenches, enemy wire, enemy aircraft, enemy artillery, enemy machine gun posts, enemy snipers etc. etc. This made a hit with the staff and they immediately put out the forms in print for us and it simplified the work. I did not get a great deal of sleep during the year and a half that I was on this triple job steady. Towards the beginning of 1916 I was pretty well run down, being saturated with rheumatism from constant exposure to wet. I suppose the gentle art of crawling in the dark all night with nerves strung to piano wire tightness did not help to fatten me up any. I told you of a few of the incidents on a few of the patrols just to give a rough idea of what it was like. It was not really the work that wore me out, it was the hostility along with constant suspicion shown by the o. c. and the adjutant with the knowledge that no matter how good or how hard we worked we would never get any credit for it. As long as they were in the unit I could never get any satisfaction from the work. It dragged on this way until I eventually gave it up in the autumn of 1916. After being a brigade observer for about a month I went back voluntarily to the ranks and took up sniping for a change and a rest. In the autumn we did quite a few crude surveys behind our front lines. Knobel now captain led us in this work, it was preparatory to a lot of digging of support trenches and communications.

One time in the late fall we took over billets from a Calvary unit that was being broken into trench routine. I forget whether it was the c.. m.. Mrs. or some other unit. At any rate they had stabled their horses in our sleeping quarters making an awful mess of them. On coming out of the lines we had to work for several hours carrying horse manure out on rubber sheets and in biscuit tins etc. before we could get a place decent to sleep in. We were in a sort of shed or annex to a barn with a clay floor and brick walls. After we got the place dunged out we spread fresh straw in a strip along the walls making our beds on it. In the centre we left the earth floor bare and built a sort of crude fireplace. Here we had a fire we sat around on small boxes or biscuit tins which served as chairs keeping us off the damp clay. The o. c. was looking for something to use as a pretext to entering a crime against me and here he found his excuse. We were moved from this to another and when we were packed and cleaned up ready to pull out, the men who were to take over the quarters were waiting to get in, seeing this I did not remove the half dozen small boxes and tins that served as seats around the fire. There was a junior officer detailed to inspect billets when you are leaving and see that they are left clean. Our billet was a palace by comparison to what we found when we came there. The inspecting officer had been posted by the o. c.. His eyes hit on the seats around the fire and he put up a great fuss about it, and got busy right away. He put me on the crime list for a dirty billet giving the seats for a reason for it. It was a very flimsy excuse for a crime sheet, and I knew it well. I also knew that the seats were not the cause of this fuss.

I was told the time to appear, and marched in like a felon. Right Turn! Left Turn! Halt! There they were, a grand array of all the legal lights. It appeared that he had selected his crowd. There was not a friend of mine in the lot. It was a circle of hostility for sure including some new draft officers that did not know me at all but had my pedigree from the o. c. This was the first time any officer had ever found the occasion to yank me up on the carpet since I had entered the service. The horrible details were all polished up and read out in a way that would have made a shyster lawyer prosecuting attorney green with envy. Then I was asked what I had to say for myself. I replied that it would be a useless waste of words for me to say anything for I knew that this thing was all well (cut and dried) before I came in. There was no direct reply to this, only cold stares of hostility. Then the o. c. Presiding Judge cleared his throat-Ahmed!

Relieved himself of a lot of petty stuff that had itched him apparently for some time back. They proposed to relieve me of one of my stripes. They stepped beyond their authority right there for the stripes had been given me in the field, by (Col. Lipsett) and could not be taken away without a court martial and so on so forth. I took them all off myself, and went without any for a while. I think we had another week in the line. Then it came my turn for my first leave or furlough to Blighty. The Battalion was to be out two whole weeks on rest, and I would not be needed so I got away on leave to the England as a buck private for I had not decided to put up any stripes yet. I never would have put them on again except for a peculiar set of circumstances that cropped up, and made it almost impossible for me to quit my job at the head of the scouts at that time. This condition cropped up during the two weeks I was away and I will tell you about it later.

First Leave To Blighty

Just now we are off for Blighty on the first leave. I don't know where I am going, but I am on my way. Across the Channel on the old channel boat, fog, cold, and mist to Folkestone and London. Put up at a little hotel just off the hub of the world or Trafalgar Square. Took in Choo-Chin-Chow at His Majesties. Tonight's The Night at the Alhambra, A Little Bit Of Fluff at the Gaeity, a musical concert at some place also and another play called The Truth and Nothing But The Truth at Kensington, Made the rounds of the town with one Dink McLean or D. J. M. Dink, he was some guy and could certainly show one around. We went to a lot of odd corners. Ye Olde Cheshire Cheese, the Coal Hole, Dirty Dicks and an eating place in the basement of a big hotel where you could get a real feed and were liable to meet anybody. We met Herbert Asquith himself and Dink being able to talk with anybody in any company, Butted in and we had a feed with H. A. along with an ex Commissioner of the n. w. m. Police vis-a-vis. We ran into another government man at the Ches' Cheese. A commissioner from the East India Service. With Dink to break the ice we had a couple of pleasant drinks and a chat with this gent. We took in a flash to the Oriental Restaurant just off Piccadilly Circus and had some marvelous vegetable get-ups the like of which I have never encountered before or since. We had a look in at the Royal Cecil but this did not appeal to me very much. It was too exclusive for me by several miles though Dink professed to like it. We walked the (Strawnd) at even-tide. We went to see a film that was being tried out by the inspectors and censors before being put on the regular screens. Took in the Zoo Gardens and some of the museums. Leave didn't last long, we only got seven days all told in England.

The afternoon of the fifth day I ran plumb into an adventure, right in front of the Gaeity Theatre. This adventurer was on its return from the Gen. P. O., had been posting some parcels to friends overseas, was just convalescent from several weeks of quinsy or throat trouble, was jumping up and down with little high heels on the pavement and raring to go. It was dark, it was Irish and I only had two more days left before going back to the gates of Hell yawning wide. We chummed for two days and nights and then I took the plunge into the dark again.

I never felt quite so lonely in my life as when I went through the iron gates at the depot at Waterloo Station on my way back over there. I missed the pitter-patter of those little feet. Ye Gods! You have to live through it to know the sensation of the sheer drop that was at those iron gates where so many went, went in their hundreds and thousands and did not return. Dust and silence in their eyes.

Man's inhumanity to man with some unbelievable exponents in London during the war years. They were legal sand baggers, Legalized lead pipe artists. Big husky brutes, that loafed around London when elderly men with families, other men far from physically fit, and mere slips of boys were wading in mud, and blood and fire in the trenches. How they got their jobs and why they kept them is one mystery that certainly should be solved. A man would arrive on leave, perhaps exhausted, he would have a good sleep and start to look around, He might be accompanied by lady friends or relatives. His mind far from such things as Red Caps. One of these Gents would spot him, trump up some excuse to halt him, brow beat and insult him, roaring at him in a way that no one could possibly stand. The chances are ten to one that the victim's rage would suddenly rise to heights beyond his possible control. This was the end that the Red Caps had in view with it ending in a mix up, and the victim would be clubbed and kicked into submission or at least into exhaustion by three or four (sidekicks) or legalized fellows that were always handy to mix in when the stage was set. He would then be cuffed, kicked along to a military prison, deprived of his funds, and done out of his furlough or leave that he had waited for and looked forward to during a year or more in the trenches. I have known sober fine men who had not had a drop of liquor, were happy the moment before, and at peace with the world, to be set upon in this way. The person turned into a savage beast, without the shadow of an excuse on their first day out of the line, perhaps on their way to home to be with their folks. You would have to actually see the thing done and then would almost doubt the evidence of your senses. The Good Lord surely tolerates some awful specimens that walk around on their feet in the human image. Perhaps He never heard of them, but the British Army Officials should. To croak one of these things would be doing the world a grand good service. To put them in the trenches and keep them there would be a lot better.

I had a narrow escape from these boys on my first trip out from the hotel on my first day on leave. I had been warned about this game by a victim who had gotten back to the trenches before I left. This was all that saved me from falling into the trap with both feet. Having walked about two blocks from the hotel and pausing on the curb to get out my pipe and fill it for I felt like a smoke, I had naturally unbuttoned the front of my great coat to get at tobacco matches etc. There came a roar behind my elbow that would have stirred the wrath of the best Angel that ever sat around the Golden Throne. I instinctively just rose on the point of my toes with every sinew tautened in a pivot swing that would have been a jaw buster if had been let go with all the rage behind it. In that moment I had a glimpse of red and it came to me in a flash in that fraction of a second that here was the game I had heard about. It was old stuff and all this thing wanted was to do me out of my seven day leave and have the pleasure of helping a gang of red tops to beat me up and throw me in the clink. It must be a strange mentality that can get pleasure out of things like that. Certain departments of the army are about the only place where a depraved nature of that brand can get play and exercise of its natural bent. With the military police it is all one way with no come back possible for the victims. Here this type thrives and grows fat. I had remembered in time but it was hard to keep on remembering. Somebody should have played them at their own game. You could have concealed about a platoon of leave men from the trenches some place handy sending out a decoy victim to walk up and down. When the dirty work was under way you could ring in the platoon and beat the up red caps to within about a 32nd of an inch of their lives. A branding iron would not be a bad rig to use on these guys, and it might leave a permanent impression.

Return To The Messines

I forget if it was Calais or Le Havre where we landed and were marched out into the country about eight miles to a sort of distribution point. On this march out we fell out by the side of the road for a ten minute rest at the end of the first hour. I had my few personal belongings in the packsack, including a prismatic compass, some good razors, spare clothing, photos, personal letters etc. On starting out from this place I accidentally exchanged packs with an imperial who had been next to me.

At the distribution camp they woke you at daylight with the officer standing on a soap box calling off all the different divisions. You fell in with the men for your division when it was called and were shipped off to the railway point nearest to your unit. On arrival I found that the battalion was all ready to go into the line. Their rest period had been cut short by emergency orders.

When we had pulled out on rest, our line had been taken over by the c.. m.. r s. They were new and green at the job then. Fritz got wise to it the first day and began to try what he could do to demoralize them and to put their wind up. I think he would have made an attack if they had been in there a few days longer. I was sent to form the advance party that always precedes a battalion going in to take over dugouts and quarters etc., and on strange ground guide them in. We heard plenty of bullets whistling as soon as we stuck our noses around the end of the hill a mile back of our line. Working our way into the front trench we found things in very bad shape. The trenches were full of water with the mud knee deep and more than that in spots. The dugouts and shelters were flooded out and they had been using rifles and two x fours, or anything else that would serve as props for the floors in these shelters.

The said floors now consisted of sheets of corrugated iron propped high enough to bring them above water level. Drainage ditches, saps, and sump-holes were plugged up from neglect, and full of mud and water. Along the front trench we came to numbers of hip rubber boots that had stuck fast in the clay with the wearer being unable to pull them out. He had walked away without them and there they were sticking up out of the soup. They had not had any listening posts out beyond the parapet for nearly a week. Fritz had been over tossing bombs right into the front trench. At Messines Road the Germans had come up to within 120 yards of our trench and here had dug a trench out across the road and some distance on either side. They had strengthened this with breastworks and wire. They were occupying it now in force evidently intending to connect it to their main line by trenching across. They were keeping up a constant ragged rifle fire day and night to further harass the greenhorns. Fritz had sure made hay during the two weeks we had been out on rest and had the poor old c. m..rs going-going and nearly gone. This is what I found when I got back from leave. Here I was up against it. I had made resolutions mentally that I would not put up stripes again, or try or carry on the scout etc, under our present o. c. I had decided it was a thankless and very uphill job. Here was a state of affairs that made it impossible for me to quit the job until it was straightened out, and no mans land was again under control, and the enemy snipers tamed down to an attitude of respect and quiet. It had been a rare thing for an enemy bullet to come over our lines. As to the ground between the lines it had been ours at nearly all times right up to fritz's wire. He had even put all his listening posts inside strong wiring and had abandoned moving patrols entirely on account of the aggressive tactics of our scouts. Now this was all changed and the shoe was on the other foot with a vengeance. I could not very well quit the section under those conditions.

The first night in there we swept no-mans land clear of any attempted enemy patrols. The following day my bunch of snipers got to work and before nightfall, it was like old times. You could hardly hear an enemy bullet over our lines. The following night was very dark and very windy with a squall of rain at intervals. We decided to make a cleanup on that German breastwork that had been built across Messines Road. We threw bridges across the support trenches where they crossed the road behind our line. Then we used a motor truck and hauled an 18 lb. field piece straight down the road to the front trench. We fixed the gun up here ready for business then removed the sand bags of our parapet from in front of it. The fuses were set at zero and the gun traversed a certain distance after each shot. The gunners put some 30 rounds rapid fire onto that breastworks at 120 yards range. A raid which netted some prisoners and disclosed about 18 dead followed this treatment. We occupied the site of this barricade with a patrol during the hours of darkness for a week or more but fritz did not show any inclination to try to reoccupy it. The next task was to re-establish a line of listening posts, overhaul our wire defenses then drain, and repair our trenches and dugouts. There was lots of work for everybody for a couple of weeks.

We were at Bulford Camp a couple of miles to the rear for Xmas. The company cooks put up a good dinner and everybody passed the day in good spirits. Of course there were lots of parcels sent from home at this season and they helped immensely. Paddy Reill got to celebrating Xmas and had a few more than was good for stability. A dance got started in one of the wooden huts. Paddy was in the middle with a dozen or more men getting formed in a circle around him and they started revolving in a sort of war dance. They made a few revolutions alright until they came to the end of the hut. They went right on through taking the end of the hut and Paddy along with them. Paddy was under and got two broken ribs. He had to stay at the dressing station for several weeks while the ribs knit again.

There was a joke going the rounds about Paddy during his stay at the dressing station. The rum issue for the battalion came up that far by G. S. wagon and was left there until darkness. It went up to the line with the carrying parties when they came out for rations. Paddy had the bright idea of filling a jar with water and substituting it for one full of S. R. D. Later on the next day he spotted a friend passing and beckoned him to come in. He led the way around to the back pulling the cork with many Oh's and Ahs! poured out water. In some sad and mysterious way the switch had been bungled. Paddy nearly fainted that time. Paddy was quite a character and a good sniper to boot.

When our right hand platoon was run over and captured at St. Julien Paddy was among them. He enquired if he could go if he wanted to. An officer told him it was every man for himself so Paddy went. How he got away and escaped death or capture is a mystery. I guess his Indian blood became useful at that time helping to melt into the landscape. Lipsett used to ask about it just to hear Paddy's peculiar style of description. Part of it went like this, "(We snuck along a ditch, and clum a tree)" etc. He made elaborate use of his hands in describing any event. Paddy was hit by a fragment of a whizz-bang shell that fritz sent over in retaliation for our shelling of Avenue Farm. Curiosity to see our shells bursting led him to expose himself and was the cause of his death. His Sniping mate Phil McDonald was killed by a shell while on his way to visit Paddy during the time he was in the dressing station with broken ribs. Phil had asked me if he could go out early so as to visit Paddy on his way. When about a hundred yards from the dressing station a shell came over and hit the cobble stone road. A big slab from this shell spinning from the burst caught Phil and very nearly disemboweled him. He died in Patty's arms a few minutes later. He used to put a nick on his rifle stock for every German he shot. I sent Phil's rifle away to Winnipeg where it was exhibited for awhile. I believe he had some 40 or more notches. It was a MK 3 Ross with a Winchester Telescope three inch diameter. There was just 12 days between their deaths.

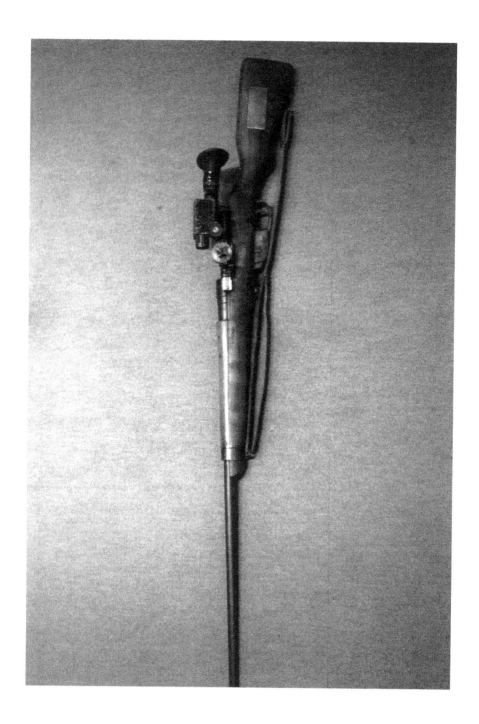

THIS RIFLE WAS USED BY SNIPER No 710. PTE P. McDONALD
90TH BATTALION (90TH RIFLES)
WITH IT HE ACCOUNTED FOR 42 GERMANS
BETWEEN March 1915 and 3 January 1916
WHEN HE WAS KILLED BY A SHELL NEAR MESSINES.
THE RIFLE WAS PRESENTED TO
BRIG. GEN. L. J. LIPSETT, C.M.G.
90TH BTN.

I saw a duel one day between these two and a couple Bavarian snipers. These two enemy snipers had a peculiar head dress by which you could distinguish them. They wore a cap something the shape of a Glengarry, of a brownish bronze color and with a large tassel drooping from one side. One of them had thrown the sand in my face that morning. I was watching for them and so were Paddy and Phil. At last those two succeeded in spotting the enemy snipers standing with heads full above the parapet, screened by a dense tuft of willow that grew from some stumps that had been built into their parapet. We were certain they would not remain there for more than a few seconds. There was no place right along there in our trench where two men could shoot from cover. I acted as observer with the telescope. Paddy and Phil set their sights and adjusted and cocked their rifles while under cover. On the word "go" they both stood up at once, aimed and fired. One of the enemy snipers slumped down and rolled out of sight. The other one spun around like a top with his rifle describing a circle over his head while still gripped in his hands. Then he came down on the sandbags with a whack that raised the dust. His rifle was discharged while its muzzle was making that circle in the air.

A sniper who is in good training only needs three seconds exposure of a target. Phil had a good post up in the loft of an old barn. The top floor was loaded with tobacco stowed in there like we would stow loose hay in a mow at home. I was on my rounds one day and went up to see how Phil was getting on. I could hear him chuckling to himself about something that appeared to amuse him. When I climbed up he said, "here! Take a look at this damned thing will you". At a distance of 800 yards up the slope toward Messines and on the front slope of a trench parapet, was what appeared at first look, to be a man working with a pickaxe. He would stoop and straighten moving his pick up and down. Then he would move forward and back a bit. It was a dummy to draw our sniper's fire and disclose their position to the enemy observers. They would be watching from two, or perhaps three, fixed points thus being able to get an intersection and map the location of our sniping post. They did not mind using a few shells to dig out a sniper. That dummy could quite easily fool anyone looking at it without glasses or a telescope. They used to go to all manner of tricks and elaborate rigs to draw us out in this way.

I watched one time for a good three hours while they tried to draw my fire. They would open and close a loop hole. Move a dummy figure back and forth behind it. They would put a stick out through it to represent a rifle barrel and move this slightly every once in awhile then stick a dummy head over the parapet moving it in as natural way as possible. They would also stick the end of a shiny tin through the loop hole to represent the end of a telescope. They used to have an empty square box set behind such a loop hole, and if you fired, they could later get the line of your bullet through the box and locate you very closely that way. I have seen them put up a big turnip and a mangelwurzel with a cap on it etc.

We were treated to a beautiful concert one evening on this part of the front. It was a still clear summer night and a German in their front line sang for some time a number of yodeling songs or Swiss mountain songs. He was a dandy at it and during the time he sang you could not hear another sound from either side of the lines. We applauded him with a good will. It was a treat. During the first couple of months we were there it was quite common to pass compliments back and forward between the opposing lines by word of mouth. There were numbers of Germans who had lived in Canada and the States who could to speak our lingo like a native. There was one especially, who had been a barber in Calgary. He used to remind us that he had shaved us B— many a time and of course regretted the fine chances he had let slip to cut our throats. There was some shouting back and forth over the news about Cradock's Squadron, and again when fritz got caught in the Falkland Islands. Any outstanding event was the signal for a few comments to be handed back and forth. It usually ended in hot words followed by a shower of bullets.

Sometime after Xmas the machine gun section of our battalion got busy building reinforced emplacements for their guns to fire from. They would make the roof of a solid mass of steel girders or rail and on top of this would pile sacks full of loose bricks that they brought from ruined buildings nearby. The sides would be banked up with the same material, and then covered well with earth and camouflage. We of the scouts had our front line home at this time in a wine cellar of an old estaminet that stood close to where the road crossed our right flank. We too wanted to reinforce the roof so it would withstand the burst of ordinary field gun shells or whiz-bangs. The machine gunners had filled a large number of sacks with bricks from a heap nearby but had not yet carried them away. Some of the scouts eyed this fine collection and then told me to go someplace, or in other words, to depart from there for awhile. I obliged, and strange to say, our roof was a lot thicker and stronger when I came that way again. Now it did not matter whether we were guilty or not. The scouts always got the credit if anything went missing or if any tricks or mischief was pulled off. The m. g. crews didn't forget to howl about their bricks. Right after that, if it was a special dirty rainy cold night there would be a couple of reports go to battalion headquarters, from the m. g. posts that such and such a number of Germans had been seen moving at such a place in no mans land. Of course the o. c. would immediately order out a couple of scout patrols and we would get a grand soaking out there in the rain in the swamp on a goose chase. This went fine as long as the present officer was acting adjutant at battalion headquarters. But one time he got a vacation or something and a Capt. MacKenzie was put in his place. MacKenzie was one of the original eight officers and had known me from Valcartier. I told him about the little game that was being played. Iszatso!! All right old timer we will see. There came an extra dirty wet night and sure enough the fritz patrols got thick out in front of those m. g. posts. MacKenzie enquired as to the exact place they had been seen. Then he ordered a m. g. with a full crew to be put out there until daylight with a relief every two hours. I guess that hurt the feelings of the scouts when I explained it to them.

The next day our observers who had been up in a big bushy tree reported that you could look into a trench where lots of Germans passed up and down. We suggested that a m. g. up there would be a good rig. The o. c. who was quite willing for somebody else to try anything, ordered it done. Now they had a character in the m. g. Section. One Nobby Clark. This was the one and original man of that name and fame. Nearly every brigade in the corps sooner or later produced a phony edition under the same name, but there was but one real Nobby Clark and he was a dandy. He feared neither God, man or the devil and would fight at all times willingly with gusto. He was tagged with nearly every medal except the V. C. He was as crazy as a bed bug in some ways, but always cheerful. He manned the gun up in the tree after it had been put up there during the night. He fired it, and got down, alive and well too. You could not break his luck anyway.

One time there was a battalion of Scottish highlanders on our right. They had thrown out a listening post that was a little too far over in front of us. Nobby happened to be on duty there, and hearing or seeing them out there he crept out to investigate. I guess he couldn't make out the broad and guttural lingo they were muttering and mistook them for Germans. He got busy and made an attack on them all by himself. The Scotties beat him off with a shower of bombs. Nobby swore some great oaths and ran in and got his machine gun returning with it to the attack. I think the scots had a near squeak before we lassoed Nobby and brought him home.

One night we heard a thumping and pounding noise out in front mixed with curses and the jangling of barbed wire. We crept out cautiously to see what in Hades was going on out there. We found that Nobby and one of his mates had fallen out about something and had gone out in front to fight it out. One time he went on leave to London. While there he dolled up in officer clothes, tacked on all his medals and made violent love to some general's daughter, marrying her too before they got wise to him. He left us joining the Calvary taking part later in some of their escapades and winning some more medals. I remember seeing him stripped to the waste one cold wet Christmas and fighting in pouring rain and about six inches of mud and water seemingly quite happy.

We had another character in the scouts. Joe Millan, an ex-pugilist from the Pacific Coast, originally of Glasgow. He was a patrolman and got over the ground like a cat. He was out one night on a sort of listening post during a spell of rainy weather when the shell holes and all the depressions were brim full of water. He spotted a lone enemy scout and took after him with a big 45 colt revolver as his sole weapon. He had three or four rounds in the revolver and that was all. He opened fire on the German forcing him to take cover in a shell hole full of water. Millan was now out of ammunition and could not figure out what to do next. He called to the nearest man on duty at the listening post trying to get him to come out to his aid but it turned out to be a new draft and he was not willing to come.

There was this German in a shell hole armed with a mauser rifle. Joe beat it in to get a rifle or bombs or something and when got back his German was across to the left on his way home. He left a distinct trail of mud and water for about a hundred yards from the shell hole. This fritz must have been in bad humor for he fired a pot shot at the listening post on our left flank as he passed. Joe got into an argument in an estaminet one day getting hit on the head with a pick handle. Old Doc. Mothersill m. o. told him it was lucky he had no brains or he would have suffered from concussion. When Joe had a few drinks he would start to give a representation of a bear eating blueberries. He could certainly make some unearthly noises during this performance. At a certain stage of inebriation he would start to talk on theology and he had a surprising and wide knowledge of the subject, he and Alick Gunne had adopted a wayside Shrine, a sort of stone archway with miniature figures of the Saints decorating the interior, where the devout wayfarer in pre-war days had been wont to offer up prayers. They, he and Alick had taken this for a home and bed as it was conveniently located on the support trenches. Joe called it the Jesus Box.

During the time they used this as sleeping quarters they had an accident. Coming in off patrol they were cleaning their pistols, with Gunne in some way discharging his and was badly shot in the knee. Our loving o. c. immediately suggested that the wound was intentional and self-inflicted. Now Alick Gunne was not by any stretch of imagination a man likely to do a thing of that kind. He had a nasty wound but got a more painful one through the efforts of the o. c. who persisted in his lowdown idea putting it in writing that followed poor Gunne to hospital and through the stages of convalescence. Now it was far from a joke to get put along with a bunch of self-inflicted cases for they were subjected to a lot that would break the heart of a self-respecting man of the caliber of Alick Gunne. He recovered but did not come back to his own battalion. Probably he could not trust himself to spare the o. c. if he had to come in personal contact with him again. He went to an officer's training school coming back to the line as a lieutenant in the 44th battalion. He was killed while leading his platoon in a bombing attack up a trench on the face of the Green Fosse or Green Crassier at Lens. I never saw a man more unsuited to command and to be a judge of men than that o. c. His ideas of discipline took the form of petty personal persecution that he carried to disgusting lengths in many cases of sorrowful memory.

I had an odd experience with one of his junior officers one day. At our extreme right flank there was a bend or corner in the front line trench. At this corner stood a huge thick willow stump some nine to ten feet in height and crowned with a thick brush of withes or willow sprouts. There was an English unit on our right at this time and one of their men was shot dead, while taking observations from this tree. This happened early one fine morning. I had been in a o. p. of my own since daylight looking for any new earth works or wire work along the enemy front. I was told of the man that got sniped from the willow. In a few minutes I got word to come to company headquarters as the junior officer mentioned wanted to see me. On my arrival he at once gave me orders to go to the willow tree at our right and take observations on new earth that had been thrown out at a sap in front of Avenue Farm. He specified the location of this and I informed him that I had already taken the location of this work. I had already taken observations of it and found it to be earth thrown up by a couple of shells when a battery of ours had registered there the evening previous. I did not bring up the subject of the man just killed. I waited to see if he would, as I knew he had been informed of it. Regardless of my observation report he still insisted on observation from the willow. I was a wee bit surprised at the cold-bloodedness of it for he thought I had not yet heard of the fatality at the willow. I was also confident that I could take a peep from that willow by using enough caution and experience to not get shot. I got directly behind it and eased myself up so slow you could not detect movement. It was a Zulu trick used on exposed ground, and we had practiced it often. I brought my eyes just far enough up to slide a telescope through the dust, leaves and twigs on top. On putting my eye to the lens I found myself looking straight at the muzzle of a mauser rifle. I could see the front lens of a telescope sight above its shiny muzzle and the outline of a pill box cap behind it. I took note of the big elm tree that partly screened the fritz sniper, then let go sliding straight down into the trench. I decided to come back later for my telescope. The junior officer had failed this time. We had more than Germans to watch at times. This same officer had rather odd tendencies. One day he was on a patrol along what was known as the (International Trench) just to the left of the bluff in the Ypres Salient. One of my scouts, Mitchell was with him. In the course of their patrol they came on a lot of rifle grenades that had been fired but had not exploded on account of the soft mud where they lit. While Mitchell was some distance away with his back to him, the officer seized and threw a rifle grenade at Mitchell with all the force he could muster by swinging it by the end of its rod. It failed to explode again for which Mitchell was of course duly thankful. They were alone in that section at the time.

Not long after the willow tree incident, this officer was detailed to go out on a patrol with me. We had an objective near where the Petite Douve River crossed the enemy lines. To get there we had to follow a long ditch fringed with willow stumps that ran on a long slant toward our objective. When we were over half way there he called from behind and asked where I was going. I told him and he said "I guess we won't go over there now, we will cross this open ground to the left. "there is some of our wire that I want to look over." Alright! Away we went parallel to our line, till we came to the old ditch down, which we had made the patrol to the creek (when the flare was a dud). At one side of this ditch was a large square sump hole that had been dug to drain the front trench and it was full of muddy water and dirt of several kinds. In his prowling around he succeeded in catching his foot in a trip wire and immediately there was a jingle and rattle of tin cans. They used to be hung in pairs on the wire to serve as alarm bells to the sentries. Fritz must have heard it for he opened with a burst of machine gun fire that snapped very close throwing blue sparks from the wire on both sides of us. The junior officer went to step back to take cover in the ditch and fell plump into the big sump hole full of filth. He had a new uniform from a famous London outfitter and that did not improve his feelings, or sweeten his tongue. Why didn't you tell me that hole was there? I asked him in turn, why he had not climbed a willow stump that was right near the hole? I know you have great faith in willows.

We still had some of the old colt machine guns that had come from home with us. It was a problem at night to screen the flash from their muzzle so that it would not be visible from a flank as well as from in front. One lad had a bright idea. He riveted some brackets on the end of a length of ordinary stove pipe so it could be attached, just ahead of the muzzle at night and thus screen the flash. They attached one and tried it out. You never heard such an unearthly racket in your life as that gun made in that valley with its stove pipe muzzle attachment. They could not use it on account of the noise if anything being worse than the flash. They used to hang up blankets or burlap for screens shooting through them at night. The old colt was not (too good) for some purposes on cold nights. It had too many long flat sliding surfaces of metal against metal. The oil would stiffen up on these slides and it was hard to get the gun started to work freely. Maybe you had been on patrol and located a fritz wiring party at work. You went in and gave the location to the m. g. crew. They would work the old cocking lever under the barrel and pull the trigger. Plunkstop- cocking lever again, then plunk-plunk-click-stop a couple of times. By the time the old colt decided to start regular work the enemy wiring party had taken warning and scuttled to cover and your fire drew nothing but some blue sparks.

During the first months in the line a wiring party was quite an expedition. You were supplied with a lot of wooden posts exactly like the fence posts at home and also a big maul to drive them with. You would go out in the open field at perhaps 100 to 200 yards in front of the enemy trench, string out your posts, and then start driving them in. Whack-Whack-Whack with the big maul. It sounded as loud as a field gun out there in that open place. There would also be the men carrying the wire on spools with a stick shoved through the centre of the spool being held by a man on each end. All told, there would be quite a large and noisy party out there. Fritz might want to do some wiring on his own side, and if this happened to be the case it would be the signal to start to Whack-Whack. It would then be a race between the two wiring parties to get finished first and then turn the machine gun on the other fellows. If fritz didn't happen to want to do any wiring himself he was apt to make it very interesting for our party by shooting up plenty of flares to make them quit work, and by sweeping the ground with m.

124

g. fire or shrapnel. Later on we were equipped with iron screw stakes patterned after those used by the Germans. They were made out of a round iron rod about tree quarters of an inch thick. At the bottom end this had been twisted to a corkscrew shape. Above the corkscrew there were several single loops or turns at intervals of about a foot till you got to the top which had a loop. They were cut in lengths suitable for the kind of entanglements to be put up. You used a cross stick through one of the loops to screw them into the ground. The wire was run direct from spool to loop in stringing it on the stakes. The scouts were often detailed to furnish a screen or a line of outposts beyond the wiring party. When a bunch of new draft men were being broken in to listening post duty they used to give us trouble. They would lie there and watch the wire posts at night until they really thought they were moving about. Then they would firmly believe they had seen some Germans. Some times they would give the alarm and have the whole works (standing to) at the parapet, but usually it only meant more orders for patrols from the o. c..

At Petite Douve Farm the enemy evidently had a battalion headquarters, and lived in style somewhere in the basement. Paddy Riel was watching that place from a high spot one day and saw the chef or cook for the enemy headquarters outfit step up around the end of a traverse for a look around. He had on a regular white chefs suit and cap. Paddy shot him without delay, and said he figured the fritz officers would be pretty sore about that. Jack Ballendene shot a fritz sniper out of a tree one day some distance to the left of Petite Douve, or up near Verbrandenmolin. We used to hold the line alternately to the right and left of the Messines Road. The position to the left of the road gave the best observation and sniping facilities for you could command a view of more enemy country.

There used to be a British airman that flew a fast monoplane quite a bit on this part of the front and he used to entertain us with some hair-raising stunts in the air over the opposing lines. He was reputed to be the famous mad major who was supposed to have a field battery of his own and was doing his own observations for the battery. He certainly could handle that machine. When he wanted to look at a target he would pretend to be falling until down very close, then straighten out, and away.

During the latter part of our stay at Messines we got a new cook in the scout section. He was a real old lumberjack cook who had fed the timber beasts in some northern lumber camp at home. He was long, lanky, and dark with a stringy drooping mustache to match. He lived up to the reputation of his breed, for all bush cooks, are supposed to be cranky. When he first arrived it was a spell of especially wet and drizzly weather, and the wood we rustled from ruined buildings for his cook fires was pretty soggy. He had to cook in the open air any place that was handy along a communication or support trench. On the first day he fogged up with the soggy wet wood. He made an enormous cloud of smoke that soared skyward and rolled up and away like a miniature forest fire. Seeing this pillar of smoke from afar I suspected that the new cook was getting into action and hurried along to caution him that fritz would shell him out. Better cut down on that smoke or fritz will sure shell it. Huh! Says he. Hope to God he hits it. This front line stuff was all Greek to him as yet. In about a minute's time a whizz-bang lit on the paradox a few yards to the right. This was a trial or ranging shot. A small piece of metal soared high up from the burst and then came down out of the sky with a peculiar whine and went splat!! into the mud close to where we stood. The old timberbeast looked upward and all around skyward with a comical physog and remarked (Snortin old Jesu!!) what do you suppose that was? Of course the next shot was a lot closer and jarred the old fellow out of his calm and conceit considerably. It also splattered his outfit with some mud that was not so clean. He soon got wised up alright and was just as ready to watch his smoke as the rest of us. He was a real cook though putting us up good meals considering the handicaps. He liked to show his back woods type of independence and would often get fed up with the constant rain, mud and wet wood. At such times he would throw his tools and pots in all directions, put his coat over his arm and march off down the trench and swear by all the Gods of the north-shore that he was quitting and we and our old dixies and pots could go to Hades. If you left him alone you would generally find the meal cooked o.k. when the time came around for eats. Battalion headquarters got wind of the fact that I had a good cook for I guess some of the boys must have been crowing to the machine gunners and others about our swell feeds.

The noble adjutant got busy eventually and beguiled him to quit us and go to cook at the headquarters dugout. They got him down there and the officers chipped in and supplied him with funds to go down to the French village for fresh green vegetables etc. and they planned to have a real setup at headquarters. The timber-beast was a real one and of course took that money and bought booze getting gloriously drunk and did not return for a couple of days. When he was brought back he was, of course, not in the best of humor. They got uppity and official with him on top of that for they could not savvy the mysteries of a lumberjack. He came strolling along the trench where I was and says "Hey–Frank, kin I have my job back"? This cooking for the staff may be alright for some but you can't quit when you feel like and tell them to go to the devil. I said O. K. and suggested maybe he was not suited for mixing in society and such like. He cooked for us for quite awhile until the staff trying to get even, transferred him to a platoon. While on his way out to a listening post at night he fell into a sap and ruptured himself and was sent away on that account.

During the late winter of 1915 and spring of 1916 I got saturated with rheumatism and also contracted a heavy cold from exposure to constant wet while on patrol work at night. I decided I would have to quit that work if I wanted to retain a measure of health. I had been at it now steadily for 13 months and had led most of the scout patrols made in that time. There were three men now in the scouts quite capable and willing to do the work and I decided to let them go to it. (He was a good horse but he done broke down). There was Warner T. Bole, W. Maitkin and Eric L. Powell. Anyone of these three would and could do the work right. I had quite enough to do at any rate without patrol work. I had also lost a lot of my keen interest in it since the present o. c. and adjutant took charge of things at battalion headquarters. Those two were worse than the rheumatism. During the balance of our stay here on the Messines front Bole, Maitkin, Powell and Jones did most of the patrol work bringing their reports in to me. We would make them in the regular forms before forwarding them to brigade headquarters. This brigade headquarters also instituted a group of observers on their own and Eric Powell was taken from my scouts to take charge of them. I began to lose my trained men. Sutton was taken by brigade and kept steady at draftsmanship work, mostly maps. Carson also was used frequently on this work at headquarters. Taylor was sent away on a training course and so on. Early spring found us moving out of Messines and on our way north into the Ypres Salient once more.

Ypres Salient

We had been supplied with some of palmer's knee-length oil—tanned shoepacks for winter work in the trenches but only a very few of them had been issued as yet. They were an ideal foot gear for the front lines but were of Canadian make and of course the (powers that be) were studying out a way to discredit them and prove that they were not any good. I give them credit for working this out in a shrewd way. The shoe-packs were kept in stores all during the cold wet months in the trenches while we waded around in filthy water with wet feet. On the first warm spell of sultry spring weather they were brought out and issued to the whole battalion. We were started off on a long route march on a hot day with the new issue. There had also been an issue of heavy woolen caps along with other winter wear in stores. All this stuff was issued at the first of the hot weather. Away we went in all the glory of full winter duds on a day that was as hot as July. As a natural consequence the men became badly over heated, encased in the high-topped oil-tanned larrigans, were virtually parboiled, becoming a mass of big blisters and raw meat. That was the finish of the shoe-packs, as it was intended to be, their finish. We went in eventually by way of White Swan Chateau, and Chesterfield House on the left of the Ypres Commines Canal taking up a position at what was known as the bluff. This was a high bluff overlooking the canal, from its highest side and sloping away more gradually to the north. On our left flank was the famous international trench where the Princess Pats had gone through some rough times. Powell was away and I was temporarily given the overseeing of the brigade observation work as well as sniping etc.

The o. c. worked a good one on me during the week we were on this front. It was part of his plan to discredit my work at brigade and division headquarters. Brigade had asked for a detailed report of all our wire defenses on this part of the front. Any instructions to me had to first go through our o. c's headquarters on the way up. The request for a wire report was sent from brigade on a Tuesday morning so that I would have time to do the necessary patrol work entailed. The ground to be covered was badly exposed on a slope toward the enemy. Our o. c. did not deliver the order to me till the late afternoon of the following Saturday and we were to move out of the sector in a couple of hours, or as soon as darkness made it possible. As soon as I received the order I started in to do the best I could in the short time left to me. I detailed a couple of observers to overlook the sector and get what they could in that way in the short time left them. I had one old eighth officer still with us and I knew he would help me out if at all able to do so. I consulted Capt. Smith and he advised that several junior officers had made wire reports of their sectors on the night previous. He obtained copies of these for me and with what I had noted myself along with what the observers picked up, we knocked together a wire report that covered the ground fairly well in spots. Darkness arrived and time to go out with the relief and attend to billeting arrangements for my unit, scouts, snipers and observers. Now the o. c. had figured some more on this thing. He had sent a wiring party out the previous night and they had strung some eight rolls of accordion wire on a piece of rough ground where I could not possibly see it. He had this card up his sleeve all the time. My report had to go through his office on the way to brigade. He waited till most of his officers were in the battalion headquarters dugout and then decided the time was ripe and the stage set to give me a couple of hard knocks. He called me in and started a venomous tirade about the wire report. He soared to some heights and did succeed in making me look pretty black to some of the new draft officers who had recently come to the battalion. Capt. Smith was present and witness to all this drama. I suggested that the inefficiency was not limited to me and could well be laid to his own door for he had kept the order for a wire report in his dugout all week. Whether through design or carelessness I had no means of knowing. This was the sole cause of the hasty and incomplete report. I had done the best possible in the short time left to me.

During the first night in here we had started to establish some sniping posts. The bluff gave a fairly wide view to the right and in front. On the right shoulder of the bluff we found a disused trench with an old French sniping plate set in the parapet and commanding a good view. Fred Minty and I worked nearly all night to reinforce and repair this putting it in shape for use during daylight sniping. Next morning Minty went there to take up position and watch for targets. When he came in sight of the new post he saw two of our new draft officers standing head and shoulders above it pointing, waving their arms and having a fine time taking in the view of the enemy lines. Why they were not killed during this performance I don't know for they stood in plain view and at point-blank range of the enemy lines over a wide front. I guess they had fool's—luck for they sauntered away presently when told they were in a very exposed and in a dangerous spot. This little display of happy ignorance cost us our sniping post and might well have cost the lives of a couple of good snipers for fritz soon after turned a machine gun on the post boring away at it till it was practically demolished. All of our hard work of the night before was thrown away by the exhibition staged by the two with fool's-luck. The slope in front of the bluff proper was a very exposed piece of ground. We patrolled it at night. Bill Maitkin was severely wounded on one of these patrols. He was in a stooped position with his back toward the enemy lines, returning from patrol when he was hit under the shoulder blades by a rifle bullet. It traveled up and forward breaking the shoulder blade. He was ruined for life by that shot and took no further part in the war.

There was an observation post tunneled out of the highest point of the bluff from which we used to take observations. This was thinly roofed and subject to shell fire at all times. We made patrols along what was left of the old international trench. It was a hard-looking place. The old trench had slid in during wet weather gradually filling with mud and water until it was a mere shallow trough through the desolation of wire and shell holes. This trough was seeded very thickly with the bodies of soldiers of some six nations. They were sticking up through the mud along the whole length of it. That is how it got the name (International). This place was very exposed and you had to crawl flat along it to prevent being seen and shot by the enemy.

After the session with the o. c. at the headquarters dugout I hurried out to see about billets for the boys. We were put in what had been the racing stables in connection with the White Swan Chateau.

While here I lost a good sniper, Jim Ballendene, brother of Jack Ballendene who was transferred to us from the cavalry in order to be with his brother who was one of my snipers. At the east end of the stables there was a sort of barn with single brick walls and this was full of hay.

Jim was in the yard just west of the barn when a shell came through both walls and burst near him. He was hit in the side by a piece of the shell and sustained a very serious wound. I never heard whether he recovered from it or not.

There was a large pond in the Chateau grounds with a small island in the centre with a rustic bridge across to it. The whole grounds were shaded by fine large elm, willow, oak and beech trees. The pond was stocked with white water lilies. Also there was a lone white swan still swimming about in it. His mate had been killed during the war in some way and he too had suffered the loss of an eye but still sailed majestically on his rounds of the pond. I took a swim one day in the pond and picked some of the water lilies finding that they differed from the ones at home in that they had absolutely no scent. The officers had their quarters in the basement of the chateau. There were several chateaus scattered through this part of the country. Among their number was the famous Talbot House or (Tock. H.) where a society of officers was founded that still holds meetings and re-unions in different parts of Canada. (Tock. H.).

I had an odd experience here one day at the n-west of the grove of high elms that enclosed this chateau of the white swan. I had been sent up during the afternoon from billets in some wooden huts further back, to act as an advance party and take over trenches and dugouts for my unit, guiding them into the front trenches when they marched in after dark. Another man accompanied me, we were traveling along a foot path across country that led us past the corner of the elm grove. When some 150 yards from the corner I seemed to sense or feel some impending evil, stopping and saying to my mate, wait a little, we will sit on that old log lying there for a few minutes and have a smoke. I felt that I was expecting something to happen. Sure enough, over came a five point nine inch shell hitting directly on the path at the corner of the elm grove. Had we kept straight on we would have been just in time to connect with the shell. I experienced this sort of premonition on numerous occasions during my three years and seven months of front line duty. We went in at what was known as the Ravine, a strip of trench in a rough piece of ground with the canal (Ypres-Commines)on our left flank in a deep cutting. We could overlook quite a bit of enemy country from this sector. We built a few sniping posts and used them regularly. We began to have trouble with some of the new draft officers. When we were absent from one of our sniping posts they would go into it, work the shutter looking out of it and even in some cases sent privates from their platoon to shoot from the post with regular short Enfield with bayonet attached. Now a short Enfield is an awkward thing to shoot with from a sniper's plate especially with the bayonet attached. The barrel is so short the gas blast from the muzzle strikes the earth in front of the loophole, raising a cloud of dust that is a sure give away of a sniping post. In addition to this, an untrained man will wave the rifle about and in other ways court sudden death. Perhaps we would return to the post quite innocent as to the performance they had been pulling off in our absence and fritz would be laying for us with several varieties of sudden death all set to wipe us out. We worked all one night making a good concealed post in a support trench close behind the front trench. It gave a splendid enfilade view of the enemy lines to the east along the valley of the canal. I suspect that one of the new junior officers had monkeyed around this post in the manner described. I went in this post at daylight together with R. L. Stutt an ex-school teacher and ex-preacher from near Prince Albert, Sask. We usually had a board placed across for a seat, a light roof covering and a curtain at the rear to exclude light from that way, so it would not shine through the loop hole in front betraying us. I had a long Ross rifle with a Winchester A5 scope.

This scope gave a fairly wide clear field and we used to put the rifle on rest, watching for a target through the sight itself when there was no place handy to use a signaler's telescope. We painted the rifle barrel with wet clay to keep it from flashing in the morning sun. We were always under a disadvantage in the morning hours from having to face the sun. Fritz had the sun at his back and was often able to see the lens of one of our scopes or glasses shining like a star when the morning sun was reflecting from it. We shaded the lens as much as possible but the sun in your face is a serious handicap in several ways. On this particular morning I had sat at the rifle some three quarters of an hour without obtaining a shot. It became chilly in that damp drafty place and I wanted to move about a bit to restore circulation. Getting down from the seat I told Stutt to take a spell at it for awhile. He no sooner was nicely seated than fritz opened up on the place with a machine gun. I was slightly lower down at the back when I heard the roar of the machine gun bullets and saw the streaks of blue flame and sparks from the sniping plates. Stutt being rather new at the game probably did not at once grasp what was happening. I saw him leaning backward and thinking he might be hit I reached up to his collar and yanked him down out of the line of fire. I then led the way out of there as fast as our legs would carry us. Fritz had a habit of following up such a burst with a shower of trench mortar shells, whiz bangs, rifle grenades. pineapples etc. to make sure of cleaning up on the snipers. I went back after some length of time and recovered my rifle from what was left of the post. I had started recently to put double plates in the sniping posts for fritz had acquired a new type of amour piercing bullet that made a clean hole through a single plate about the size of a 22 caliber. The double plate saved us on this occasion alright for the forward plate was riddled like a sieve with the back or second plate being badly dinged and nearly punctured as well. I saw one of these armor piercing bullets hit a tree one day after spinning from the trench embankment. The jacket was stripped from the core which fell down and rolled into the trench. The core was of tempered steel with boat tail and sharp point and about the size of a slate pencil or a 22 caliber bullet. Before being fired this core was enclosed in the ordinary nickel jacket of the standard German 8mm service caliber. The complete bullet was no different in appearance from the regular service bullet. When it hit a steel plate the jacket stayed behind and the steel core went on through the plate always taking a thin round blister off the far side of the plate about the size of a dime. I noted that nearly every plate in our parapets along this part of the front and northward to Hooge had been punctured in this way.

Fritz threw over some of the heaviest minen werfers I ever saw on this part of the front. They threw up a black column of smoke and debris to a great height leaving a very large crater. The concussion from them could be felt for some distance and felt like a huge hand giving a push downward on the top of your head.

This part of the line had a weird and gruesome look that seemed to whisper of death and devastation. The very ground here seemed to speak and the night wind seemed to pluck at your sleeves and counsel you beware. You could feel the pulse of the thousands of the dead with their pale hands protruding through the mud here and there and seeming to beckon to you. The ragged stumps of torn trees stood like sentries looking over a scene like the aftermath of an earthquake. You could feel the presence of something not of this earth. Akin to goblins.

On the first morning in this sector I started from the right flank accompanied by a new draft man who had been trained as a sniper in some depot (18th Reserve) in England. I was to take him around and show him how and where to start to work on his gruesome job. I started early in the gray light just proceeding the dawn, and when about half way along our frontage came upon a new draft man who had just finished his first night on sentry duty in a front trench. He had gone stark staring mad. His reason had fled and left him a pitiful driveling object wracked by sudden fits of raving. It took four men to lead him away back of the lines. Fritz was putting over rifle grenades at the point where he had been stationed and they made a weird whine and a whistling wail as they curved over to him in a high arc. These had been coming over at intervals for a long time and may have given the final touch that snatched away his reason and left him in a shape to match his surroundings, a thing of stark madness. He was a short thick set man with an extremely prominent roman nose. He looked to be about 30 years of age.

After he was taken away we went on toward the canal cut on the left flank. In the bottom of this cut we had a machine gun stationed to be used in an emergency in any sudden attack on the cut. The regular crews had not been in the habit of firing this gun at night as such action would give away its position at once and defeat the purpose for which it was put there. A new draft officer fresh from England had been detailed off to take charge of this gun crew during the night and he was brim-full of bright aggressive ideas, (mostly aggressive) about what should be done with a machine gun and when. He had ordered his men to fire bursts of so many rounds every so often all through the night. As we approached the place in the growing light fritz had just made up his mind to wipe out that gun and crew. We were just in time to get into the edge of the inferno that burst upon the bottom of that cutting. Fritz sent over every kind of explosive at his command and we spent some time flattened against a zigzag portion of the trench wondering when the storm would be over. The two of us escaped without anything more than a shaking up from concussion but the gun crew were not so lucky. Some of them paid with their lives for the re-education of that new draft and over aggressive (Hoffiser). The old n. c. o's on the crew had protested in vain and were told they knew nothing.

This sector was in the vicinity of the famous St. Oloi Craters where the 27th and 28th battalions had a rough passage. During the time we were on this part of the front the scouts came across one of our airman that had fallen or been shot down in a wood. They picked him up and notified the proper authorities. As a result we all got an invitation to visit the aerodrome a few miles away. An officer was detailed to show us around the place and all together we were treated in a very courteous way. We spent a whole afternoon very pleasantly in this way. We were shown the workings of an apparatus they used at that time to drop incendiary bombs onto captive balloons and other targets. It was a sheet metal affair of the shape of a large wash boiler such as women use to boil clothing in on wash day. It was without a bottom and contained a number of vertical sheet metal tubes about the diameter and length of ordinary stove pipes. The bombs were hung in these tubes and could be released from anyone of them or all of them by tripping levers. The whole business was hung or suspended beneath the body of the plane and operated from the cockpit. We also had a look at the apparatus used in aerial photography. It was bracketed on the side of the fuselage in such a position that the aviator could sight and time his film exposure by leaning over, and sighting over a rig that automatically gave the right angle and time with respect to speed and elevation. Speed, and elevation indicators together with a dozen other gauges and gadgets were directly in front of him on the forward bulkhead of the cockpit. On the heavier planes used for bombing and observation work the machine guns were mounted on a sort of circular rail or track that went round the full circle of the cockpit on which the gun was mounted. With this arrangement the gunner could shoot in almost any direction at any time. It was necessary to be able to do this, for these heavy awkward machines were often pursued by faster planes and would have been helpless prey with a fixed gun mounting. The fast single seated fighting planes such as the Bristol, Spad, Sopwith Camel and others were armed with fixed or rigid guns and the plane had to be aimed at the target. There was a telescope sight mounted on the fuselage in front of the airman and by leaning slightly forward he could press his forehead into the cushioned eye piece of this scope. At the same time reaching straight up overhead he could grasp two hand grips that operated two Lewis guns mounted directly above on the top wing of the plane. These guns were of course sighted in with the telescope mentioned above. While doing this the plane was guided with feet and knees by means of treads and the (joy-stick) or lever that sticks up between the aviator's knees when he is sitting on the seat. Some planes had a single gun mounted on the fuselage in front of the cockpit. This gun shot between the revolving blades of the propeller. It had been worked on the basis of time with the speed of gun and revolutions of propeller taken into account. It seems to run in my mind that they could fire about 49 rounds in a burst without hitting the blades at that date. If more than that number were fired at one time or without pause they would begin to cut into the blades. This may not be exactly the workings of it but it was figured out somewhat in that way.

While we were out at the aerodrome, planes were coming in going out on their way to and from the enemy lines. I had an opportunity to see what manner of men that were pulling off all the hair—raising and breathtaking stunts that we witnessed daily over the front lines. I noticed the most of them were tall in build and slim or comparatively slim. Most of them were of dark complexion, dark hair, and rather inclined to be quiet deliberate and slow moving types. There was the occasional short man and an occasional blonde. These were also the quick nervous kind and quite young. The tall dark ones seemed to run in age from 20 up to near 40. I guess the nervous ones lasted quick and died young on that job. We were told that any quick or jerky movements in the handling of a plane at speed were apt to be fatal. The cool and steady going man was the type that was really doing the work in the fighting areas. On later trips to other aerodromes at Mt. St. Eloi and other places we noted that this rule held good as to the types.

One night when we were being relieved by another battalion at the Bluff fritz blew up a mine on our right flank causing several casualties on account of part of the two units being there at the same time. The scouts and snipers had just gone out and were on their way to billets at a place just south of Chesterfield House, and known as Home Farm. We had small shelters built in the south side of the old buildings facing on the Commines Canal. During the evening R. L. Stutt and myself were sitting in one of these shelters talking. Stutt was lying on a single bunk against the wall and I was sitting on a bench close to the foot of the bunk when a shell came through an open window casing on the n-e side of the house and then through the brick wall at the back of our hut. It then plunged into the earth directly under where we sat so the earth floor bulged upward about six inches. There it stopped but did not explode. (Another Dud).

We had a term in the front line on the top of Mt. Sorrel, a sort of small hill of sand and loam covered with the stumps of what had been second growth of pine. This hill was to the left of and over looked the naiad of Hill 60. We got some sniping at this place as we had a view of the enemy communication trenches etc. on the side toward Hill 60. I found an old mass of bricks a few yards to the rear of the front trench and on the highest point of the hill. I burrowed into this from the back and discovered a tiled floor. I heaped the bricks on either side to make a path across the tile floor to the fragment of wall on the side toward the enemy lines. From here I had a splendid view to the east and south. I fixed a telescope rest and used it as an observation post for several days.

Immediately behind this river there was a curious apparatus known as a roman catapult. There was a long wooden arm about 10 feet long that swung on a pivot or fulcrum at the base. A short distance above the base there were powerful coil springs attached to the arm. It was used to hurl bombs etc. into the enemy lines. Using the long arm or sweep as a lever and pulling it back or away from the enemy lines you could stretch the coil springs full out. The arm now lay back flat and was secured there by a latch or trigger. You placed the bomb on the outer or tip end of the sweep then released the trigger. The coil springs did the rest. We used to play a joke on fritz with this rig by putting a stale tin of bully beef on, in place of a bomb, and letting it go over. When nothing happened he would cautiously investigate the bully beef tin. We always heard some fervent curses and yells with a strong sauerkraut flavor. He could never seem to see any humor in it at all.

One day I was in the o. p. in the brick pile. During the previous night our people had started to dig a new support trench along the top of the hill on a general line with my o. p. They had thrown up quite a bit of fresh earth. I suppose fritz had observed this and during the afternoon decided to register some of his guns on it for future reference. He put over three shells. One of them hit in the brick pile directly in front of my face and I was buried in bricks getting a rather severe concussion from the burst. I had a partial plate of false teeth in the roof of my mouth and a round piece the size of a shilling was broken out of the roof of the plate. I had three gold fillings in my front teeth and these were knocked out and lay loose on my tongue together with the disc out of the plate. This concussion blew the partition out between my nostrils. It was still out in 1933. My left eardrum was also damaged considerably. My watch was in my pocket and sustained a fracture of the dial in two places and some dents in the case. I got it repaired some six months later and it is still on duty in 1933. I crawled out of the brick pile and found the empty case of one of the three shells. It was of five inch caliber and a very odd-looking shell case. I sent it into brigade for identification and they told me it was a Russian howitzer shell. These Russian guns had been captured on the eastern front and were being put in service here.

While observing from the brick pile one day I spotted an enemy range finder that was being trained on the next hill to our rear or what was known as Observatory Ridge. This rig differed considerably from the ones used by our infantry. Ours is known as the Bar and Stroude consisting of a straight pipe or tube of a diameter of perhaps three inches with a length of about four feet. This tube has a lens set in at either end but at right angles to the axis with each of these lenses throwing onto a reflector set at a 46 degree angle. These reflections in turn were thrown onto the receiving prisms in the midship of the tube. One of the lens-prism arrangements at one end of the tube is made to swing on an arc that has the objective or target as a fulcrum. This moving lens is activated by a sort of reach rod connected to an adjusting screw amidships. The two reflected images are made to slide past one another in the usual way and the range is thus reduced to numerals by means of a proportionate scale rigged like a vernier showing in the reflector under the eyepiece that is located on the top and midway of the tube. (Adoption of the triangulation system). Fritz had gone one better as usual. His was a more clever adoption of the same principal. Instead of a straight horizontal tube that must be raised bodily above the trench and exposed together with the operators head to the enemies fire, he had two tubes radiating like wheel spokes from a hub consisting of a cylinder shape. The tubes could be spread fanwise when a long base line was required or closed fanwise to a shorter base. The prisms threw the pictures to the centre where they were reduced to numerals in the same way as in the Barr Stroude. The operator could stay below the parapet and the only thing necessary to be exposed was the two lenses at the top ends of the tubes. The whole thing was painted a dull grey non gloss finish. The one I saw was fully exposed above the parapet for some reason. I tried to hit it with the sniping rifle and may have done so. I did not see any dust fly from the parapet near and it was immediately taken down out of sight below. The range finder did not reappear in the vicinity.

The month of June was drawing near and we knew little of the furious times impending for us along the east side of the salient. The whole salient was to be rent and torn and bathed in blood along its eastern front. Our o. c. had procured a lieutenant from some other unit who was to supersede me as head of the scout section. This man Harrower had hailed from the vicinity of Glasgow. He was a small pink and white person with a weasel cast of countenance and a shrill piping voice but equipped with an abundant supply of self assurance and what is known as push fullness. He started in to run things while we were at Mount Sorrel. I was in the brick pile o. p. one day and happened to take note of the way he was working. There was a (rifle battery) an arrangement of about six Lee Enfields set rigidly in a steel frame being ranged and set to fire on a fixed target. He was using this as a rest for his prismatic compass and had a sheet metal helmet on his head. as well there was a plentiful supply of other iron and steel lying about. From this position he was trying to get intersections on some object in the enemy lines. The final result from his deductions was sent in the form of an observation report to brigade headquarters. It fell to the lot of Sutton an ex-surveyor from B. C. (and one of my scouts) to try and establish the position of the target from the compass bearings sent in by Harrower. It worked out at a swamp some quarter of a mile to the rear of our lines and in close proximity to a light horse artillery battery that was placed there for emergency use. It was evident that his natural intelligence was not on par with his aggressiveness and he would have to lean heavily on what was still left of my old scout section if he wanted results.

The scout section had now won its spurs and become an indispensable asset to all the units on the battle front. The 8th battalion scouts had made this by two years of steady and hard work that started at Valcartier Camp. It was now established out through the corps as a recognized unit in every battalion. An officer was detailed to take command of the scouts in each battalion and it was named the intelligence section. The snipers were still under its wing and on its ration list. Our o. c. had selected Lieutenant Harrower to take charge in our battalion. I was relegated to the scrap heap and the ash can or, in other words, pushed over board. The first intuition I got was when a company sergeant major from no. three company came around and notified me to take charge of a platoon of his company. The o. c. had assigned me to that job on his own hook and had not taken the trouble to tell me. Orders are orders in the front lines and you don't stop to argue about them.

On the first opportunity I went to the o c office and requested to be relieved of my new job. He passed a lot of (buck) about the good work I had done for the unit in the past and proposed to regret the action he had taken and so-on-so-on. I told him I had no ambitions or intentions of becoming a platoon commander in one of his companies. He admitted that he had no authority or grounds for reducing one to the ranks. He finally asked me what alternative I would prefer. I could not know he was soon to leave the battalion, and thus cease to spite me. So I told him I would rather be a private in the snipers. He went eagerly to the task of transferring me on paper to that status. It was a voluntary choice of the least of two evils.

That is the way it looked to me at the time. It may have been my (guardian angel) on the job too. You could not have carried out your duties as a scout officer in the next two years of heavy fighting and lived to tell the tale of it. From the records taken later, the average life of a scout officer in the front lines was eight days. Some of them lived quite awhile but they were the ones that leaned very heavily on the men under them and did not try to do the work assigned to them but passed it on to subordinates.

This work fell to the lot of Warner T. Bole, in our section. He did not last long but went away disgusted and severely wounded to England. He later recovered and took out a commission in the 44th battalion as scout officer. He was killed at Passendaele.

My experiences with our o. c. made a very deep lasting impression on my whole nature and outlook which will persist in effecting me to my grave for I cannot shake off the influence of his work. I find myself constantly looking for and expecting something from others that is like it, or on par with it. It has given me a sour and untrusting outlook that handicaps me in many ways still. Try as hard as I like I cannot shake it. It was a wet blanket.

"And-back he turned our feet, back to the twilight paths of time, To jungle wraiths, fang confronting fang. And thick coiled venoms. Against our wills he drags us down to his own hellish depths. Back to the age of tooth and claw he hurls all me and mine, and on a startled soul imposes his low creed, and even in death shall not be worsted. Spitting in our teeth his spites triumph, leaving in our hand a blood stained sword and wonder in our eyes".

I never worked as hard or took as much real interest in anything as I did in that scout work. It was a creative and pioneer work to a great extent in my case. It could not be judged by past or altogether by later standards. The sole reward is in the knowledge of things done well. The satisfaction of starting something that went far.

One fine June morning we were in the front lines opposite Hill 60 and from our left flank could overlook Mt. Sorrel. The 5th battalion was next to us on the left. The morning quiet and there had been very little bombardment since sunrise. You could hear song birds tuning up and see them flitting about, busy with their nesting season. I was just thinking about how foolish it seemed for men to be dug into the ground and striving to kill one another when all nature seemed to breath of peace and life.

Suddenly the stillness was broken by a tremendous roar of concentrated drum-fire that seemed to be falling on our line to the left of Mt. Sorrel, and beyond toward Hooge. The barrage was very heavy and gradually increased in volume until you could not distinguish the reports of individual guns. The whole was blended into one sustained roar that swelled until it developed a growling undertone that indicated a very-very heavy delivery of shells. A splatter of enemy shells began to fall in our sector like heavy rain drops on the fringe of a western thunder storm. The drums of death rolled and rolled till Mt. Sorrel was blotted out from view in a tempest of smoke and flying earth. The stumps of the trees in Square Wood and Sanctuary Wood could be seen rocking in the drift of smoke till it reminded one of a bad forest fire in northern Ontario.

One platoon of the 5th was caught in that storm and badly cut up. Every thing to the left of them was a shambles. The front trenches from Hill 60 to Hooge were practically blown of the map. Together with a large percentage of the men occupying them. This drum-fire had fallen upon the newly organized 3rd Canadian Division. The c. m. r. s and the 52nd were among the worst sufferers in that hail of death. We came in for quite a strafe but what we got was as nothing to what was going over on our left. I certainly pitied the men that had to lie under that hammer that day. We did not know how far the attack was going to spread south, having to (stand to) and be ready for anything.

After awhile the shell fire eased down a bit so the scouts and snipers took advantage of their roving commission and began to dribble over to the left flank. There was a slight hill or rise in the ground on our left that gave a view of the whole south slope of Mt. Sorrel. I had not been there long, when happening to look around, I saw that nearly all the scouts and snipers had come too and were spread along the old trench that led back a short distance at right angles to the front line. The German barrage had lifted or moved ahead beyond what was left of the front line on Mt. Sorrel and the German troops were coming across there in hundreds. They evidently intended to stay for they were carrying all manner of equipment, tools, and barb wire etc. We could have brought a deadly enfilade of rifle and m. g. fire to bear on them from where I stood. I enquired of an officer about this but was ordered not to open fire. I suppose it was just as well for if we had enfiladed them they would have simply turned that tornado of gunfire in our direction blowing us off the map.

No troops in an open trench could live through a fire of that volume. It seemed queer to stand there idle with thousands of square heads passing in full view and within easy rifle range. We got shelled that day by our own guns. I was told it was some territorial unit of artillery newly out from England that was firing short. I had a close call from the burst of one of their shells. It was shrapnel and they sent over quite a few of them. There was a Belgian battery of 75's also firing short. We watched the Germans while they reversed the trenches they had captured. This is done by shifting sandbags and earth from the original front to the back and reinforcing with a certain amount of new sandbags. This could only be done where the old trench happened to be on a line chosen by them for holding against our counter attack. They were wasting no time and worked feverishly like a huge colony of ants to get themselves dug in and ready for the counter attack that was sure to come as soon as our people could prepare it.

This fritz drive on the east flank of the salient penetrated at one point to within two miles of Ypres City. They were not able to hold all they took for we were pulled out of the line that night and rushed up together with other units of the old First Canadian Division in counter attacks that pushed fritz back beyond Maple Copse and into Wood Square and Sanctuary Woods just to the west of Mt. Sorrel. We landed on the n. e. slope of the Observatory Ridge and could overlook a lot of the ground fritz had overrun in his surprise attack. From this location in hastily thrown up trenches we got some good sniping practice. It was a desolate looking mess in front of us with the smashed and broken remnants of trees mixed with fragments of wire and trench revetting sticking up through a welter of mud and water-filled shell holes. Among this mess of scattered downed timber and wreckage we could trace here and there the alignment of the new enemy defenses and their communications leading back over Mt. Sorrel and around each side of it. The new enemy salient was heavily manned and they lost a lot of men here when the final counter attack by the old first division swept them back again over the crest of Mt. Sorrel into their old line once more.

Some of our higher command had taken most of our artillery away from the Ypres Salient with the idea of using it for some attack they were planning to pull off in the vicinity of Arras, away to the south. Fritz had in some way become wise to the fact that our artillery was nearly all away so took advantage of it to make the drive described above. What few guns we had left were mostly light field and horse batteries. They did great work in the few days when every thing depended on them hanging on. Some of them were out in the open fields with the limbers bringing ammunition to them at the gallop all day. In this way they were badly exposed, suffering accordingly, but kept up the good work holding fritz in check until more heavy guns were rushed up from the south to reinforce them. One of the first artillery reinforcements to arrive in the salient was a battery of South African howitzers. I saw them in action near the Ypres-Poperinge Road. They were of about eight inch caliber.

We alternated between the temporary front and the dugouts along an old railroad embankment south of Zillebeeke Halte and Zillebeeke Farm. The communication trenches from Zillebeeke to the front were very shallow exposing us to enemy fire. We had some hard and thrilling trips back and forward over that strip of country while acting as guides, and messengers, as well as carrying parties on numerous occasions. Outside of a flurry or two in the vicinity of Maple Copse and Square Wood fritz did not make any serious attempt to push his attack further. Our artillery was being rapidly reinforced, with things being shaped up to throw fritz back to where he started. Our heavies began to pour shells onto the new enemy lines and their tenancy there must have been rather unpleasant for a couple of days.

When ever a battle of this kind started we were put on emergency rations known as x rations. The rations consisted of bully-beef and hardtack. If I lived on this fare for a couple of days it would always give me a serious attack of dysentery. About the third day of this battle I took bad with it and suffered tortures from it all through the remainder of the season into late autumn it stayed with me from June onward through our trip into the battle of the Somme in September and October.

It is a very trying thing with one becoming very weak, nervous and generally run down in a short time. I became so weak I could hardly keep up on the march and so jumpy under shell fire that it became an agony at times. One day I went up to the exposed communication trench from Zillebeeke to the front line in daylight on some errand. I forget now what we were sent for. I was bad with the dysentery that day and in a very weak nervous condition. I was so jumpy from the fire that I had to stop, take shelter, and rest up recovering some semblance of equanimity before we got more than halfway to the front line. Mitchell and Powell were with me, and I can remember the queer looks they gave me when I would jump, dodge and take cover from shells or machine gun sweeps. They went on at last leaving me sitting in the trench. I was there some little time before recovering some steadiness.

After returning from this trip with Powell and Mitchell I was lying in the dugout under the old railway embankment just below Zillebeeke Lake and Zillebeeke Farm feeling pretty shaky, and weak both morally and physically when who should come along but Col. Lipsett my old commander. He came and hunted me out in my dugout personally requesting me to go up the line again on a regular suicide mission that would take me right through all that badly exposed and fire swept zone that extended north east for six miles. When I think it over sometimes now I don't believe I would have been physically able to carry out his wishes at that time. I declined his request with excuses.

Now I have not got so very much out of life since the war and often wonder why I did not go as he asked me to. It is a practical certainty that I would never have returned from that trip. He looked at me when I declined, looked at me long and hard and Lipsett could look at a man (so he could). I had gotten pretty low when I could refuse to even make a try when he asked me to do something that he was having difficulty in getting done. Attrition is the only answer I can figure out for it now. I had been gradually worn, dragged, and hammered down until I was but a shadow of what he had once known as his sergeant of scouts. Many a time I regretted that I did not go. Lipsett is dead now and he was killed on just such another trip as the one he requested me to make that day.

After he became a corps commander with the imperial troops he asked for a reconnaissance up front on some badly exposed ground, and his junior officers declined to go.

He went himself and was shot through the head by an enemy sniper. Now he told these junior officers of the imperial unit that he never was refused a patrol while with the Canadians. I am here to state that I refused him that time at Zillebeeke or my shadow did. Any old front liner who may read this will perhaps understand the condition I had gotten into at the time. If they don't understand, well then I guess they never had a long enough or hard enough siege of it to make them understand how I felt and still feel about it. In that case a prolonged siege of it would probably enlighten them a bit.

In 1917 and 1918 I had pulled myself up a bit by my boot straps making a fairly decent comeback morally and physically. On numerous occasions I was able to buck into it again with a spirit that helped me to partly forget the time I turned Lipsett down cold when he needed my help. They say confession is good for the soul. The long grind had pretty nearly got my goat. That was the lowest ebb. I had now come to realize that I was in bad shape and would have to control myself by willpower and try to shake off the effects of long continued never-ending exposure to all manner of shocks and nerve strain. From that day on I never got so bad and by 1918 I had fought it down and was almost back to normal condition. During the time I was in this bad shape I would wake from sleep shaking with convulsions, like ague chills. It did not matter where I was, whether I was in the line or in comparatively safe billets in the rear. If awakened by the sound of gun fire I would shake from head to heel. I have seen my bunk shake and vibrate violently for perhaps 20 or 30 minutes before the spasms would pass. I have lain that way many a time cursing and setting my teeth trying to stop it. I have known my heart to take a leap as though it would jump from my body, followed by three or four heavy thumping strokes, then stopping altogether for a period of several seconds at a time. At times like that it was physically painful and left me feeling queer. My bodily, or physical courage, was getting badly shaken but morally I was still able to be boss and could call up hidden resources of that kind of strength and go ahead. Many a man was suffering in the same way as I could note by their actions. I suppose very few of them would admit it or write truthfully about being in such a condition. I knew this was not due to natural cowardice, or weakness of that kind, but had been brought on to me by over-strain long continued combined with dysentery.

At last the counter attack was ready. Mackenzie at brigade headquarters asked me to establish an observation post and watch the progress of the attack. Our people had established a code of flare signals. These rockets or flares were carried by our attacking troops, and were to be shot up as signals to headquarters and the artillery as our men attained each specified objective in the counter attack. Different groups and colors of flares, each had their meaning. My job was to keep constant watch from my o. p. and transmit the message of the flares by wire over the field telephone to our brigade headquarters in the railway dugouts. South of Zillebeeke Farm. I got busy with a couple of signalers and we strung the wires to an old dugout that was just below the crest of an elevated embankment from which you could get a view of Mt. Sorrel. At dusk I went to work and built a small shelter of sandbags right on top the embankment. I figured that the sandbags would give me some protection from shrapnel and also from machine gun fire. It was no protection from a shell. One hit with a whizz-bang would have wiped me and the o. p. right off the embankment. The signaler was directly below me in the dugout, with me shouting the messages to him while still keeping a lookout. The hour for the counter attack was set for one a. m. of a dark stormy night with thunder, lightning, and some rain, mixed with the thunder and lightning of the guns. The ground to be covered by our boys was very rough, broken, and churned up by the heavy guns that had been hammering it for two days and nights. Huge shell holes dotted it thickly and these holes were brimful of water. Some of the ground was a natural bog or swamp covered with smashed and broken remnants of trees mixed with an assortment of barbed wire entanglements. To all this was added the darkness and the rain. It was truly a wild night and the imagination could not picture a worse inferno than was there during that attack. The German flares had not been taken into account in our people's plans and when hell broke loose out there in front it was a severe test of anybody's judgment to form instant decisions about which group or groups of flares, had been, or were being sent up by our boys. A mistake might cause the gunners to get wrong information. I did not know what use brigade was making of what I was wiring in or to whom they might relay my messages. The fighting lines in front were lit up like a huge fire-works display. There were dozens and scores of flares in the sky at one time and in as many groups and colors. I did the best I could to figure out our signal flares from among the others and made my messages short and as clear as possible. Fritz must have thought there was a field battery or a concentration of troops behind my embankment for he started to slip salvoes of whiz-bangs over it. Those shells were just clearing the top of the bank and no more, bursting in the low ground close behind me. He kept this up all through the counter attack. Some of those sifters passed so close to me I could feel the heat of them and smell an odor of scorched metal as they shrieked past me. I was expecting a direct hit on my wee pinnacle at any moment. Owing to the nervous condition I have written about, it became quite trying to stand there steady with the breath of these hell scrapers fanning my hair every few seconds. There was quite a lot of high angle machine gun fire also coming my way, together with the ragged and aimless splatter of rifle bullets. All things came to an end and in a remarkably short time. I saw the group of rockets go up on the crest of Sorrel that told us the boys had reached the final objective, at or near where our old front had been, before fritz had made the drive. Soon after this our guns put down a barrage just beyond this and our boys were now digging in on the new alignment.

During all these operations there had been a steady and rather cold drizzle of rain. This rain continued through the next week. In order to keep warmth in their bodies while lying out in the wet our boys had to wear their great-coats. These coats became saturated with water and loaded with a plaster of wet clay until they finally got so heavy that they weighed the men down and very seriously impeded them. Cases were known that night of the attack when men stumbled in the dark into big shell holes full of mud and water and perished there from shear inability to climb out again. Over the top of the great-coat there would be full web equipment. This equipment included 120 rounds of ammunition, bayonet sheath, trenching tool and handle, haversack with rations, two spare cloth bandoliers of ammunition, some mills bombs, some flares, water bottles etc. In some cases the man had a shovel or pick tied on his back or perhaps a couple of panniers of Lewis gun ammunition or a sandbag full of bombs etc.. The clothing taken off of one wounded

Canuck at the end of this fight was weighed on a scale and tipped it 118 pounds. This weight was mostly in absorbed water and clay stuck on the clothing or boots. All of the other equipment was extra weight added to the above.

I was over the ground early next morning and it was a very gruesome looking mess. There was a zigzag line of trench from Square Wood leading toward Mt. Sorrel. This trench was a solid mass of dead Germans. They were packed in it from end to end like sardines in a can. They must have got crowded here in the dark and been caught by machine gun fire and shrapnel. The whole place was thickly strewn with the dead and wounded of both sides.

We had three nights carrying out wounded from that front. There were some wounded that had been lying there since the first day of the battle. The fire had been so heavy it had been impossible for stretcher parties to get over the ground. It was pretty bad yet. Crossing the dip or valley to the left and behind Mt. Sorrel you had to run the gauntlet of machine gun fire from some enemy guns that could sweep the valley. Our battalion was pulled out the day after the counter attack. I was sent up to guide a party of stretcher bearers and we carried stretchers all night back to a small village in the valley north of Zillebeeke Halte. Halte means station or stop on the railway line. It was nearly three miles of a carry from the top of Mt. Sorrel. We had a mile to go before we struck a road and this mile was across the low ground where the fighting had taken place in our counter attack. It was a mass of shell holes filled with water, thus very soft and boggy. Sometimes we would sink into the ooze nearly up to our hips and have to rest the stretcher on the mud while we pulled our feet out of the clay and water. Before morning I was soaked through and through and so exhausted my knees would keep giving out on me. There was a cold raw wind and drizzle of rain with some enemy machine guns sweeping the ground across which we were struggling back and forth until daylight. I was sent up again the following night on the same job. I was afraid I would get pneumonia from the wet and told R. S. M. Harry Neighbor about it. He was a good old scout and gave me a full bottle of rum.

On this second night there were two stretcher parties sent from our battalion. I guided one and Mason Button, a Kenora man, was sent up to guide the second party. On our way up we had to pass a bad spot known as shrapnel corner. It was an old level crossing of the turn pike and the rail road. There was quite a bit of traffic here at all hours. Fritz knew of this and shelled the spot systematically. I got across o. k. with my party but

Mason Button walked plumb into a salvo of shells on the crossing and was himself hit badly. He lost both of his legs. This night and the next were repetitions of the first night. When I reached the stage where I became exhausted I would take a swig out of my water bottle of rum then keep going, till it worked off, when I would take another.

Those who advocated taking away the soldiers rum, little knew what they were babbling and chattering about. Could they have gone through even one hour of what we experienced on those three nights? They would have forever ceased to babble and would have been shamed into silence.

Lime juice would not be much use to man under conditions such as were there. I would have been in the hospital with pneumonia before the finish of the third day of that grind. The dysentery did not help much to buoy me up during these three nights work. One night we carried 27 men from the old line on Sorrel all the way to the small village north of Zillebeeke or a distance of about three miles. Among this lot was a colonel who had been in command of one of the battalions of the 3rd division. I helped carry him a good part of the way from where we found him. I believe his name was

Phillips or Woods. I am not certain. After the taking back of our old line we held this part of the front for awhile, and alternated it with periods in support at the railway dugouts south of Zillebeeke Farm. While here R. E.

Brash was taken sick with a bad attack of lumbago and was sent down the line and did not return to us.

A new colonel came to our unit at this time for our o. c. was getting pretty sick of the job. There was too much fighting in it these days. One day at Mt. Sorrel he decided to leave us for good. I was at headquarters dugouts one day on some message. The smell of rum down in that hole would knock a horse down. The machine gun officer drank himself into the snakes or willies and had to be carried out and given medical attention. Major Raddell was the most sober one of the lot and may have been leading the bunch of them on with the view of gaining command of the unit himself. He did obtain command eventually.

They did not forget the scouts. Perhaps it was because the scouts had to visit them frequently in discharge of their various duties as guides, runners etc. They did not forget the scouts. Oh no! They gave orders for raids into the enemy trenches with a lot of details of what was to be done there by the raiding parties. The plans they made for the scouts and bombers to carry out certainly lacked nothing that would go to make the raid exciting and suicidal for the elected victims. Bole would attempt anything almost, but expressed his doubts to me about the outcome of this venture. He said goodbye and told me he did not expect to come back. He asked me if I wanted to come with him on the raid. I was no longer supposed to be a scout. I had been put in the discard previously. I did not feel like digging in now. Bole went on what he knew to be a fool's errand and escaped with his life, but sustained a serious bayonet wound through the upper part of his leg. Some of his mates were not so lucky. They did penetrate to the enemy trench but were thrown out and suffered heavily. The survivors were lucky to get back at all. Bole did not have the moral courage to say no to them as I had done when they tried to make the suicide attack on the wire at Avenue Farm. He had an abundance of physical courage, more than I was ever given. This sort of business went on for a number of days. We were shelled by our own artillery during this period. Not by the Canadian artillery, but some new territorial unit that was green at the work. They dropped six inch naval gun shells into our support trench about 50 yards behind the front line and killed one of our best c. s. m's and a couple of other men. There were several other heavy shells dropped short that day.

Captain Mackenzie got wind of how things were in the front line. He came up and saw for himself how things were and to say "no". Presently there was a clean up and there was a shuffle of the pack. This may seem like strong talk but the half is not being told. Our adjutant left us before we went into the next big fight. He left us while we were on the way in to take our share in the Battle of the Somme about two months later. He never came back either. We had a term in the line to the south of the Ypres Commines Canal and just to the north of the famous St. Eloi Craters where the 2nd division boys got their first taste of real rough stuff.

While on this part of the front I found an old Ross rifle lying in the trench. It had a name written on the stock Ypres Lizzie. I adopted Lizzie right there and then. On trying her out I found that she was a beautiful shooting weapon. While in that sector we put up some targets on a range at Dickebusch. I shot with Lizzie using the peep or aperture sights only. In a competition against four others equipped with telescopic sights, I held the top score. I used that rifle for a long time in the line making many a hit with it too. I often wondered who the original owner was. It was probably some sniper of the 2nd division.

We were in at different points along the east side of the salient for awhile without anymore fighting or occurrences of note beyond the ordinary trench routine of daily strafes, and reprisals by trench mortars, stokes guns, flying pigs, aerial torpedoes or sausages, rum jars, pine apples, various forms of rifle fire and hand grenades. There was some crude devises used in those days, one especially, that was used by our people. It was in the form of a ball or sphere attached to a piece of two and one half inch pipe about two feet long. The ball was of iron and contained a heavy bursting charge. The whole rig weighed some 60 pounds and was fired from a sort of mortar. There was a flat nose cap with a detonator on the side of the ball opposite the handle or pipe. These often failed to explode on landing. We called them footballs. Fritz had a sort of aerial torpedo that was thrown from some sort of catapult. This was called a sausage on account of it's shape. It was a creepy sort of thing to see coming over for it wobbled and wavered about in the air and you never could determine which direction it was going to take in its downward plunge to our trench.

You might start to run in one direction to escape the burst and the sausage would seem to turn and follow you. You never could tell just where it was going to land. The rum jar was another fritz affair made of thin sheet metal with a wooden block base. It resembled a rum jar in general size and shape. They were about ten inches in diameter, and in three different lengths. The biggest ones were about two feet long. They were filled with a coarse explosive of a yellow color and loose like sawdust. I saw one of the wooden catapults that they were thrown from but did not have the time to examine its workings or dope out where it got the power to hurl these things so far. The minen werfer or mine thrower was a sort of heavy trench mortar or howitzer that threw over a very heavy shell that left a huge crater. I never saw a dud from a minen werfer, they always seemed to explode. We had a flying pig or huge aerial torpedo, some of them were ten inches in diameter and up to five feet in length. They were fitted with fans or rudders at the back end of the pig to assist them in keeping a straight course. They were erratic in their flight and apt to fall short. There was often a case of a premature burst that had the effect of wiping out the crew of the mortar that was firing it. The explosion of these was very heavy. The pineapple was a fritz affair with a slight resemblance to the above named fruit. The casing was corrugated or cut in notches all over the outer surface. This had the effect of causing the case to fly into small bits when it exploded. The bursting charge in these was of some kind of quick explosive that gave a wicked crash and drove the fragments with great velocity. There were more R. I. P's than blighters from them. R. I. P. means a wooden cross. A blight is a wound.

The battalion pioneers had the job of sewing you in a blanket when you became a R. I. P. case. There was one of our old pioneers who would tell you (if you got into an argument with him). Huh! I'll get even with you. Every man to his own trade. I'll sew you in a blanket yet. Somebody at about this time thought he had got even with me. At the corner of Maple Copse and Square Wood one of my former scouts, Archie St. Louis, came upon a grave with wooden cross and all, bearing my name. He supposed I had been killed in the fighting there. He was surprised when I stepped into his dugout at the rail dugouts near Zillebeeke Farm.

Archie was now in the wireless section and was on duty at a key in a dugout with a set of aerials set up overhead. He let me listen in with the ear phones while a German operator was sending a lot of routine stuff 153 in the ordinary commercial code. St. Louis said that this fritz was a very smart operator and used to talk to them giving them lip in the commercial code. He was a fast sender alright making that old key fairly hum. All this stuff was copied down for comparison with other stuff picked up along the whole allied front. Collectively and by comparison with other stuff gleaned from widely separated fronts they were able to make deductions by sifting the wheat from the chaff, gaining fragments of real information from the mass of stuff that was broadcasted daily from widely different points.

I don't know how I came to get a wooden cross as noted above. There was a man from Kenora in the 52nd Battalion. He was killed in that fight. His name was Louis Sampson. We had been writing to one another. He may have had my name and regimental number on a paper or letter in his pocket when killed. This may have been taken for identification by the party who buried him. He was blown to atoms by a heavy shell or trench mortar. This is only conjecture, there were other Kenora men in his unit, and it could have been any one of them. I was over that ground in one of the counter attacks made after fritz's first drive and might have dropped something from my tunic pocket that was found close by the remains and mistaken for the name of the victim. I never had a chance to go there and view it myself.

Training for The Somme

In the mid-summer of that year we were taken out of the front line and went into training in preparation for a trip into the Somme. We were taken on some long marches ending up at a couple of small villages by the name of Houlle and Moulle. Here we were drilled and put through various kinds of training. The unit was now largely made up of new drafts. This applied to the staff of officers as well as to the rank and file. All this new material had to be got into shape. The old hands needed a bit of rest and a chance to get a new grip on life for our length of front line service was more than normal. I now took no further part in the organization or training of the scouts or observers. I was now a private in the snipers and had nothing to do with other work. The scout work was being carried on by Lieut. Harrower assisted by a couple of scouts, Taylor and Carmichael.

During the time we were here in training we were sent to a rifle range belonging to some British unit. This range was short with all firing done at ranges of 100 or 200 yards. It was located in an old sand pit. It was in charge of an old English officer. I guess he was too elderly for front line service. He was training his own men here in the use of the short le Enfield. The best he was getting for groups with new barrels equipped with English made telescopes was three and four inches at 100 and 200 yards. We were using the MK. 3 Ross equipped with a Winchester scope. He started us in to shoot at 100 yards. Jack Harron an ex-Alberta Ranger was my shooting mate. We two put on successive groups of five shots in one inch and three quarter inch circles at 100 yards. The old imperial officer was flabbergasted. He took our rifles and put a testing plug through the bore to measure them. He told us they tested out better than the brandnew barrels that he was getting from the Enfield works. The rifles we used had been in front-line service for nearly a year and a half. I myself shot with old Ypres Lizzie. I had had her equipped with a Winchester scope by the battalion armourer. He asked if I had ever been to Bisley. I told him I had practiced on moose and deer and such-like in the woods country. This was all new and strange stuff to him and he was real interested about it. We had quite a yarn together about rifles and such.

We drilled and route marched around that part of the country for some weeks. During the time we were here we were joined by a brass band from some unit in the old 90th that had been in training in England. This was the first time we had any band of our own since coming on active service. It was quite a band and used to give concerts in the evenings at the officers quarters. There were several other units in the near vicinity and a sort of military sports day was organized. There were football, and base ball games, horseback wrestling and a prize fight in which Joe Millan, the ex-pugilist gave us a sample of his wares. There was a horse show and in connection to this there was a steeple chase over hurdles, water, hazards etc. Canon Scott our Padre, rode in this doing very well too for a man of his years. He was a great old sport. Two of my old scouts made the best showing in the wrestling on horseback. Jack Harron and Bill McLean. They were both good horsemen having been at it for years in the west. Jack had been an Alberta government ranger in the mountains for some years before the war so was an old hand on the pack train route, diamond hitch and all that stuff. McLean had come from the prairie and had grown up among horses. There were other sports such as tug-o-war, foot races etc. The (crown and anchor) man did some great work in the weeks we were here and you could hear his spiel at quite a few spots around the corner:" Roll right up gentleman. Try your Luck. They come here in shoe-packs and drove away in motor cars. What price the old Sergeant Major. How about the old Mud Hook. If you don't speculate you can't accumulate. Roll right up" and so-on. Then there was Housie-Housie. Top-o-the House–Kelly's Eye, and its spiel. For a few short weeks we had a taste of the life that the men on the bomb-proof jobs led all through the period of the war.

The Somme

Then we were off on our way again to the Somme. We marched and we rode on London buses, also by rail. We marched some more and landed in a rain storm on an open side hill to the north of the town of Albert. The spot where we camped was called the Brick Fields. We were supplied with small canvas tarps or fly's that we pitched like tiny tents. Both ends were open with the wind driving the rain in on us and the surface water swamped us out below as it crept up through our flimsy ground sheets or blankets. The whole place was soon a sea of mud from the trampling of many feet. The officers pitched a big marquee tent in the middle of the works and were sitting around tables with nice camp chairs to sit in. They set the jars of rum that were supposed to be issued to us on the table in the big tent helping themselves liberally while we stood about in the rain on the open hillside trying to shiver ourselves warm in wet duds. Nix! Not a bit of it from that gang.

Harrower had a very high pitched, shrill, sort of squeaky voice and while on route marches he used to get behind us and frequently yell, "Cover Off". It was sort of a habit with him and the squeaky sound always brought a chuckle from the officers as well as the men on the march. Some wag in the section was able to imitate him, to a little more than perfection, when all were trudging along quietly there would come a squeak somewhere amidships. "Cover Off".

When on the march to the Somme we had our first meeting with Australian troops. We met them on the road one day shouting greetings as they passed in motor lorries or trucks. We were soon to see them in the line at Muckuiet Farm to the right of Thiepval. It fell to our lot to take that place that the Aussies and several imperial units had been unable to wrest from the Germans in several weeks of hard fighting. Big Durand who commanded the platoon on the left at the battle of St. Julien, came back to his old battalion before we went to the Somme. Shorty Weld, or Pinky Weld also came back. These fine officers were relegated to junior ranks and such riff-raff as our o. c. had picked up, were kept on the strength with a senior rank to these old warriors.

Since Lipsett had left us there had been no place for any real men on the staff of the 8th. Fawning parasites were the type now in demand and this type predominated. Imagine a man like Harrower being senior to Durand in the latter's own battalion. It was enough to make the dead at St. Julien rise up out the mud and curse. Soon after arriving at the Brick fields there was an aviator landed in the field close to us in a biplane, two seater. There was a wide gap of five or six feet shot clean out of the upper wing directly over the aviator's seat. One of the two pilots was dead and the other severely wounded about the head and shoulders. He had flown his plane in that condition for about 20 miles and made a good landing and then lost consciousness as he reached the ground. The fuselage and the tail rudders were completely painted with his blood to a brilliant red from his seat backward.

We marched through Albert passing under the famous Leaning Virgin. Eventually we were quartered in the town in some ruined buildings for a few nights. Fritz was dropping a few shells into the town all the while we were there. We were moved farther forward in a few days to some huge craters that had been made in the chalk that under laid most of the country here about. These craters were close to and on the south side of the Baupaume Road a few miles east of Albert.

They had been made by the explosion of mines under the front line trenches in the start of the Somme fighting earlier in the summer. We made shelters as best we could on the sloping sides of the craters. A graveyard or cemetery had been here and the loose chalk was inter-mixed with skulls and other bones. Some of our boys took a notion to horrify some of the imperial officers that were riding by on the road daily casting curious glances at these wild colonials. They took some skulls that were kicking around underfoot and stuck them up on sticks at the margin of the road. You should have seen the blimeys stare at us wild and untamed savage "Canidians" after this decoration was set up.

During one stage of our trip to the Somme we were traveling by rail and stopped in a railway yard for sometime. We were kept in the cattle cars as it was only a temporary stop. While we stood there a train load of English tommies pulled in on the next track stopping abreast of us. Somebody wanted to get a rise out of the tommies and shouted across, asking if that was a leave train or if they were going on leave. It was great to see the look of disgust on the faces of the tommies and one of them replied with great vehemence and very broad dialect "(Some Bleedin Opes)". He of course made it a little stronger than that, As sogers will. Our boys of course roared and laughed at the reply with this only puzzling or disgusting tommies all the more. I bet they thought we "Blawsted Canadians" were a ballyhoo lot of rotters. Probably thought we were plumb daft. We sympathized with them for we all knew that they, as well as ourselves, were in for a rough time in the near future.

From the craters we were sent up the line on working and carrying parties to the vicinity of what was known as the sugar trench. There were a number of trenches in this area to the left of Courcelette and to the right of Thiepval.

In the middle of this area was a place known as Mouquiet Farm that had been a bone of contention between the British and the Germans for a number of weeks. Our people had attacked this place several times being thrown back each time. The Australian troops had tried their luck and failed. Sir Arthur Currie was now in command of the Canadian corps and the old first division was put in this sector and after several attempts succeeded in throwing fritz out of it, nack and crop. Currie tried the same methods the other troops had used, several times at first and did not succeed at doing anything except to nearly annihilate the highland brigade of the Canadian corps. There was a row over this with a lot of pretty stiff arguments among the staff of the corps. The troops had been sent up against wire entanglements with no proper artillery preparation with the usual results. Under a little better management we succeeded in taking the place alright moving forward to a trench that was within 500 yards of the Zollern trench. This put us in front of one of fritz's strongest lines of defensive works. There were the Hohenzollern and Hessien trenches in which were incorporated the Stufftt, the Shuaben and couple of other strong redoubts.

We eventually were set the task of storming and the taking these lines of heavy earth works. The battle that took place when these defenses were taken was one of the fiercest and hardest fought of the whole war, but for some mysterious reason this epic fight seems to have passed almost unnoticed by the people who have taken it upon themselves to make a record of many great battles of the war. Courcellette was a greater fight by far than (Waterloo). The storming of the Zollern and Hessien lines and the four redoubts on the 26th and 27th of September 1916 by the 1st Canadian division was a fight that easily outranked the battle of Courcellette. I figure that one of the reasons that its story has never been given to the world is because the most of the men in that terrific onslaught never lived to tell about it. The 8th battalion came out of with a strength of less than 40 men. A number of the other units engaged did not fare much better than we did. I don't believe that mankind in all his striving on earth ever saw before or since quite the equal of the savage and scientific storm of fury that swept that piece of shell-churned ground that day. The concentration of all man's fury that had been gathered through the ages seemed to break, and tear loose there that day. The earth rocked dizzily with the force and fury of the meeting. The sky above was a seething tornado of fire and steel above which again there were locked in death grips the fighting squadrons of the air forces. The eastern and western horizons were a solid sheet of dancing vivid flame while the thousands of great guns from both sides poured their rivers of heavy metal upon that tortured strip of ground. The concentration of machine gun fire brought to bear by both sides at one time got so heavy it actually drowned the roar of the artillery on the disputed ground. The troops from the north of Ireland, or the Ulsterman, had some heavy fighting on our left at Thiepval. We could hear the roar of the battle for a number of days. The whole country was completely churned up by shells on the front that we went over. You could not see a bit of green sod clear to the horizon in any direction. All landmarks were gone or blotted out and it was difficult for the artillery to get anything to serve as reference points from which to lay their guns. Infantry moving up at night became lost and strayed in the vast sea of mud and shell holes.

There had been a couple of villages or small towns along the Baupaume Road just east of where the big mine craters were. These towns had been built of brick, stone and chalk. You could not find even a fragment of a wall intact. You could not even trace the place where the cobble stone paved streets had been. Just in front and some yards to the left of what had been the Sugar Refinery at Courcellette I saw the half of a horse lying on a fragment of road. The horse had been cut in two vertically endwise from nose to tail. It was as though he had been set on a lumber carriage in a saw-mill and sawed in two endwise by a band saw or huge circular saw. The right half of the horse was totally intact with the left half missing. I have never been able to figure out what hit him, unless it was a huge slab off one of the 15 inch or 13.5 inch shells. I have seen steel slabs from the burst from a shell fly 1100 yards from the place where the shell burst. Occasionally one of the big shells would fail to burst and perhaps ricochet or spin end over end after hitting a cement redoubt or gun emplacement. The noise they made when spinning was something to remember and would try the strongest nervous system. We made eight trips or did eight terms in the front line during the time we were on the Somme. One time we were on the way up the line and were delayed from some cause. I never heard what the delay was. The shell fire became very heavy and to save loss of men we were sent into a big German dugout that had served as a shelter for the crew of a fritz field battery. The guns were still there in the gun pits. On the foot path in front of this battery we noticed a small leather strap sticking out of the mud and, on pulling it out it was the sling attached to a Winchester A5 Scope Sight in a leather case. I cleaned it up and it turned out to be a very good glass. I used it in sniping until Xmas 1917. I then went on leave to Swansea in Wales and shipped the sight home from there. I have it now in 1926 and use it on a .280 caliber Ross. While we were sheltered in the dugout at the battery fritz began to shell it with a heavy gun. He was trying to cave in the roof and kept slamming away with delayed-fuse shells that dug deep and then drove deeper when they exploded. While he was at the roof with the heavy gun he kept a barrage of shrapnel sweeping the exit and the path outside. The last shell that he put over while I was in there very nearly caved in the roof. The timber revetting cracked and sagged and a lot of loose chalk, small stones and a thick cloud of dust came through it. The concussion very nearly knocked us out as it was. I decided not to wait for the next shell and went outside and took a chance with the Shrapnel in preference to being buried alive down there. I don't know whether he succeeded in caving in the roof or not but I don't believe it would have survived another direct hit.

We had a man in the scouts who believed in fatalism, or was a sort of fatalist. He always insisted that a mans conduct or personal efforts had no effect in delaying or hastening his demise. If his time came, his end came, and not before or later. He often argued along this strain and his conduct showed that he had come to believe in this theory. Some time after leaving the old battery position we were standing in a narrow trench that was about breast deep. There were several of us strung along the trench and fritz was slamming it pretty regular with shrapnel. We would all duck down flat in the trench and escape the sweep of the lead balls from the burst of the shells above and in front. I said all, (but no) there was the fatalist, he would not take the trouble to duck his head, said it didn't help any, twas all preordained and caution was a waste of effort etc. The rest of us escaped without a scratch but he was riddled like a sieve and killed as dead as a mackerel. That was a lesson for the rest of us and I for one did not forget that little demonstration. I saw other cases where believers in his doctrine threw away their lives needlessly. As a theory and a belief (it is the bunk).

While on this front we saw the first tanks go into action. There were three of them and this was the first time they were actually used in battle. They were named Cordon Rouge, Crème de Mentha and I cannot recall the name of the third one. They were queer looking object on first sight and fritz didn't know how to take them. In some cases the Germans took panic and fled from them. In one case they surrounded a tank clambering all over it with bayonet and bomb looking for vulnerable spots in its armor. The first tanks were able to do a lot of execution on account of the enemy not knowing their nature or capabilities for slaughter. They went up the line on the old Albert-Baupaume Road. These first tanks had a pair of wheels sticking out behind for steering purposes. Later models were made without this attachment and were steered by independent control of each caterpillar tread. Fritz was soon wise to the tank business and concealed special guns to be used only against them at point blank ranges. These concealed guns made short work of many tanks in later engagements such as Passchendaele and in the fighting along the canals at Cambrai.

I later saw huge rifles that fritz had made to penetrate the plates of tanks. These rifles were almost a duplicate in oversize of the service weapon, with all parts enlarged in proportion. They had a kick that any army mule would envy being about six feet long or thereabouts. Later he built an auto-loading or automatic field gun for use against tanks. I heard one of these guns firing on several occasions and its speed of fire was just a shade slower than our old pom-pom gun that was used against aircraft in 1915. The pom-pom was a dandy but was too small and could not reach high enough to be of any use against modern planes with real climbing ability. Its limit was about five or six thousand feet elevation. The Pom-Pom ought to be ok for use against the smaller types of tanks that are in vogue now, providing it has punch enough to drill their armor. The German auto-gun is a much heavier weapon to judge by its sound and the burst of its shells.

Transport became a serious problem on the Somme in the area immediately behind the line. Light rail tracks were thrown down in the mud in some cases and mules were used to haul small trucks on these irregular tracks across the sea of mud that stretched for miles back of the line.

We went in the line one night and it was planned to make an attack at five a.m. of the following morning. The snipers were given instructions to go out in pairs and dig in no-man's land and there await zero hour. In the attack we were instructed to follow the third wave and be prepared to snipe down the enemy while our boys were digging in at the final objective line. R. L. Stutt was detailed to go mates with me. On the way in he took a notion to visit an ammunition store where he had seen some particular brand of cartridges that he liked to use. I told him he was liable to get lost on account of the lack of landmarks and wander around all over the place. That is just what he did. When the time came to go out at about 9 p.m. he had not showed up and I did not know whether he was lost or became a casualty. I waited a while and then went out with Fred Minty as a side kick. I remember seeing Pinky Weld or (Shorty Weld) in the front trench when going over the top. That is the last time I ever saw him. I don't now if he was killed, wounded or what. Minty and I went out to a place about halfway across to the enemy lines then got busy with a trenching tool to dig a funk hole deep enough to give shelter from machine gun fire or shrapnel. It got quite chilly during the night so we kept digging a bit every little while to keep warm.

We were in a position to watch the gun fire from both sides. It was an awesome sight and sound all through that night. The whole complete circle of the horizon was one unbroken glare of dancing and fierce up leaping flame. You could tell the different classes of guns by their sounds and the color of the flash from their muzzles as they lit the sky. There were the long range high velocity naval types, the huge 15 inch, 12,inch, nine point two inch howitzers, the six inch naval, along with all the smaller fry, six inch howitzers, for and one half inch, a few eight inch along with a swarm of 18 pounder field guns and some French 75s. The ones that used cordite for a propellant made a crash like the slamming of huge iron doors and lit the sky with a bright orange flame. The ones that used nitro-cellulose made a sharp vicious hissing sort of a roar lighting the sky with a bluish white flame not unlike a short circuit on an electric cable. In this bedlam of heavy weights the chatter of the whiz-bangs and the 75s sounded like rifle fire by comparison. The bigger howitzers seemed to bark hoarsely like huge mastiff dogs giving forth a great coughing roar followed by a sucking sound like the intake of a monster breath. This sucking sound that came close on the first roar was always accompanied by a deep and subterranean sort of thud or bump that seemed to come from the bowels of the earth. The big naval guns gave the loudest and most intense sort of explosion lighting the sky with a bright white blinding flash. They hurled their shells across that sea of mud in a flat trajectory. When they passed, you felt as though you could reach up and touch them. The breath of some of them felt very close for they were plunging into the enemy line only about 150 to 200 yards in front of where we lay. The big howitzer shells were tossed high up in the sky, curving over and coming down almost vertically. The last downward swoop is a wicked sound. When they burst there is a wide geyser of vivid flame and the earth rocks and wobbles from side to side in a way that is like nothing except perhaps an earthquake. This particular wobbling of the earth under one has a sort of nauseating effect on the stomach as though you were going to be sea sick. The sudden changes in air pressure that take place in the vicinity may have something to do with that feeling.

In the enemy redoubts in front of us they had shafts 40 feet deep or more equipped with hoists. They could keep their machine guns at this depth hoisting them to the top for use after the barrage lifted and our boys started to go across. The heavies were trying to put these guns out of business but a number of them were not hit, for you could hear them fire short bursts every few minutes from different points in front. They seemed as though they signaled to one another in a sort of code that they played on the machine guns.

The enemy artillery was not idle during this night by any means hurling a lot of metal with the bigger part of it going behind and beyond where we lay and plowing up the ground along the line of our front trenches. Troops moving up lost heavily from this fire during the night. I unearthed a big shell of about nine or ten inch caliber while digging in. It was a dud or one that failed to explode. I rolled it out on the bank of mud in front thinking no more about it for some time. Toward morning fritz began to sweep the ground with machine gun fire and I heard the rattle of a shower of bullets hitting the casing of that dud and suddenly bethought myself that a bullet hitting that nose cap would be liable to set off the big shell blowing me to kingdom come. I hastily reached up turning the shell so the nose pointed to me and away from the machine guns.

The grey misty light of early dawn began to creep up from the eastern horizon as well as the hour that had been set for the final assault. Fritz began to get nervous sweeping the ground with storms of shrapnel and machine gun fire. He also sent over a scatter of gas shells on all the low places and sags in the ground. You could see the yellowish green vapor oozing from the mud where the shells had landed. The night dew seemed to hold the gas vapor helping it to get in its work. Sunshine and wind would dissipate it to a great extent. Darkness and dampness were more suited to its use (like other evil things). These shells came over at what must have been the extreme range of the guns for they were going very slow and some of them wobbled, and key-holed or turned end-over-end before reaching the ground. They made a mournful sort of wail in the air. When they landed they made a hollow sort of putt. Examination showed that they were fitted with a nose cap of some material resembling hard rubber or black vulcanite.

With the approach of dawn the heavies seemed to slack off from there prodigious labors of the night now firing slowly and intermittently as though wearied from the long grind. I suppose they were saving shells, and cooling their guns in preparation for the final savage storm of death that would burst out at the zero hour and continue to the end of the battle. Some English battalions were on our left and they failed to get ready in time for the assault. Word came along the line that we would have to lie in our holes in the mud until one thirty in the afternoon.(No grub, no rum). It had been nearly 24 hours since we had eaten anything. We had to lie close in the mud during that forenoon for it would not do to show too much movement along the line where we had dug in. If Fritz got wise to where we were lying he would be able to shell us out pretty badly before the time now set at one thirty p.m. for the assault. The shell fire and other fire kept up fairly steadily in all this time, and just after noon there seemed to be a pause as though both sides were holding their breath.

It was the calm before the storm. A creepy and suspicious kind of stillness. Men looked at their watches, shifted, and fidgeted about. Time never seemed to drag so slowly. As the final minutes began to slip away we heard a battery somewhere in the rear let out a spluttering salvo.

This seemed to be a signal and the whole skyline burst in flame with a terrific roar. Everything beyond a range of about 50 yards was blotted out of sight in a blizzard of dust clouds, smoke and flying earth. We could then see the first wave moving forward and though it had been a calm day the men seemed to be leaning forward as if against a stiff gale. The gale was real and must have been caused or induced by the terrific storm of shells and machine gun fire that was sweeping across that strip of country. You could not hear anything and could see very little. The roar swelled and swelled becoming more intense. All of the numerous machine gun units on both sides cut in with their hundreds and thousands of guns. The roar of bullets became so loud it actually drowned out the sound of the big guns and the nearer bursts of shells around us. We were trying to distinguish the third wave of attack as we were supposed to follow that bunch forward. The barrage came down heavy on the line where we, were dug in. I saw a whole machine gun crew wiped out by the burst of a shell about 15 feet to our left. Minty was dug in just to my left and was sitting up in the bottom of his hole in the mud with his feet toward me. I had just made a sign to him that it was time to go forward. Then there was a blinding crash and I knew no more for awhile. Minty said he was buried up to his chin in the wet clay and could not get out. A lone survivor of the machine gun crew dug him out. He took a look at the place where I had been and saw nothing but a big shell crater with the smoke coming out of the cracks and fissures in the ground. He figured I had been killed or perhaps blown up and did not trouble to look for me then. I do not know how long it was before I came to, and before my mind began to grope its way back to consciousness. It was a queer feeling. I did not know what to expect. For awhile I could not figure out if I was still on earth or not. I thought I might be some place else for there was a strong odor of sulphur that seemed to choke and strangle me. Then I got the smell of gun powder, strong, and began to hear and feel the burst of shells very close. I decided I was still on the Somme. After a bit I sized things up and found I was on my left side and about four feet below the surface of the mud. There was a crack or fissure directly above my head and I could see daylight shining down through a thick cloud of blue smoke that seemed to come out of the earth all around. I tried to move but found that I was packed in that clay so hard it was like a plaster cast or a setting of cement. I could not budge my body or legs by exerting all my strength. I then reached upward with my free arm trying to get a grip on the packed clay above so as to pull myself up. When I did this the earth began to tumble in on top of my face so I lay perfectly still for a bit for fear my breathing space would be closed up. The thick ooze of smoke and gases still came out of the ground and I began to go off to the land of nod again. It smelled sweet and sickly like ether or chloroform. I woke again after a time. I guess it was the shock of a shell bursting close to me in the clay that jolted me into consciousness again. There were three more of them in quick succession and every one dug in deeper and hit harder than its brother. The burst of the fourth nearly broke my back for it hit directly behind me in the mud. I held my breath waiting to see if there would be a fifth. Five-gun batteries had become quite common of late. The fifth one did not come.

They say a person who figures his time has come thinks of all his past with everything passing before him in quick review. I did not experience it that way. My thoughts were strictly on the present and

I was trying to figure a way to survive or get out of that hole. I do remember thinking about people at home and friends in Kenora. The gas fumes soon put me away for another term. This was repeated a couple of times. In a subsequent period of consciousness I heard voices. There was someone talking close above me.

I woke up at this and made all the noise I could in an endeavor to draw their attention. They must have heard me for I can remember a couple of men holding me and talking. Minty was still there with another man. They got one on each side dragging and pushing me along toward someplace. This part of it is not very clear in my memory. They told me the next day that I was telling a long yarn about some sergeant major during the time they were helping me along back to where we had come from before the start of the attack. I had been below ground from about 1.30 p.m. to 5.30 p.m.

They shoved me into the stairway of an unfinished dugout leaving me there to get over it or croak, just as I saw fit. Fritz put a shell into the trench just above the entrance to my shelter some time during the night giving me a bad jolt from the concussion. If you are in a small hole with only one entrance or outlet you get the full benefit of the concussion from a shell—burst. I got it. Now I had been suffering from a recurrence of the dysentery since arriving on the Somme due to a return to X rations, or bully and biscuit. I had not eaten a bite for about 24 hours before being buried. You can guess that I was a bit weakened by the combination of dysentery, hunger, gas poison, and shock along with three bad doses of concussion from shells. I lay in that hole all that night, the next day, and at sundown somebody looked in and said we were to march back to Albert. I hobbled out and started off with a lot of other crocks that made up the 40 odd that was the sum total left of the old 8th battalion at the finish of that fight. It was dark and we splashed and stumbled through mud and water mixed with corpses and barbed wire. After a long period of this we came to the narrow gauge track where the mules hauled the small trolleys up the line. The cross ties were too far apart to be used as steps so you stepped high, then on the next step you went kerplunk down into the deep holes the mules had dug with their hooves in the soft mud. The holes were full of water. There was several miles of this sort of travel before we came to the Baupaume Road. I was in a sort of trance or stupor by now with it seeming as if I had been plodding, slipping and plunging along for ages. My limbs seemed to work automatically like some sort of machine that was only dimly and uncertainly connected to my mental apparatus. We arrived at the Baupaume Road and here I got the only free cup of coffee that I ever saw dished out by the (YMCA) in all the time I was in the army. They actually did not want our money. I was beyond the stage where I could feel any shock or this would have finally floored me. They did not try to march us directly to Albert. I was told they did not want to march such a slim remnant of a battalion back past the incoming troops. It would not have a tendency to cheer them up for the work ahead.

We were kept at the old mine craters where we had been on our first trip up to the line until a new draft was brought up from Albert to march in with us so it would not look quite so bad. During the time that we were at the craters fritz succeeded in making a hit on a huge ammunition dump that was some 500 yards below us in a valley at the south side of the main road. The explosions were transmitted from one huge pile of shells to the next, and in this way the whole mass was set off. The roar was terrific and it continued like a concentrated battle all thru the night. I was too feeble and all in to take much notice of it at the time but was told by others that it was a great spectacle. I know I was wakened several times by extra heavy bursts of explosion. Some of the shells that were down below in the piles and thus confined to a certain extent attained quite a velocity and flew long distances. There was certainly some money burned in that dump.

I got knocked out too early to see much of the battle described above but heard something of how it went from some of the survivors. R. L. Stutt who was supposed to go out with me got lost on the evening before the attack and finally went out with Shepperdson. Shepperdson didn't like it and said so. He told Stutt he was going to get out of there and sure enough away he went to battalion headquarters going down into the headquarters dugout, staying there doing what he could to help drink our rum and furnish entertainment for the officers. He had a good line of hot air and he did make it stick and got away with it too. He could get away with most anything especially other people's horses. He had been a cow-puncher in the west for some years. When he spotted a good horse he would revert to type and the nag would go

171

missing. Some one of our officers generally would benefit by securing a new saddle horse. I guess Shep benefited too in a way. The headquarters dugout during times of storm and stress for instance.

Poor old Stutt was left on his lonely lonesome having to rustle mates and find a job on his own hook. He ran into some of our scouts and got plenty to do as a runner or messenger under heavy fire. One of the parties he was on had a rough passage.

Just before we went into the Somme there was a young lieutenant, a new draft of Manitoba Icelandic extraction attached to the scouts under Harrower. Now when the attack went forward Harrower was asked get information about the sector to our front and opposite our left flank. This area was under heavy fire and Harrower gave the new lieutenant his own compass, raincoat etc. sending him out to get the information. The new lieut. was accompanied on this patrol by a couple of my old scouts. When near their objective the new lieut. was shot and killed and it was of course impossible to fetch him in from there. A couple of other scouts were killed and wounded. When we got back to the first camp for reorganization Harrower was right there on parade wanting to know where the new lieut. had gone with his compass and his rain coat. He shouted and kicked up quite a fuss about the loss of these articles but not a word about the lieut. Some of the older officers were somewhat taken a back by this demonstration of callous selfishness.

As our attack had overrun the enemy first line the troops on our left, some English battalions, had failed to make it and fell back. Our boys went right on another 500 yards past the Hohenzollern trench and also took the Hessien trench. These two trenches included three redoubts or strong points. The Stuffitt redoubt to our left was still in the hands of the enemy together with the trenches in that part of the front. Our boys were badly off for they were enfiladed from the left. They bombed their way along the enemy line right up to the walls of the redoubt on our left. Fritz threw in heavy reinforcements pressing them back a little. It was in this heavy fighting that our battalion was nearly wiped out. The 7th battalion sent some help and they succeeded in putting a wire block in the trench and held what they had gained. This hard fighting and heavy loss was due to the troops to the left of us falling back and failing to make their objective. A couple of my old scouts, Campbell and another, went forward some 600 yards beyond the Hessien line as far as the wire entanglements of the Regina trench. The barrage was lifted a few minutes to allow this patrol but they did not have time to get back, and had to come through some of our own barrage. They got back however.

It was a wonderful piece of work that the old 1st division did that day and they have never, so far as I know, been given any credit for one of the fiercest and hardest won fights in all history. Victories of far less importance have been highly lauded while this seems to have been overlooked by the historians. Moving pictures were actually taken of one part of this battle. They would be worth seeing. It was certainly a bit of the real thing.

We had an old machine gun sergeant, Watkins, who had been with us continuously from Valcartier. I don't remember how many gun crews he had led and had seen killed off. I believe he survived three gun crews in this fight alone. He came out of it again and now he was busy again training new drafts to man his guns in the next fight. He was a small man and stooped, of a quiet, and very cheerful disposition and an unassuming person. He had been asked several times to take out a commission but I guess his retiring disposition led him to decline it. He seemed to prefer his old line of work on the guns. It is a pity that he could not write the history of his guns and their crews from Valcartier onwards. It would be a great tale of high courage, sacrifice and achievement. The real stories of the real fighters on the tempered spear point of the fighting forces are very seldom told and all the world usually gets is a sort of second-hand summary by people who never were in the rage and flame on the actual bow-end of the nation's fighting machine.

After we got back out of this fight and were being patched up ready for the next one we were just outside of Albert. I heard that some new battalions from home had arrived. There was a man from Kenora in one of these units. I think it was the 78th. Harry Hives who had boarded with me at home before I enlisted. I went over to their lines one day to see him and was just in time to see him falling in to go up the line with a working party. I did have a word or two with him before he marched off. He was captured by the Germans a few days later while out with a patrol and spent about three years in Germany. The o. c. of his battalion was Kircaldie and had been one of the officers of the original 8th battalion. I had the pleasure of meeting him too when on the visit to the 78th. He was a very capable officer. A tall raw-boned, quiet man, rather stern and strong on discipline.

While recuperating here we obtained some Winnipeg papers of a recent date and had the doubtful pleasure of reading of how the home folks saw the war. It appears they were trying to organize a battalion of college students around Winnipeg and were only wanting fellows of a certain social status to fill its ranks. No common stiffs need apply. The paper went on to set forth the advantages of joining this unit. Your boy will be associating with chaps whom they could associate with in civil life. They went on to say," The time has come when the class that from which this unit is to be recruited, must begin to think about doing their bit". November 1916 mind you! I guess they figured that the common stiffs might be all killed off if they didn't do something soon. The mamma's darlings had all been in various officer's training schools and camps in Canada until they all became officers, and there were no soldiers left for the making of an army. They had used family influence, patronage and coin to enable them to jump and transfer out of every unit that threatened to be sent overseas. Now it was getting near to a showdown and they figured to herd them all into the yellow whole as a unit and start them off for someplace, a quiet place preferred. It would be a pity to mix them with rude fellows. Some of the old 8th men relieved themselves of some heartfelt curses when they read this mess of twaddle. A couple of the n.c.o's said they hoped it would be their luck to get some of those classy birds in a draft to our unit. They sure would be pleased to have charge of them for awhile. Ye Gods, democracy—what things are done in thy name.

During the operations on the Somme we were under command of a newly promoted officer named Raddell. He had come out with us from Valcartier as a Sgt. major of machine guns. He was a peppery and very soldierly sort of gent who had gotten his early training in the British army and retained a lot of the ideas drilled into him while in that service. We made another trip up the line to a wide valley that extended away to the north east toward a small town named Pye. The Regina and Kenora trenches had been captured by Canadian troops while we were being refitted and filled up full of new drafts. The enemy troops were badly shaken in this area by long—continued artillery bombardment. I saw some of them in this valley jumping on all fours like frogs from one shell hole to another in an abandon that was no longer human. To see them was to pity them. They must have passed through an ordeal that would wreck them physically and mentally even if they did survive.

They used to boast that the verdommed Englanders could not put down a barrage. They did not know how. The Somme was really the first taste that fritz got of his own medicine. It was the first time in the war that we had artillery to put up a barrage that was real. He was beginning to go through some of what we had been getting continuously since 1914. His men did not have it in them to stand up under it and keep their morale for long.

While on this front we came in contact for the first time with an enemy corps of marines. They had been used as reserves principally up to this time and that was the reason we had never come in contact with them. One of these units had Gibraltar written on the facings of their uniforms. They were superior physically to a lot of the prisoners we had gotten of late. A lot of the German units were filled with drafts of men that had been recruited from mills, mines and factories to judge by the look of them. They must have been at indoor and sedentary jobs for several generations. Almost without exception they wore thick lenses, glasses or spectacles. A majority of them were bald-headed. Their heads and bodies were in a majority of cases misshapen and of abnormal aspect. They had a queer pallor, and a grey mouse or rat-like aspect that gave you a queer feeling when close to them. They were well educated in their way seeming to be of an intelligent disposition. It is a hard thing to define. Their intellect seemed to have been machine—made and their ideas seemed to travel in grooves. Many of them could talk English quite well.

Some had previously been to Canada and the U S, others had been in England. The Germans of the marine corps previously mentioned were superior to these drafts in every way and were full of spirit. Some of them put up a fight with the bayonet in one case. Our own marine corps had been used previous to this in the attempts to take Mouquiet Farm. South African, and Newfoundland units, as well as some Australians were used at that place before it was taken by the 1st

Canadian division. The soldiers knew the place as "Mucky" Farm. I don't remember if any of the new Zealand troops were used there or not. We had eight terms or periods up the line in the Somme, and our unit was practically wiped out four times while there.

Lens

We were finally pulled out and went up to Bruay in the coal mining district in the vicinity of Lens. We held a lot of different sectors along this part of the line during the whole of the following winter. We were at nearly every point from Bully Grenay, and Fosse 10, to Ecurie. We were in at Suchez, Vimy, Leavin, Cite Moulin, Cite Collone, Cite St. Pierre, Moroc etc. At every new place we went through the military baths. The baths were some institution. There was usually an old stationary boiler that had been patched and made to stand a few pounds pressure of steam. This was used as a heater and from it pipes, were run along the ceiling of the bathroom proper. Here the pipe line was fitted with short branch pipes that had a tin can perforated with nail holes to serve as a spray. We would disrobe in one room, throw our underwear through a window to an attendant and pass on naked in Indian file into the spray from the tin cans. After a very short time there you would hear a yell from the Sgt. in charge of operations. Then you moved out and a new suit of underwear was thrown to you as you passed another window. You had to take pot luck on what you got. If you were tall and broad you were sure to get an outfit to fit a runt and viceversa. Sometimes we were able to trade off ill-fitting garments with some small guy who had drawn a big suit in the lottery. These clothes were supposed to be free from lice or vermin but it was only a dream. The first dose of lice I got in France was on a new suit taken from a pile of stuff that had never been worn since coming from the factory. It had been stored and handled over the floors of these baths, in close contact with infected clothing until it was literally loaded for bear. You did not notice anything wrong until you got warm or started to perspire. Then things got lively and interesting all at once.

The French folks in Fosse 10, Bulley Grenay and the Bruay District were glad to welcome us back for we had been through and lived in this area before going south. In the French army there was a ruling at this time to permit a man with four children to support to be taken out of front-line service and be given employment in mines, mills or other comparatively safe work at some distance from the actual fighting area. Now one of our boys hade been around Bruay before. There was a grass-widow in that town who had presented la Belle France with a couple of husky twins just before we returned from the Somme. The man of the house had been at Verdun for about two years. The double addition gave him the required four and he came home joyfully. We were dubious about it fearing there would be some complications. Nothing doing! The war-weary French patted the Canuck on the back, treated him to numerous shots of Vin Blau and Vin Rouge etc. and proclaimed to all and sundry. Tres-bienkanadien- comarade tres-bien! Every body was happy including the twins. Oui-messieurs. A real case of (all's fair in and love and war). Oui-oui madame. Oo-la-la!! Bon sontay soldat kanadien se-merci bucuip. Oliveoil- san-fere-ann; we-we; encore-maybe?

> Oh! Madame have you any good wine, Parles Vous
> Oh! Madame have you any good wine, Parles Vous
> Madame have you any good wine
> Fit for a soldier from up the line
> Inky-Dinky-Parles-Pous
> Mademoiselle from Armentieres, Parles Vous
> Mademoiselle from Armentieres, Parles Vous
> Mademoiselle from Armentiers
> She hadn't been kissed for seven years
> Inky-Dinky-Parles-Vous

When we first returned from the Somme we went in the line near Bully Grenay and Fosse 10. I think we had a term at Moroc next. This place was a desolate looking heap of ruins to the west of Hill 70 and was swept by constant shell fire and machine gun fire. We were in cellars and shelters among the ruins. We traveled up and down the front at Angre going into the line at a point on the north west shoulder of Vimy and directly in front of the ruined village of Suchez. If ever there was a place that breathed of death and spooks it was that ghastly-looking skeleton of a once pretty looking village. You seemed to feel the presence of its 175,000 dead. The ground was seeded with their bones for at least ten feet in depth. We dug some new trenches on the crest of the ridge going down to a depth of eight feet or more, and the soil was still was still thickly seeded with bones, clothing, equipment, rifles, bombs, boots etc.

It was here that Joffre made his determined attack on Vimy and failed. The fighting in this spot was fierce, and terrible and long drawn out. The evidence is there to show it. It was said that the French used a deadly turbinate gas (liquid explosive) here in the final fighting. It was supposed to be the only time it was used during the war. They had lost something over 100,000 men in the desperate onslaught. The evidence showed that the French were fully justified in the use of the gas. The only pity is that they did not make more extensive use of it. The two pinnacles of the old convent towers still stood up tall and ghostly in the valley like grim sentries over this grim record of man kind's savagery. The wind seemed to moan, sigh and whisper in these ragged towers with the broken trees groaning and creaking in the night wind.

About in the centre of our battalion frontage I was looking for a spot on a high bit of ground close to our front trench that would serve as a sniping post. Crawling along an old French trench I came upon piles of bleached bones and crawled through a space ten or fifteen feet in length that was nothing else but human bones, piled like a mass of firewood on either side and in the bottom of the shallow trench. There was no soil mixed with it here, the sides and the bottom of this bit of trench was entirely composed of bones. You had to crawl through on hands and knees for the parapet had long since been washed away by the winter rains and the spot was exposed.

At our right flank there was a sort of re-entrant in our line with a corresponding salient in the German's. Here the Germans had an advanced post. This post had been shelled heavily recently by our trench mortars and flying pigs. The enemy trench was demolished and the relief's to and from their forward post had to take chances and jump across the open in spots. I made a sniping post on our right in a heap of chalk-filled sandbags that had been taken out of a miner's sap and piled here. It was something over 100 yards from where the enemy showed themselves when coming out to the post. I went into this post one morning just before daylight. In a short time I saw three Germans jump out of a hole in the ground coming over a sort of mud bank directly toward me. I shot one while he was on top of the bank and another as he leaped down into a trench. The third got into the trench alright. There was a low spot about fifteen or twenty feet to the right of this where he would be exposed as he passed. I lined on this spot just in time to see the profile of his head bobbing across the low part of the trench. I pulled the trigger just as his nose was coming into line with the crosshairs in the telescope. All three had gone out off sight and I could not swear as to whether the last one was hit or not. I knew that the alignment for him and lead were right, and saw no reason to suppose he escaped. About an hour later a couple of our observers, Taylor and Cook, saw three stretchers carried back from the enemy front trench. I suppose these three were the ones mentioned above as they came from that vicinity. Fred Minty occupied that post the next morning and had one shot.

We had a term in the line further to the right in front of Mount St. Eloi and opposite Farbas Wood to the left of Ecurie. Along this frontage there was a line of craters where mines had been blown up under the front trenches at different times. There was a lot of this underground work going on at this time. You never knew when you might take a trip skyward along with about a hundred yards of your trench.

There was old Bavarian sniper along this part of the front who had become famous for his killings. He had accounted for several officers in our brigade and the week before he came into this sector he killed a couple of snipers of the 7th battalion. The post where they were killed had been given away by a new draft officer who did not understand what it meant to send his green men into a post of this kind, and having them banging and shooting at the landscape through it. I questioned this officer about it and he said the snipers did not use the post enough so he thought he was being efficient in sending his men in there to shoot. It takes all kinds of people to make up this world. This officer was one of a kind. The bullets that killed the two 7th Snipers came directly in through the loop hole hit the timber and iron sheeting in the roof and glanced downward. This had been a good post and had been in use for a long time before the bright officer advertised it to the old Bavarian. This grizzled old Bavarian had been glimpsed on several occasions. He wore a beard appearing to be a man at least 50 years of age.

After the incident of the two 7th battalion snipers I quietly set myself the task of hunting for the old timer. Keen and artful from all accounts he was a pretty fly one and it behooved me to step light and go easy if I wanted to keep my scalp. I started out from our right flank into a maze of disused trenches that had changed hands several times and now were between the opposing lines. They were filled with wire blockades or entanglements to prevent their use by either side in surprise attacks. The ground was rough and made up of heaps of earth that had been thrown up by the explosions of mines and shells. I worked my way forward cautiously till I thought I must be close to the enemy outpost positions. I could see a straight piece of trench ahead leading toward the enemy trench. At the far end and about seventy yards away it formed a T or a junction with another trench. There was a wire block, or mass of wire blocking the trench about halfway down, and beyond that a few yards, was a sniping plate of the French pattern set in across the trench with its face toward the T junction. I crawled through the wire block and up to the old plate, cautiously taking a peep through it to the trench beyond. There was no light screen behind the plate so I had to be very cautious and slow in putting my eye to the hole so as not to show movement or sudden darkening of the hole. I had just got placed where I could get a good view ahead when a Bavarian n. c. o. stepped into the lens of the glass and seemed so close I involuntarily drew back. I fired but the recoil threw the glass out of focus and I could not be sure of what took place. The Bavarian had just paused in passing the junction to look my way. The suddenness of his coming caught me off guard. He must have been hit for we were not more than 20 yards apart. I did not waste any time around there but hurried to get back beyond the wire block to the far end of that straight trench, for there was no cover or shelter until you got to the first jog or traverse perhaps 50 or more yards from the old plate. When out of bombing range of the T junction I stopped under cover listening for awhile but heard nothing. Trenches ran at all angles here with most of them leading into the enemy lines direct. I worked my way back a bit more for I was in a good place to get cut off or surrounded, and bombed out or worse. I don't know what branch of the service that enemy n. c. o. represented. His uniform was grey with a slight purplish tinge and he had red facings on his shoulders, collar and cuffs. He wore a wide—topped cap with a sort of patent leather visor and red band.

That evening I was out at the beginning of dusk among the wire in a piece of rough ground that gave a view across number 500 crater. These craters were numbered and known by their numerals on the maps. A short distance behind our front line in this sector there was a machine gun emplacement and the guns in this emplacement had been doing considerable firing for a couple of days. It must have been giving trouble to fritz at some point back of his lines, for while I was at the crater in the dusk, an enemy single seat battle plane of the Red Devil squadron came sneaking over low down to the ground just high enough to clear wires and stakes etc. He was passing directly over toward the machine gun position.

When opposite to me I could see the pilot sitting in his cockpit. He couldn't have been more 200 yards from me. I fired three shots at him with each of the bullets throwing a blue flame some feet in length where they glanced off the armored fuselage on a line with the pilot. After the first shot he tilted his plane to turn to the left and the last shot was at the bottom of the fuselage as it rolled up toward me. He spurted away to the north east and was out of sight in a few seconds. This is where a .280 with armor piercing bullets would have been the real goods. I don't know whether I did him any damage or not.

I was still on the lookout for the old Bavarian sniper half expecting to be shot at while exposing myself in shooting upward at the plane. 500 crater was his favorite hang out on an evening and it was near here that he got the two 7th battalion snipers. Looking north east across the crater you could see a mass of tangled wire in a sag or depression in the rough ground beyond. When it was quite dark I caught a glimpse of a movement among that mess of wire. I did not make anything definite out of it that night. The following night I was back there again and set to watching that sag with its mess of wire coils. Dusk crept toward darkness and I was thinking about going in and calling it a day when there was a distant flare light. It lit up the skyline beyond that sag full of wire. There was the unmistakable outline of the head and shoulders of the old Bavarian. He had not taken the distant flares into account and he was outlined in a light that just enabled me to pick up the cross hair in the old Winchester A5 Scope. I fired before the light flickered and died out, then shifted my position off to one side a bit waiting for awhile to try to catch another glimpse of the spot by the aid of another distant flare. I expected a trench mortar shell, or pineapple, or a few rifle grenades to come my way, for the Ross had made a bright flash in the growing dusk and any of the enemy who were on the lookout would now have my location very nearly. I did get another glimpse across that sag full of wire. There was clear sky behind and I could not make out anything by the contour of the earth below. We never saw the old Bavarian sniper again, nor did I ever hear any more about him in the time that we remained on that front. The only thing that could have saved him would be the glancing of the bullet from the tangle of wire in front of him. I did not see any blue flame and it always shows when a bullet hits wire at night

I have given these few samples of sniping events in order to illustrate as nearly as possible the nature of the work and the reasons why you could not always be certain of hits from the evidence showing after the shot. We registered or tested our rifles at marks every day to make sure they were adjusted perfectly and in our own minds we were not in much doubt about the results of such shots as I have described above. Sometimes we were accompanied by an observer with a telescope to check all shots made.

While on this front we alternated between front line and support duty. One time while in supports we were billeted in a building that had been used as a fair or agriculture show-house in peace times. We had two or three wild Irish guys in our battalion who made trouble at all times and at all places. The whole battalion often had to suffer on account of the fool stunts pulled off by this drunken trio. Perhaps we had been on a long route march from some place and arrived at some small town or village in the evening. We would like to stroll around for a change or relaxation, getting acquainted with the natives and perhaps having a few drinks of wine or beer at the local pub or halus. We would no sooner arrive than the trio of wild Irish would get busy and create a disturbance or insult some of the women, damage some property, steal something, or get into a drunken brawl and immediately the town or village would be put out of bounds for the whole battalion. The whole outfit would have to mope around billets spending a miserable and cheerless existence while there. The same thing occurred in dozens of cases and it is a wonder the boys did not knock the trio on the head some night with a shillelagh or something giving them a quick transfer to Irish Heaven. One of the trio on one occasion had been drunk and absent when the battalion went into the line and was now under arrest pending a court martial trial. One of his side-kicks succeeded in getting on as the guard that was detailed to act as general caretaker and wet nurse for him while he was in the clink. The guardroom was upstairs in the south end of the building and when the drunk pretended he wanted to go outside to a latrine or something. He and his mate went down stairs and around the back of the building. Here his mate got hold of a billet of wood hitting the court martial case a wallop on the arm breaking the arm. He explained that the drunk had fallen when going down the stairs. He was sent down the line to a hospital and in that way escaped court marshal. We were relieved to be rid of him regardless of how he got away. We were soon moved out of the fair building and into some wooden huts in the edge of a big hardwoods on the south slope of Mount St. Eloi and north of the village. While here some of our battalion staff were caught selling rum and clothing such as socks and shoes to the French people. Some old charitable lady in Winnipeg who looked upon herself as a sort of mother to the battalion used to ship out a lot of good wool socks etc. to be distributed among the boys. We found that this stuff was being peddled and converted into cash by our admirable staff. The battalion post office staff was no better for they used to smash open dozens of parcels that folks at home sent to the boys in the line, looting them of anything they fancied they would like to have. The things that I just mentioned did not come to my knowledge by hearsay or second hand. I witnessed it myself. I was sent on some message to battalion post office one day while we were in the old Chateau at Gueay Servins. The P. O. was at Petit Servins. On my arrival the place looked a wreck. The floor was ankle deep in wrappings and fragments of soldier's parcels. I saw one of the clerks smash a couple of unopened parcels across the corner of a counter to see if there might be a bottle concealed in them. There was a ready sale and good price at all times for McDonald's Chewing Tobacco. It was very seldom that any of this stuff got through to the boys in the front line. There were cases where the Sgt. majors (quarter masters) applied and got special leave to go to England to bank their cash profits. They were a grand and glorious lot those boys in q. m. stores. They certainly made hay while the sun shone. They got medals for this kind of work. There was not one of them that did not sport a machonachie medal. (military medal). It got so bad that the officers had to (crime) the front line men before they would put up or wear one of these medals, and then they only wore them under strong protest. The sight of seeing the p. o. staff and q. m's. sporting these decorations was too much for the boys who had to earn them honestly.

We moved from here to Cite Collone, a suburb of Lens, and held the front line there for about a month. During the time we were at this place we had a regular western winter. The snow stayed on the ground with it staying clear and frosty for about three weeks. Our front line ran along in front of a mine and a railway spur among ruined houses. The railway close behind our front line was on a fill or embankment and there was a subway through this fill. Our communications ran through this subway. The mine buildings were behind our right flank. Just to the right of the subway we had a sniping post in the railway embankment close up under the crossties and rails. We entered this post from the back side of the fill. Fritz used to bombard steadily with a heavy minen werfer and the shells from it used to skim close over the top of our post bursting behind the railway embankment. It was a creepy place to stay with those heavy pigs flying close over us all day. Occasionally there would be one that fell short too. We got several jolts of concussion from heavy bursts. The ground rose gradually in the front of our lines to the top of a low ridge some six or seven hundred yards distant. We got quite a few targets along the enemy support and communication trenches on this ridge. Most of the shots were at ranges from four to six hundred yards. To the left of the subway and behind the embankment there was one of our flying pigs dug deep into the ground in a two compartment dugout. The pig was located in the front compartment and shot its huge torpedoes up through an inclined shaft or slot. The crew was wiped out one day by the premature explosion of one of these pigs. After this they made it ready and then retired to the second compartment while the pig was fired. I don't believe this maneuver would have saved them if it had exploded again for the concussion in these closed underground passages would have been terrific. Fritz never seemed to get the location of that pig for he kept on throwing his minnies over on the right side of the subway directly over our sniping post. Our people tried out some kind of a high velocity field piece on this front one day. I never heard what sort of a gun it was but the shells from it tore across that line of ours at a high velocity. The only thing you could compare it to for velocity was the famous fritz rubber heel gun, the nine point six inch Naval piece that he used to shell us from positions about 18 miles away. It was during this winter that our people tried out the sound locator for enemy guns. Some eight months previous to this time the enemy had shelled a mine head that was located close behind our present front line. Fritz had been in the habit of shelling it for a number of months and had apparently taken the gun away. It was a gun of about eight inch caliber. During this winter he brought the gun back to its old position and again opened fire on the mine. A sound locator was hurried up and the position of his gun taken. A shot was then fired on that location by one of our guns. The drop of our shell was registered on the locator and a correction of range immediately made from it. In 20 minutes from the time the German gun fired, our battery had made a direct hit on it and it was silenced.

The mine mentioned above was worked by the French during the night. The boilers were kept alive through the day with banked fires and no movement or smoke shown during the daylight. I went into the boiler house one morning to get some hot water from the French stoker in charge of the boiler. My French was a bit mixed and when intending to ask for water asked for milk instead, at the same time pointing to the injector under the boiler. The frenchy thought I was asking him to milk the boiler and took it as a great joke. I guess it did sound funny to him with him thinking I was quite a joker. I never let on keeping a sober face and letting it go at that.

While at Cite Collone we one day saw an aero plane fall nearly all the way to the earth from an elevation of over 20,000 feet. The plane was a Farnum Pusher type, square built like a box kite with an open skeleton frame between the wings and tail. Some of the controls must have jammed with him starting to fall over, and over endwise, side wise, head first, tail first, and spinning as a wheel down, down, down. Men ran, climbing up on any convenient elevation, to watch breathlessly what we thought was going to be another fatal tragedy played out before our eyes. He fell so near to the earth that he was hidden by our view by some tall buildings.

At the last possible moment the pilot succeeded in righting that plane, straightened it out and flew away. Now that was not a stunt. It was a real fall, an exhibition of cool-headed bravery along with a few other things, it ranks as high as anything I ever saw, heard of, or read about or ever expect to hear about. You should have heard the roar that went up from the thousands of fighting men who witnessed that battle and its outcome.

It was comparatively quite and uneventful on our front during our stay at Cite Collone. There was one small raid pulled off by fritz and a counter effort by our boys but neither of them amounted to much.

I had a hot time with an undershirt that I got one day. Just before we came into the line, we were rushed to the baths and then went directly from there into the trenches. I had drawn a very tight-fitting under shirt of heavy wool at the bathing house lottery and it was binding me in the armpits. I marched about a mile with full equipment and began to perspire a bit. Talk about (coming to life), I'll say that shirt did nothing else but. I thought my skin was on fire. The thing was literally alive and moving. I had to strip right in the communication trench and get rid of that shirt quick. I flung it as far as I could in the snow and went shirtless until the next bath day.

Suchez

We left Lens and went in for a term in front of Suchez. There had been some sapping and counter-sapping going on here on the shoulder of the hill over looking Angre and Lens. We had been expecting our miners or fritz to blow things up for some time. There was an enemy machine gun up the valley towards Lens that swept the valley in front of Suchez every night. We had some losses at night from this fire as it swept directly across our supply dump and ration dump where the battalion transport came up nightly to deliver rations and ammunition etc. to the carrying parties from the front lines. The guns were firing at long range and the bullets rather spent being very nasty things to get hit by. They would keyhole or spin when they hit, tearing an ugly wound.

We had an old roman-nosed Clydesdale in the transport that was a veteran and had been with the battalion through many battles. He had been wounded, shell shocked and gassed. Now when he was taken to a bad place that was under fire, he knew what to expect. He would shiver, tremble all over, and break out in a sweat and whinny softly for sympathy. That old Clyde had real courage for he never balked or refused to go nor did he take panic fright like some of the horses and stampede. It was one of the most touching things to be experienced to have to watch these animals exposed to bad fire and to see them wounded. It seemed to get your goat worse than seeing men cut up. The men have an idea what it is all about but the horses have to take it as it comes and say nothing. Simon Gourevitch, an old Kenora man, used to drive the old horse mentioned above. Simon had transferred to the transport under command of Foghorn McDonald. Foghorn was a character who became widely known through his odd ways, doings, sayings and his sterling qualities in a tight corner or on a hard trail. He was a real diamond in the rough–(very rough). He was not adaptable to the polished ways of the staff but never the less came to be widely and favorably known among them.

The snipers had a sort of shelter or sleeping place on the top of the hill a few yards back of the front trenches. This shelter was partly dug into the side hill and partly built up with sandbags filled with loose chalk. The whole hill was chalk with a very thin layer of loam and sod in spots. The shelter had a frame work of two x four's or scantlings with bunks made of the same material with wire netting strung on them to serve as a mattress on which we slept. The roof was of corrugated iron sheets covered with a layer of chalk. Right in front of its door I saw a case where the old tin hat or sheet helmet saved a man's life. Jack Haron and I were standing there one day talking. We were facing each other about three feet apart when a piece of steel came straight down out of the sky from the burst of an anti-aircraft shell hitting on the back rim of Jack's helmet. The rim was bent straight down and the piece of shell hit him on the spine at the base of his neck. He went down as though pole-axed, shivered, quivered and straightened out. I thought he was killed for a minute. We examined him and sent for a stretcher. He came to in a little while and was taken down to the dressing station recovering alright. The rim of the hat broke the force of the blow saving him from instant death without a doubt. I had shrapnel and spent bullets even glance off my old tin hat leaving nothing worse than a dent and scar. Your ears would ring and buzz for a few hours, that was all.

I was at the old snipers shelter one day when I got another sort of hunch or premonition that it was time for us to get out of it. I could not explain why but the conviction was strong and having profited by these hunches before on several occasions, I decided to sit up and take notice. I told Smith, another sniper, about it. He had seen my hunches work out before and was ready and willing to get busy moving out of that place quick when I told him the hunch was working again. We hunted all over the side hill for a new home. Near the base of the hill we did find an empty dugout. It was the only one to be had and did not look very promising. It had a great weight of chalk above the roof as it was dug right under a steep part of the hill. The roof timbers were old, and cracked, and sagged in the centre so that it did not look very safe. We found a short timber to put upright as a post under the cracked roof timber and then decided it might stand quite a bit before caving in on us. The floor was under water. There seemed to be a spring or seepage of water coming out of the hill here and I guess that is why it was not being repaired and occupied by someone else. We used poles and two x fours throwing them across the bottom. On top of these we laid corrugated iron sheets and in this way made a dry floor above water level. When all set we went to collect our bedding, and equipment and moved into the new quarters. The rest of the snipers moved in too when they found out the reason for it. There was one old fellow from the States who had come in a recent draft and could see no reason for moving declaring his intentions of staying put. He followed us too at evening for he said it was lonely in the old hut by himself. During that night fritz blew up two mines at what was known as the Pimple. Both sides made a rush to try to capture the huge craters that were left by the explosion. The rims of these craters were quite high due to the large mass of chalk thrown up and would be a point of vantage from which the possessors could command or overlook quite a bit of the surrounding frontage. Fritz got the biggest crater alright in this case. I suppose he was prepared and ready to rush it as soon as the explosion settled. This bit of rough stuff woke up the artillery on both sides as well as well as the trench mortars, flying pigs, stokes guns, minen werfers, pineapples, rum jars, machine guns and a few other things. It turned into a very wild night, things did hum, rattle, and roar in that sector until daylight. We lost a number of men. I saw an officer named Mitchell get killed as he was making his way with the rest of us to the centre of the disturbance at the Pimple. We lost two of our best bombers, a sergeant, and a private who were on the bow end of the mix up. There had been a large amount of amminol, a sort of high-explosive used by the miners left in the open at the base of the hill and about 50 yards from the entrance of our new home in the wet dugout under the hill. This pile of explosive went up when it was hit by an enemy shell. The force of the explosion very nearly caved in the old dugout. When I looked in the roof timbers were sagged a bit more and the floor was covered with a scattering of loose stones and chalk. The men who were in it at the time of the explosion got quite a concussion and also a fright for they thought the roof was coming down to bury them alive under tons of chalk.. Daylight found things quieted down a bit. I was up in an observation post about 900 yards to the right of the Pimple on a pinnacle formed by a huge heap of chalk-filled sand bags piled here when taken out of the underground saps by the miners. We had built an o p in the top of this mound and from here could get an enfilade view of the Pimple.

Taylor, one of my old scouts was in the o p watching the Pimple. Two German officers came up from the rear of the largest crater and stooping slightly walked up the back incline towards its crest. They were evidently taking observations to see how things looked after the wild night. They had on ankle length greatcoats and were carrying field binoculars on a short sling strap around their necks. They evidently had not figured on the high spot where we were. We could see their every move. I had a sniping rifle that had been zeroed at 100 yards just before coming in the line this trip. The telescope had not been tested or ranged yet for any higher range. I asked Taylor if he had established the range of the Pimple from here. He had not done so as yet. It was some thing of a problem to solve. A rifle sighted in for 100 yards and a target nearly a thousand yards away over broken ground. We all made a quick estimate of the range and averaged up the whole of the guesses and finally decided it was about 900 yards. I recalled that a .303 MK 6 bullet had a curve of about 29 feet over 1,000 yards with an Lee Enfield. We were using .303 MK 7 cartridges with a lighter bullet and higher velocity and a Spitzer instead of a blunt nosed bullet. I compared notes mentally and decided on about 24 to 25 feet for the curve of a M K 7 when shot from a Ross. Using this as a basis I took the height of the German Officers as a measuring rod and spaced off his height four times on the vertical hair in the telescope trying a shot at the sky some 25 feet directly above him. At the shot he spun around grabbed with his right hand at his left arm or shoulder indicating that he was hit somewhere about the left arm or shoulder. He dropped out of sight behind the pile of chalk. His mate also took cover at the same time but immediately came to the top of the chalk pile and resting his elbows on the chalk looked directly our way with a pair of binoculars. I had no measuring rod this time to space off the feet on the sky but guessed at it and fired again. The bullet threw up a spurt of chalk dust a couple of feet to his left and about three feet low. He then withdrew out of sight and we saw no more of either of them. It was a long chance and a chance shot. I worked and figured for it though and always felt a lot of satisfaction from having made a hit at that range by a sort of dead reckoning with an improvised sight. There was not a breath of wind at the time and that was one less unknown quantity to consider when doping it out. I found that the front thumb-screw of the dovetail block of the scope mounting had jarred loose. That accounted for the second shot being off to the left.

Fritz tried to make a raid on the crater in daylight that morning. We saw them start forward along a piece of trench. There was a spatter of rifle fire and a few bombs were thrown but the raid apparently fizzled out for some reason. He did not make another attempt. Our boys planned a counter raid to go over at three points on the battalion front. The right hand party got there alright meeting with stiff resistance and were beaten off with the loss of several men. The centre party was led by a young lad about 18 by the name of McDonald. He was one of the scouts. A lieutenant was supposed to be in command of this centre raiding party. McDonald guided the party, largely made up of new draft men, to the German parapet alright and sat astride the parapet pointing and showing the men where to get into the trench. They seemed to hesitate about going forward and were inclined to look around to see where their officer was at. That worthy was well behind the rear end of that procession and, after McDonald he had tried a bit to get the front of the party to jump into the trench and failed. Word was passed up from the rear to retire, and the scouts saw them go heading back on the double to their own lines. The men in the rear of the party said they got orders to retire from the lieutenant, and passed the order along to the rest of the patrol. McDonald was left astride the enemy parapet cursing in good Canuck cuss words. These happenings leaked out and McDonald being still angry when he got back to battalion headquarters to report, told a true tale of just what had occurred. This looked pretty bum for Mr. lieutenant and they called McDonald up again and cross questioned him severely to try and shake his evidence. This they failed to do at all. They only made a bad matter worse for they unearthed more facts. It was a case that had to be squashed some way and squashed quickly or the officer would be up on a very serious charge. They got around the difficulty by sending McDonald away from the battalion altogether. He was told to pack his turkey and was shipped off to a labor battalion that was on road construction some place behind the lines. He never returned to us. Thus was the honor and glory of the society brand class of officers that our old colonel had imported, kept bright. The left hand raiding party was led by another scout, Sandy Carmichael. He got into the enemy trench and down into a big dugout, shot a German officer with his pistol and in his prowling around came upon some sort of an electric device. A small dynamo or generator, and a switch-board with a lot of wiring. He demolished this outfit as best as he could in the short time available. This party kept the enemy off with bombs and bayonet and got back to our lines ok in the appointed time. They are given a certain number of minutes to get into the enemy trench, do what damage possible and get out again before our barrage comes down again on that part of the enemy's front lines. While the raid is actually in the enemies front trench our guns put down what is known as a box barrage behind the enemy front trench to keep them from sending reinforcements forward and to keep the front line men from escaping the raiding party. These raids are often sent over for the purpose of getting a prisoner so as to find out what enemy unit is holding that part of the line.

I was near to forgetting the sequel to the (hunch) business and the dugout shelter we abandoned on the hill in front of Suchez the day before the Pimple blew up. I went to take a look at it on the day following and there had been some doings there in the night. Three shells of the small whizz-bang variety had gone through the roof. There was a fair sized crater in front of, and close up to the door. The two x four framework was collapsed, and shattered. The wire netting beds were filled with wreckage, large lumps of stone, and chalk. It was very doubtful if anyone could have lived through it, had they been in that shelter during the night. Truth is often-times more strange than fiction. Smitty said nothing when he saw the wreck of our former home.

Vimy Ridge

We moved out of this place soon after going into the lines again at the craters in front of Neuevele St. Vaast, or in front of St. Eloi. We were busy here for some time preparing for the attack on Vimy Ridge. A sawmill was put up and beech planking was turned out from the big wood on the west side of Mt. St. Eloi. This planking was cut long enough to make a road for two lines of wagons or guns. In the area leading up to the front lines the mud was leveled, and graded a bit. Several of these plank roads were laid flat on the mud. There was a square timber stringer or binder run along each edge and also several length-wise planks underneath to act as sills thus keeping the planking from settling in spots or sagging. When this road was hit by enemy shells it was not a very long job to remove some of the damaged section and put in fresh planks. It made the movement of transport and guns a simple matter where before it had been next to impossible to move anything on wheels across the shelled areas.

Scores of new batteries were moved in and registered on various sections of the enemy lines. The ammunition for them was stacked up like piles of cordwood all over the place and covered with a sort of camouflage material made up of a sort of burlap sacking, trimmed in different colors to blend with the surroundings. This camouflage business was carried to great lengths in this war. In some cases they did wonderful things with it getting great results. Its proper application and use was an art and it took an artist to do it right. I have seen miles of road under it. Huge heavy batteries and supply dumps etc cleverly blended into the landscape Sometimes the thing to be screened would be completely covered in. In other cases its outline would be broken by light strips of screening.

I saw a 12 inch Howitzer one day on the Baileuell Road enclosed in a canvas reproduction of a Flemish Cottage. If the wind had not waved and moved the canvas we would have never noted the deception, and were passing by at a distance of a few feet only.

To be most useful these photos must be taken when the sun is fairly low or near the horizon at morning or evenings. At this time longer shadows are thrown by any slight mound or eminence bringing a lot of detail out after careful scrutiny and a little practice in spotting essentials. There was a staff of experts working at this job. The staffs of the intelligence branch depended on aerial photos to betray battery and supply locations. this alone and their long suit was the study of light and shadows. All roads or pathways show up as a white ribbon unless it be a sunken road that throws a shadow. I had a bit of this photo study while in the scouts and it is a fascinating thing once you get the knack of it. The preparations for the attack went on for several weeks while we were holding this sector from No. 500 crater over to the north edge of Thielous Wood.

About this time fritz got to be boss of the air in this sector. He produced a fast and very effective single seat fighter plane known as the red devil. Parts of the wings and fuselage were painted red. This type of plane used to cruise over our lines in groups or flights of five machines. One of these groups was in command of a famous German airman a member of some noted family in the vaterland. I forget what his name was now. I think it was Manfred von Richthofen. I believe a Canadian pilot by the name of A. Roy Brown, a quite young airman, was given credit for bringing him down in fair fight. At a later time there are two soldiers R. Bluie and Cedric Popkin who claim they could have brought the red baron down with ground fire. At the time I am writing about, our airmen were equipped with a clumsy sort of slow traveling old (bus) of the box-kite-open frame variety. I think it was the Sopwith Camel. This machine was too unwieldy and slow to be of much use in air fighting. It was cruel to see the way the red devils shoot them to pieces sending them down in flames every day. Our airmen were a game lot continuing to face the enemy with these obsolete contraptions. I saw five of them shot down in flames in about 15 minutes one day over the enemy lines just to the right of Farbus Wood at the south end of Vimy Ridge. The fuselage of these old busses stuck out some distance in front of the wings. I have seen our airman standing on the forward nose while the bus was plunging through space in flames. They climbed out on the nose to get as far as possible from the flames in a forlorn hope that they might chance to reach earth before the wings burned off or the tank exploded. Usually they were driven to jumping into space to escape the fierce heat or were thrown off when the plane turned over in its death plunge. I often saw them spinning end-over-end like a wheel in mid air after being thrown or driven from the machine by flame or explosion. It was a heart-rendering thing to see and not be able to render any assistance. I have seen our airmen face back and give battle again in these old coffins after seeing what had happened to their comrades a minute before, fully knowing they would meet a like fate (and they did). Could human courage go any further? This slaughter of some of the finest men that ever breathed went on for some days right before our eyes and we could only sit in our trenches cursing the authorities who sent these boys up to do battle in such poor contraptions.

In England they had a plane constructed for home defense. It had three wings, one above the other. This plane was able to climb very fast. It could start from earth and climb directly up at a steep angle, keeping on going up without the necessity of corkscrewing or spiraling its way aloft. When it gained the desired height it could travel horizontally at a high rate of speed. It was also good at maneuvers, ducking, dodging and looping about. One day we saw one of these three Decker planes rise from the airdrome at Mt. St. Eloi accompanied by another new type of plane called the Sopwith Camel. The latter was a biplane of smart appearance with some speed and maneuvering ability. They were up to try out the two new machines and for a half an hour or more we watched a sham battle for position or advantage between these two new fighters. They looped the loop, zoomed, did the tumbling pigeon act and a dozen other tests. There did not seem to be much to choose between them. At times you could hear their wire stays singing like harps as they cut the air in breath-taking dives and loops. We cheered up some at the sight of these new craft. We had high hopes that the red devils would soon meet something more near there own class. Hopefully we would not have to witness any more sights like what we had seen in the previous week.

At near sundown of that evening we saw one of the three Decker rise and fly toward the enemy lines. There was a flock of five red devils sailing up and down over the lines. The three Decker flew along slowly and level at about 5,000 feet up. The Fritz planes saw this strange looking craft coming slowly toward them and you could see they were very curious to know what sort of a craft it was. They began to edge toward it in sudden spurts and circling swoops like hawks. The three Decker gave no sign but continued to go forward slowly. At last one of the red devils detached itself from the group and made a swoop. You could hear the dry crackle and splutter of his machine guns. The three Decker came to life then and its pilot opened throttle to full speed firing with his Lewis guns at the same time. The sudden show of high speed and the swoop of his gun fire gave the enemy planes a surprise. He was in through them and away at full speed. They immediately took after him in a body but low and behold they could not overtake him. This new craft could show its heels. This had evidently been a try out of speeds and we now felt a lot better to see one of our machines was able to hold its own giving our boys a chance of a fair show in the air battles that went on above us daily.

There was a long row of captive balloons or sausage balloons behind our lines with a like number floating above the enemy lines. From these balloons the artillery observers watched for targets for their respective batteries. Sundown was a favorite hour for aero plane attacks on these balloons. They were shot down by machine gun fire and also set on fire by dropping incendiary bombs from above. It was a great sight to see the observer floating to the ground under a parachute while the balloon dropped to earth with a big flare of flames and a trail of black smoke. The enemy airmen had a nasty habit of turning their machine guns on the observer as he sailed helplessly toward earth in his parachute. One night a fritz came over flying low, ran the gauntlet of machine gun, artillery and rifle fire shooting down a balloon right behind our trench. He turned about firing on the observer in his parachute. He dodged a fusillade of bursting shells and it looked as though he was going to get clear away again. The sopwith camel showed up above him gave battle and shot him down. The enemy airman was a cocky one trying to give battle with his auto pistol after reaching the ground. He was taken prisoner, though it is a wonder none of them shot him in the excitement at his landing place.

In the next three days there was something doing for we now had four of the tri-planes or three deckers as well as one sopwith camel at our airdrome. They went over the enemy country giving the red devils a taste of the real stuff. They went so far east that we could not make out the details of the battles but could see hundreds of anti-aircraft shells bursting in the eastern sky and occasionally see a plane plunging to earth with a tail of flame like a comet. Our boys all came home that night so you can see who was playing comet that day. The following day we saw one of the three decker lose its wings in mid-air crashing to earth. A young man by the name of McAllister from Winnipeg was the pilot. He had been over the enemy lines for some distance and we noted that he was under very heavy shell fire. I remember saying that he would surely get hit if he did not break away. Soon after that we saw him flying for home at a low altitude, straight and slow. Fritz was peppering him with everything he had and we knew his plane must be damaged or himself wounded, otherwise he would try to climb higher doing some dodging to shake off the hail of lead and shells. He kept straight on and just after passing over us I heard a ripping noise overhead and saw the body of the plane go hurtling to earth without a sign of a wing on it. The engine was still going and it roared like a huge shell as it plunged towards the ground. Some of the wire braces or stays of the wings had been shot away and the wings had collapsed in mid air when he was only about a mile from the aerodrome. The body of the plane struck nose first right alongside a big marquee tent full of men. The pilot behind the engine was driven against it with the force of the impact. His thigh bones were broken off and driven into his body, and his head also came in for a violent smash. He was still alive and taken to the nearest dressing station and lived for four hours. He was buried near here in a small cemetery at the cross roads of Nouevelle St. Vaast. I saw his grave with an aero propeller for a tomb stone. Larry O'Flaherty from Kenora, a half-brother of Tom O'Flaherty was buried right next to him. Larry was killed while on traffic duty at the cross roads nearby.

I met the Famous Cy Peck Victoria Cross winner from British Columbia while on this part of the front. He passed along our front trench one morning on his way to or from his own unit. Jack Harron and I were watching in the fog for Germans to shoot at. Jack was spotting for me with a signaler's telescope, seeing a group of Germans carrying corrugated iron and trench revetting material loom up in the fog to our front. I swung the old Winchester A5 Scope that way. It has a small field of view and I could not pick up the enemy party at first on account of this. While I was sweeping with the scope sight in search of them a big fritz suddenly loomed up right in line with the cross hairs of the sight. He was carrying a sheet of corrugated iron on his back. I fired and Jack said he went down like a thousand bricks. While this was going on Cy Peck came along the trench and wanted to know what was going on. I told him we had just had a shot and he insisted on taking a look with the telescope. He could see nothing now, of course, for the enemy party had taken cover instantly when one of their number was shot down. Old Cy Peck was a character alright. His men saw him go ahead of a tank in a battle pointing out the way he wanted it to go with his walking stick. It wasn't exactly healthy in front of that tank for fritz always donated plenty of fire to them.

Our people built a lot of light railways of two foot gauge and they were used to transport troops and munitions over a wide area behind our lines. They had some Baldwin locomotives for these tracks that were real engines in miniature. They had a saddle water tank and the coal tender which were the integral part of the engine. The whole weight of the tank and tender was on the driving wheels. There was no engine truck or pony truck in front. The cars were similar to the hart convertible dump used on the c. p. r. but of course on a small scale. The capacity of the cars was about ten tons. They built quite a yard or terminal in the big beech woods behind Mt. St. Eloi and it was like old times to see Canucks switching cars there just like a real railway. I enquired if they needed any engine men and an application was sent to our battalion commander Raddell requesting my services in that line of work. I could have started at it right there and then. This came under the engineering corps and they have the right to take men for special work if needed from the front line battalions. I was in hard luck for I had taken special training as a scout observer and sniper. Now Raddell used this against me refusing to let me go on the railway job because I was a specialist and held me on that pretext. He said he couldn't let the old men go. He needed them to break in the new drafts etc. That was poor consolation to me after two and one half years in the front trenches. I would have appreciated a change for a while.

About this time they started to prepare a lot of hand and rifle grenades, stokes, mortar shells etc. for the attack on Vimy. These bombs etc. came up to the support lines in cases without fuses or detonator caps. I was detailed with several others to go at the work of fitting these bombs with detonators. Some of the men that had been detailed for this work got too gay at it trying to run a speed competition with the result of a couple of bad explosions with attendant casualties. I was on this work up until the day before the attack and was detailed for it again for a few weeks before the attack on Hill 70 in mid-August of that year. While on this job I was under a unit known as divisional bombers. The artillery concentration was now about complete and everything was ready for the big noise at Vimy Ridge. I very nearly got snuffed out on the day before the attack by the premature burst of a shrapnel shell from a four point seven inch gun that was shooting over us from an emplacement some 60 yards to the rear. I was in direct line of the burst and it peppered everything in a wide circle around where I stood and the earth was filled with pellet holes, like a sieve. The guns were getting a lot of American made shells at this time. A very large percentage of them were faulty and just as dangerous to us as they were to the Germans. The artillery men had to keep a close watch on this stuff for the shells were often oversize. When they were put in the gun and fired they would burst the breech or blow up the gun. The time fuses were faulty and the propellant charges must have been loaded in with a spade for you never knew if they would drop short or go away high. This accounted for a lot of casualties when this stuff had to be used in putting down a barrage close in front of advancing infantry. The Yankees soaked us about ten prices in good money for this stuff and then tried to murder us off in the bargain.

We got a lot of American made rifle ammunition too about this time and I have often seen the bullets fly all in pieces splattering all over the ground a few yards in front. I have seen three bullets out of five fly to bits refusing to go over a range of only 200 yards. When the bullets did hang together you never knew how they were going to shoot. One would be overloaded and the next drop short. For machine guns they were impossible.

I met a cousin of mine on the plank road one day before the attack. His name was A. A. Durkee. He was a major of artillery at the time I saw him. The last time I had seen him was on his return from the Boer War in South Africa.

I had a close call from an anti-aircraft shell one day while trying out our sniping rifles on an improvised range at the south east side of Mt. St. Oloi. I set up some targets against an embankment and walked back some 200 yards to where we were to shoot for zero test on the sight. I was standing alone in the open grass field when I suddenly heard the peculiar and high—pitched whine that a shell makes when is coming straight toward you. Some will tell you that you never hear the approach of the shell that hits you. That might apply to a shell fired from short range. A shell coming from any gun at long range may be heard for a couple of seconds before it hits you. From long and bitter experience you get to be able to pick that high-pitched peculiar whine from among the sounds of hundreds of traveling shells with your ear instinctively tuned and straining for that when you are lying under shell fire. This shell came plunging out of the sky and I knew it had my regimental number on it as soon as my ear caught the whine. The ground was flat and clear. I decide I had best stand still for if I jumped either way I might jump into it instead of away. It plunged into the ground about eight feet from me and a little whiff of vapor oozed out of the hole. The force of the blow shook the ground but the shell did not explode. There was one of our anti-aircraft mobile batteries at the roadside nearby and it was probably this battery that fritz was trying to hit at the time.

The big deep dugout for general Currie and staff was now completed with wire cables dug down eight feet for communications to same and we were ready. General Byng circulated a report among us that he had an extra army corps close behind us to follow up the attack (false report). We were told the artillery was also ready to follow us forward (another false report). If anybody tells you that Byng deserves any credit in connection with Vimy just say it is just another (false report). When we went over the top of the ridge and some six miles beyond it there was no one more surprised than that same Byng. He had it all doped out that we would not get far. He made absolutely no provision for supporting us on the flanks and had absolutely no arrangements to get artillery forward. His army corps in reserve was also a myth. We went as far as our guns could reach and a little further. We held onto Fresnes for four days and being exhausted by then, we turned our line over to the British troops and they turned it over to fritz inside of four hours from the time we pulled out. Lens City was evacuated by the Germans for 48 hours and the British troops on our left made no sign of a move to occupy it but lay in their line letting us look after our own left flank. On the right toward Arras we had to detail some of our sorely needed men to go and stiffen the attack of the English troops on that flank or it also would have been left open on us. Don't try to talk about Byng of Vimy to any Canadian soldiers that went through the fight and noted how it was managed. Byng did not count on success for us or make any plans to help us beforehand.

Our battalion started out from our old line near No. 500 crater going straight forward through the sag or depression before the level ground on the south edge of Thielous and Farbus woods, and over the south shoulder of the ridge. Zero hour was set for 5:28 am of April 9,1917. The 2nd and 3rd Brigades of the first division were assigned to take the first two objectives. Namely Zwolfe Graben and Zwiscnen Stellung Trenches holding them until the 1st brigade came up passing through them. We had some trouble with enemy soldiers hiding in the dugouts until the first waves of the attack passed over them, and then popping up to harass them with machine gun fire and rifle fire from the rear. This led to a number of enemy troops being killed in dugouts like rats in a hole. I know of one case of the kind where one of our men, exasperated by previous tricks of this kind, came to the stair top entrance of a large dugout shouting down to the Germans below."

How many of you are down there?" Some English-speaking German soldier answered from below "nine". Our man replied, well, divide this between you and threw a three inch stoke shell down to them.

We were next to the English troops on the right and had to detail off some of our platoons to go to the right, and keep some pep in their attack, and see that they did not lag back leaving our flank exposed. We did not go with the first waves of the attack but were attached to the mopping up parties that followed the 2nd and 3rd wave. Our duty was supposed to be to snipe the enemy while our boys dug in at the final objective.

The first real pause was at a sunken road on the east slope of the ridge. I went into an enemy observation post on the crest of the ridge and it certainly was well equipped and gave a wonderful view of the whole valley from which we had started. It was all laid out in panorama and fritz must have been able to watch every move of the preparations. I could see the plank roads winding like ribbons behind our old front line and also the batteries that were firing from our lines. I cannot understand why fritz did not blow the whole layout off the map. He must have been over confident of the strength of his own position or else underestimated the speed and fury Of the Canadian attack. Below this enemy o. p. you could walk through elaborate deep tunnels, dugouts and passages. In some cases the enemy hid in these tunnels coming out with machine guns etc. after the first waves had passed as previously mentioned. This is where the mopping up parties came in. In numerous cases the Germans would refuse to come out of their deep holes and a stokes shell would then be thrown down. The stiffs would later be carried out to clean the house.

A thick blizzard of snow came down immediately after the attack making it cold, wet and very miserable for us in the little holes in the mud that we dug at halting places. A ground sheet was not much protection from the snow and water that soaked in from above, below and on all sides. Lots of us did not even have a ground sheet for protection from the wet.

The first division artillery made desperate attempts to get guns over the ridge, succeeding in getting a few over. The trail where they went up and over was a pitiful sight as I saw it later. There was a string of dead horses right from the end of the plank roads to the top of the ridge. It was a desperate effort. When a team got mired hopelessly or fell from exhaustion they were shot where they lay. A new team was hitched on and they in turn were driven to their last limit and they in turn were shot when they fell. It was a terrible road to take guns over. I saw one that had been left mired and nearly out of sight in the mud with a group of dead horses around it. You could trace back along trail and get a record of the struggle.

Among the prisoners we took in this Vimy drive were a number of Germans who had lived for years, and had farms, in western Canada and U.S.A. Most of these men could talk our language without an accent. Some of them had been living in Canada and the United States for 20 years, answering the call from the Kaiser in June and July of 1914. They told us they figured the war would be all over in a few months. One big raw boned tall fellow about 45 years of age told us quite a tale of woe about the hardships he had suffered in the German service. He had sailed out of New York in June 1914 along with about 60,000 others who went over to get in on the loot they were promised would be theirs in the sacking of London, Paris and other cities in about three months time from the start of hostilities. He told us a great tale of disappointment they were all feeling for they thought it was alright to over run other people and loot all their belongings. It never seemed to strike them that somebody might object to it. It was their (Gott) given right. They had been worked incessantly and hard. The hours had been long on the pick and shovel. The tremendous array of great dugouts, tunnels, triple lines of deep well-made trenches, saps and redoubts etc. certainly bore out these statements. Somebody had worked and worked long and hard to build all this layout of defenses. They asserted quite confidently that they were going back to Canada and the U.S.A. It never seemed to occur to them that we might object to their little effort at murdering us off. The real German is an amazing sort of cuss. (Truly).

From opposite Vimy Village and the sunken road, on to the east as far as we went the ground got level along the same nature as a plain. Fritz did not put up a very stiff resistance across this piece of ground. Perhaps the occupation of the Horseshoe at Fresnoy was a mistake for it was a bad salient. I suppose the junior officers who were actually with the advance did not have any definite or broad knowledge of how things were going on their flanks. Our business was to attack and we did nothing else but. Our line now formed a triangle with its base at the junction with our old line on the west of Lens and its apex at the Horseshoe at Fresnoy. The south end of the base was in the flat country south of the ridge. We held our gains for four days. Then we were drawn out and our line was handed over to other troops. The scouts patrolled the enemy wire for some weeks in the Vimy sector both before and after the attack. They suffered a lot from exposure to cold and wet on account of a spell of very dirty weather at that time. At Arlieu and Willerval they suffered from gas as well. Taylor, Carmichael and others developed bad coughs from these causes never fully recovering from it. At this date 1933 they are both of them tubercular cases with indifferent chances of recovery. Some of the other scouts have died since returning from the war from the same ailment.

There was something I noted in connection with field guns during the time the unit held Fresnoy and later. The German five point nine inch field gun could sit out of range of our 18 pounder field guns and still do effective work at ranges of seven to nine thousand yards. The effective range of the 18 pounder field gun was limited to 6,000 yards. Some of our lighter howitzers, four and one half and six inch suffered in the same way due to the fact they were slightly out-ranged by the enemy's corresponding class of guns. An extra couple of thousand yards is a vital factor in some situations. The salient east of Vimy gave a clear demonstration of this fact. Ours were excellent weapons in a general way, very practical and efficient in many ways. But they were nearly useless due to the fact mentioned above.

Later on the battalion went in at Arlieu a village to the right of Leavin on the north side of the triangle that had been formed by the taking of the ridge. This and also Willerval was a bad place being subject to a lot of fire along with poor communications. Later we went in at Leavin and Cite De Moulin. These two places were suburbs on the south edge of the city of Lens. The city proper lay in the bottom of the valley and all these small towns on the outskirts were on a gentle slope toward it. There were long rows of tenement houses where the miners used to live. Whole streets were built in solid attached red brick houses. Each of these individual compartments had it own cellar or basement. The walls or partitions were torn out between these cellars, and in this way, a covered semi-underground communication route was made. Along these covered ways beneath the houses you could travel for long distances. At one time we followed one of these cellar routes until we came to its end. Being on strange ground we went very cautiously and quietly. We came to a cellar wall with no hole cut through it. There had been a doorway at one side but it was now blocked by a slide of fallen bricks and wreckage. We listened for awhile with our ears to the wall.

We could hear people talking and moving about on the far side of the wall. They were rubbing something against it. There were Germans on the other side of the wall for we could make out their guttural lingo plainly enough. A couple of houses back from here we established an o. p. by using a small shell hole in the wall of the gable that faced the enemy lines.

In this o. p. I found a large book that seemed to me might have been written by an enemy agency being left for our boys to read with the object of fomenting disloyalty and dissatisfaction. It told a sorrowful tale of the sufferings (real and fancied) of the Irish regiments during the early stages of the war dealing particularly with the battle of Loos, June 1915.

If the author was not a propagandist he should have hired out as one. It was the gloomiest thing I ever read. It played up pessimism, gloom and dissatisfaction to a peak.

I had a view of a railway yard on the south side of Lens from this locality and sniped a fritz that was wandering about among some dismantled railway trucks. I suppose he must have been looking for brass fittings. The enemy troops were given so much a pound for any brass or copper they could salvage. These metals were in demand.

I was at an ammunition dump one day behind our lines and met some of the Negroes of the west India regiment. These dusky gents were handling the big shells that were piled up there, 12 and 15 inch as well as nine point two inch. One of them said "Mann–ib a shell wust-to hit dis-mess it-uud—be-sumphin-teea-ib-le. How I longs-fo-home". We asked about his home. Mann–he says. Dat place is just like paai-dice. A cockney piped and enquired if they had boots, clothes and things in their Negro country. Why–Chile dey have mo shoes, and close and tings dan you eber seed. How aa-longs-fo-home!

Speaking of the demand for brass and copper. We found that the empty shell cases all over the captured area at Vimy had been had been stripped of their driving bands for the metal. These empty cases were also used for receptacles for slops and refuse when the square heads were marooned in their deep dugouts during the week long bombardment before the attack. Some of the stairways leading up to the trench were about 40 feet long and there was a shell case full of slops on both ends of every plank step in the stair. They had wells dug in the bottom of some of these dugouts. Near the top of the ridge the enemy officers had very elaborate underground quarters furnished with all sorts of looted furniture including pianos etc. They had been keeping women in some of them. Quite frequently we found the leather whips or (cat-O-nine tails) that the fritz officers used to work off their bad humor on the backs of their underlings. We found some German whiskey in one dugout and after some very cautious preliminaries and experiments we drank it finding it was not too bad. It was not colored appearing clear like water. It was a bit new and raw or not matured. They must have bootleggers and home-brew just like Ontario.

In Leavin I saw the little store that Jacques Carpentier used to own before the war. His name was still on the sign across the store front. It was a small affair similar to one of our stores in Kenora. I was up to an observation post on the top of the Lorette Spur one day. You could get a fine view from there over a wide frontage in the coal mining districts.

In August 1917 I was again detailed off to the divisional bombers and we got busy on applying detonators to a huge supply of trench munitions. Mills bombs were now standard and we fixed up a lot of them along with a plenty full supply of stokes gun shells. There were a few Newton rifle grenades. Our workshop was in the vicinity of Nieuve L-Amiens or a short distance east of that place toward the front line trenches. The light two foot gauge railway brought the munitions right to our door. As the stuff was fitted with detonators it was piled up in huge heaps. There was a large brick building that we filled from end to end. A single hit on that building by a shell would have made some explosion. Close to the building and outside at the north end we stacked up huge piles of stokes shells in cases. Against the south gable was piled a double tier of flying pigs some eight feet high and the full width of the building. While we worked there steadily for a couple of week's fritz threw shells all around it but only made one direct hit on the building.

The hit was made by a long distance armor-piercing naval shell nine point six inch caliber. The shell plunged into the earth some hundred and fifty yards short of the building, bored its way through about a hundred yards of solid chalk coming out again and bouncing into the attic of the house. It hit a wide brick chimney that went up the centre partition. From this it glanced off spinning across to the north gable, hitting another chimney and spun out on the upstairs floor come to rest. It was a dud and did not explode. Another one of the same kind hit a few feet short of the piles of stokes shells passing through the earth beneath them, and then continued on into Nieuve L—Amiens landing in one of the streets of the town among a military brass band that was accompanying some troops into town. It burst there causing several casualties. The dud that had stopped upstairs in our magazine became an object of great interest with a number of artillery officers coming to inspect it and examine it critically. It had come from one of the famous rubber heel or high-velocity naval guns.

We were told that this was the very same type of shell that was shot into Paris from a range of 72 miles. The gun that shelled Paris however was specially fitted with a breech of unusual thickness and strength to permit a load of propellant that gave an initial velocity of 6,000 feet per second. The projectile must have been some five feet in length but the forward half of that consisted of a long sharp-pointed false nose of tough tempered steel. The body of the shell proper had steel walls some three inches thick with a small hole down the centre to hold a bursting charge. A copper driving band of about five inches wide was set into the case near the back end of the shell. The thick steel cases had been bulged and deformed, or slightly telescoped or crushed endwise. Whether this deformation was due to the high breech pressure in the gun or to the shock of passing threw some 100 yards of solid chalk I could not say. Some of it must have been done in the gun, for the front shoulder of the shell was marked deeply around a third of its circumference by a contact with the rifling of the gun on one side. This looked like excessive breech pressure and must have played the devil with the rifling in the barrel. The shell was fitted with a base fuse arrangement of the delayed type commonly used with armors piercing shells. The deformation may have interfered with its working. During the month I was on the divisional bombers, leave was opened up for the Canadian troops in Paris and we could take our furlough there instead of England if we so desired.

Paris

I applied in my turn going to Paris for 12 days. Accommodation for British and colonial troops was secured at the Hotel DE La Republicque and I arrived there in due course. Paris is a beautiful city being at its best in this, the late summer or early autumn with bright sunny weather. The city is well laid out with broad boulevards and is well supplied with parks, and breathing spaces planted with long avenues of trees. I liked the area along the Seine River with its many bridges. We of course took in most of the places with the scenic interest in the first two days in town.

The people of Paris seemed to take the Canadians to their hearts and they vied with one another in their efforts to give us a good time on our short stay. Of (wine, women and song) there was certainly no lack. The people there have peculiar ideas about some of the things of life and we found their outlook on what at home we call morality to be rather startling in some ways. I would not say we found it unpleasant. I am of the honest opinion that they are far ahead of us in some phases of it. They are nothing if not frank and truly straight forward about it. Being young and newly arrived from a section of Hell we fell into their ways without quibble, deciding to "Do As The Romans Do". Also not to worry too much about the fine points and the ethics of it, but to start making the most of the short time given us in that bright beautiful city. Plays were put on in English at the local Alhambra and at the Follies Beguiler Theatres to entertain us. In the afternoons of the last week in Paris we used to sit at the little round tables under the awnings that were stretched in front of many hotel fronts at the margin of the sidewalk. So long as you ordered some sort of refreshment every quarter hour or so you could remain there undisturbed, except by Gaston who came around with a towel over his arm to take your orders. From this comfortable vantage you could study the life and movement of the boulevards and it was always highly interesting to a stranger.

The people here are creatures of sudden moods and liable to quick excitement. We watched a native who had fallen on the sidewalk in a fit. He was evidently subject to these attacks. The crowd surged to him in an instant growing to a remarkable size in a couple of minutes. Nobody tried to lift him up or take him away. There was much betting and speculation as to whether he would come to or peg out. The police were represented by a couple of blue coats but they stood with the rest and argued to his chances of recovery. He flopped about on the pavement for some little time eventually regaining consciousness. *Tres-Bon-Tres-Bon* the spectators slapped him on the back with hearty cries of congratulation, pushing him into the hotel and treating him to drinks. Nothing succeeds like success and he was now a fine fellow. Had he died there it would have been (*Ce Guerre, "It Is The War"*) with the waving of hands and loss of interest. The crowd melted away as quickly as it had collected with many jabbering.

Some of our boys experimented on this thing of collecting a crowd. For that purpose they would stage any sort of a foolish prank and immediately the street would be a solid massed multitude. There was a French soldier accompanied by his mother. He sought a taxi to take them to the Gore Du Nord (Station). He was on his return to the front lines. A taxi driver made an excuse that he was out of gas, for it was his luncheon hour and he was not wanting a fare, but was more interested in eats just then. They argued. The crowd swept up like a tide from all sides, and when the soldier stated his case the taxi driver narrowly escaped being mobbed or worse.

They seized his car and turned it around bodily, and threw the soldier and his mother aboard starting them on their way to the station. I believe the driver would have been pulled limb from limb had he refused to go. The jabbering and arm waving was fierce for a few minutes. A horse attached to a two-wheeled tip cart fell into the gutter and was unable, or disinclined, to rise. Again the crowd surged up. One of the spectators rushed and brought a pail of water. Another secured a pillow for the horse's head etc. Amid much excitement he was made as comfortable as possible where he lay. No attempt was made to clear the street or remove the horse or cart. Here was another splendid gamble. Would he rise or would he croak? The argument was protracted and long drawn out this time and the crowd did not clear away for some time. As for the horse he seemed to think that was quite a comfortable spot and elected to stay there till the following morning. I never did hear which side won the speculation. Probably the butcher for they eat horses in that country.

I moved from the Hotel de La Republicque to the Hotel de Cussett on the Rue de Richeileu and finally to the Hotel de Athens in the Latin Quarter. We had more freedom and were not restricted so much in these places. We had been restricted or regulated for about three years. We jumped at the chance of a few days of real freedom from the constant overseeing of officials of diverse kinds. Your petite Parisian is all that is claimed for her and it would be hard to find anything to beat her in a world wide search. She was there in her thousands and there was no escape for a Canadian even were he so minded. With one of her for an escort or guide and guardian you were well-away. She could guide you to all points of scenic interest seeing to it that no-one cheated you out of a sou or overcharged you for any purpose. Honest dealing was characteristic of her plus her many other charms. We will never forget the Petite Parisian (A thing of beauty and joy forever). We ran up against customs, and standards, moral and social, that were very strange to us though seeming to be part of these people's regular lives. Strange to say, it did not seem to wreck or debauch them in any degree but seemed to fit into the general scheme of things without a jar.

While staying at the Hotel de La Republicque there used to be a young French teen-aged student come and talk with us for awhile each morning. He explained that he did not get practice in English. He had been told that the Canadians used a fairly plain type of English, more or less free of local dialects. There was a French lassie of some 14 summers running in and out daily in company with a six foot Canuck who was some sort of a YMCA. clerk. The lassie was practically a full grown woman physically and attractive to boot. We had it on reliable authority that this couple spent their nights as well as days together. This sort of jarred UCL down east ideas, and we inquired of the teen-aged student whether there was no law in that city to protect the child of such tender years. He assured us that there was none, adding that folk in Paris rather smiled on that sort of thing. The young apparently get full fling and can learn wisdom in the school of first hand experience.

Hill 70

Twelve days and they passed so quickly, and we found ourselves on the train heading back towards Hill 70 and the fierce struggle of August 15th to 17th.

It was a cruel and sudden transition from the heights of pleasure plumb down with one sheer drop to the Hell of a raging roaring tumult of slaughter the like of which has been seldom seen. Hill 70 is the low chalk ridge on the northwest side of Lens and directly between it and the Hill 70 town of Moroc. It was the scene of the (Battle of Loos) June 1915. The British troops had tried to take this ridge but were thrown back with very heavy losses. It was here that the remainder of the old "Contemptible" met their Waterloo being badly cut up. It was a very sad and regrettable affair. Conan Doyle has written a story of it that was well worth reading. It would stir the heart of a stone god.

We were set the task of capturing this ridge and did it in mid-August 1917. The fight was a fierce one. Fritz fought with a sort of insane fury to retain this ridge making some 12 counter attacks in a period of 43 hours. In the course of these counter attacks the Germans lost a host of men for they were shoved forward in solid masses, again and again over the same ground near Cite St. Pierre, being mowed down by point blank artillery and machine gun fire until the senseless slaughter turned the stomachs of some of the boys who were called upon to perform the actual killing.

The old 8th battalion was among the units selected for the spear point of the assault. We were into a very exposed position during the course of the attack and were finally held up after suffering heavy losses. Major Sanders, in command of the attacking companies here, showed some real moral courage in that he took it on his shoulders to annul the instructions of his superiors refusing to push the attack until supported in sufficient strength to be able to carry out the task that had been set for our battalion. Had he continued to go forward with the tiny remnant of a battalion that was left him we would have been wiped completely out. It might have disorganized the assault or even caused a failure. After securing assistance the objective was made and held successfully too.

I will always admire the true courage that Sanders displayed on this occasion. It would have been so easy for him to let matters take their course as many an officer of inferior caliber has done before. He chose to endanger his own name taking the chance of severe reprimand or worse perhaps irreparable disgrace, rather than to see us all wiped out in an attempt to carry out an impossible task on impossible ground. He was finally commended highly for his good judgment. Sanders was an interesting character. Small and dark with bow-legs and an impediment in his speech, a pronounced lisp, he joined us in 1914 as a private and come back in command of the battalion at the end of the war. I can remember when he was a "Lance Jack" or one stripe corporal. He used to pinch all the strawberry jam when the rations came up for the company caching it in the dugout for his own section. He used to be frequently elected to muster the sick parade in the morning when all the lead swingers lined up at the m os quarters to get their no. nine's. He would try to shout the command, fall in the sick! Owing to his pronounced lisp it sounded like clickety click, so lickety click became his name and he was commonly known by it even after obtaining the rank of colonel. He was the last man one would have picked for such a promotion being under severe handy-cap in appearance and speech but in spite of it all he rose by sheer merit. You can never tell by the look of a cat.

The end of the battle found us with a new trench line along the east and south sides of the chalk pits or chalk quarries overlooking Lens. From here the line extended through the ruins of Cite St. Pierre. There was some hand to hand fighting one morning during the period when fritz was still trying to take back the ground lost. Zero hour had been set for a minor attack to improve or straighten the line. At 5.05 am. the barrage lifted and our boys went forward in a thick fog or mist.

Fritz had planned a counter-attack for exactly the same time and the two attacking waves were surprised to meet head-on in no-mans-land. It turned out to be one of the Prussian guard regiments, and big husky lot of men too. Some of our boys reported that the Prussians put up a real argument with the bayonet, and in some cases found it hard to overcome the highly trained guardsmen who fought with a will when surprised by the head-on collision in the fog.

We witnessed some terrible slaughter when the massed counter-attacks on our front were repeated again and again over the bodies heaped up where the first attacks melted under the hellish fire of the first Canadian artillery. At one time there was a high-piled and gruesome mass of mangled humanity like a sea-wall or dyke. Some of the ones underneath were still living while the hail of death heaped hundreds more on top. At one time you could see the whole quivering mass heave up and down in queer jerky spasms and convulsions. A lot of men had their minds almost unbalanced by this and other ghastly sights that they were compelled to witness. Machine gun and rifle fire from our lines was being poured into the advancing masses completing what the artillery had started. The battle of Loos was fully avenged here on practically the same ground fought over in June 1915. Fritz finally gave up the ridge and drew back sullenly to nurse his shattered battalions. He never made a real attempt to take Hill 70 again after that fight.

We lost a number of scouts and snipers in the course of this battle mainly from the heavy shell fire before or after it. The holding of the ridge after it was taken was far from an easy task for we were shelled and pounded with all manner of high explosives from the land, the sky, and from saps and tunnels below us that were blown up in efforts to dislodge us. There had been one group of seven who used to foregather at a estaminet in Nouexies mines and sip there vin-rouge and vin-blau in hours of leisure. Of that seven there only remained two survivors to tell the tale.

Seven supple lads and clean, sat down to drink one night, sat
down to drink at Nieuve L Amiens, then went away to fight
Seven supple lads and clean are finished with the fight.
But only two at Nieuve Amiens, sit down to drink tonight

The fire fly lamps were lighted yet as we crossed the top of the parapet
But the East grew pale with another fire as our bayonets
gleamed at the German wire
And The Eastern sky was cold and grey, and under our feet the dead
men lay

Twixt Loos and Lens in the morning
A star shell holds the sky beyond shell-shivered Lens and drops
In million sparkles on the pond Green Crossier-oer-tops.
A moments brightness in the sky to vanish at a breath, and die away,
as soldiers die upon the wastes of death our comrades lay on the
shell-scarred plain, where death and the
Autumn held their reign

Like banded ghosts in the heavens grey, the smoke of the
conflict died away. The boys whom I knew and loved
were dead, where war's grim annals were writ in red

By the edge of Lens in the morning

In the week following the battle of Hill 70 I had a hunch or premonition that I was going to be wounded or killed and so it happened that I had a number of narrow escapes from various death dealing agencies during that period. I was under a queer sort of strain and suspense during the whole of the week. My first shave was from a bullet that hit the chalk about an inch from my right shoulder. The second was from a shell that burst directly in front of me in a trench. The third was a trench mortar burst on the east rim of the chalk pits. The fourth was from a pineapple bomb.

Lens

The Lens sector quieted down to some extent after we had consolidated and held Hill 70 for a couple of weeks following its capture in mid-August. We had several terms in and out of the line at different points from Leavin, Cite de Moulin to Cite St. Pierre and Moroc. The above named places are all mining towns and suburbs of Lens City proper. They lay around it in a semi-circle from south to north in the order named.

During this period I had a close-up view of what happens when nine point two inch howitzers are concentrated on cement work or concrete and iron defenses. Our front line in front of Cite de Moulin wandered through a wilderness of ruined brick tenements and about midway of our two flanks it skirted a mine head or "fosse". This "fosse" had been strengthened with cement until it was virtually bomb and shell proof. It formed a strong point or redoubt in the German forward trench system. Our artillery decided to try the effect of delayed fuse armors piercing shells from a battery of nine point two inch howitzers. Owing to the fact that there is always a chance of a shell falling short in howitzer fire, our front line of outposts was drawn back some 500 yards during the bombardment. I was detailed along with a lieutenant Burke of our battalion to remain in the top of a ruined house directly overlooking the fosse to watch and report the effect of the strafe.

The first couple of shots were a trifle high but the third was a direct hit, and from that onward it was a steady unvarying succession of hits. One shell glanced or ricocheted off the cement and went spinning end over end through the ruined houses behind. Talk about your weird and fearsome noises. You have to hear a huge shell key-holing its way through a flock of brick houses to get it. The shells appeared to come down almost vertically and could be seen quite clearly in the last 20 or 30 feet of their plunge out of the sky. Every one of them gave us a creepy feeling when they came roaring down on us out of the sky. There is a heart-stopping menace in that last fierce plunge to earth. The shrieking monster seems to hold an all embracing threat to everything that is comparatively near. In that swoop there is the snarl and shriek of a thousand tigers and lions. The pitch gets higher and more fierce until the burst that rocks the earth around you. We saw the cement work broken in huge blocks eight and ten feet square. These in turn were heaved up and tossed about by the bursting shells that penetrated down into the earth below. Any Germans that may have been down below must have been killed like rats in a hole for the concussion down there must have been terrific. We had a first hand demonstration of why our troops had been drawn back. One shell fell short by a couple of hundred yards plunging into the earth directly in front of our observation post. We had a bad couple of seconds when that one fanned the ridgepole of the attic in which we were perched lifting the tiles off it's frail roof with the hot breath of its passing. There is nothing like a heavy howitzer to hammer a hole downward through the cement, stone and ironwork. The delayed fuse lets the plunging howitzer shell penetrate to the limit of it's own power. Then the explosion comes penetrating some distance further after the momentum and weight of the projectile has been spent. When a shell is leaving a gun you may see it clearly if you are close behind the gun. It appears as a rapidly diminishing ball or sphere that is jet black. On its downward plunge it looks like an elongated shaft or bolt and jet black.

We witnessed what may have been an intended retaliation in kind from fritz. To the left of us our line climbed up out of the sunken railway yards and northward to Cite St. Auguste.

At the point where the line climbed the embankment fritz sent over a heavy strafe with "minen werfers" or heavy trench mortars concentrated on one short length of our line. This happened just as dusk was deepening into darkness. We could see a red trail of sparks with a feather of smoke trailing behind each Minnie as it made its rainbow curve over to our lines. They came over in salvos and in flocks with each sending up a column of high vertical smoke and debris a veritable pillar of fire by night. These minnies were at least ten inches in diameter and some three to four feet in length. The explosion of them is very heavy. It was a very impressive sight when viewed from a short distance. On close acquaintance one is a bit more forcibly impressed. The concussion from them is like a great hand pressing down on one's head and threatening to telescope your neck. They leave a crater about 12 to 15 feet across and over half that in depth, depending on the nature of the ground where they hit. I do not remember what our losses were from that evening's hate.

Cite St. Pierre was a miserable piece of line with shallow and badly exposed trenches, and under a constant intermittent shellfire. The same thing applied to the communication trenches to it. In the front line here we did our observation work from an old cement emplacement and from fragments of brick walls. The dead were very thick hereabouts and were built into the trench walls and parapets on all sides. It was a common sight to see part of a British soldier sticking out of the mud. On warm days the stench was a thing to remember. When we were in support lines we were quartered in a shallow cellar or basement under what had been a convent or nunnery in pre-war days. There was constant intermittent shellfire all over the area and the shelter was very visible with no protection in a real sense. Our losses in this area amounted to a considerable figure. I shot a German one evening from a post near our right flank that overlooked a low valley where fritz had no communication trench to one of his outposts. This post used to change relief's at grey-light, morning and evening. The range was about 700 yards. I used a Ross with a Winchester A 5 telescope having previously fired a ranging shot to make certain of distance and the setting of the sights. Fritz retaliated with shell fire on my post killing several of our men who were in a dugout close behind. I had previously objected to sniping from there for fear of that result. The men were killed by concussion owing to the fact that the dugout had only one entrance. It had been a German dug out and they knew its exact location. The shell plunged down the stairway bursting near the bottom with the above mentioned results. Sniping was an unpleasant job in many ways and the above mentioned incident was the direct result of the sniper being supervised by officers not conversant with that kind of work and always inclined to overrule any kind of objections.

Colonel (later) General Lipsett was the only officer I met during the period of the war who seemed to have the proper conception of how scouts and sharpshooters should be handled. I was in charge of the triple unit (scouts, snipers and observers) while under his command and he made it clear that as long as we got results in our line of work he would not insist on too much supervision. He stated that men who were suited to that kind of duty were at the same time unsuited to routine work and apt to chafe under too strict discipline. He let me pick my own men, plan and carry out the work in my own way getting results aplenty along with the cooperation of the men concerned. He would not insist on a sniper working from a machine gun post, bombers post, or from a spot where a bunch of men were quartered. The sniper could cause a lot of casualties by drawing enemy fire to the place.

The Autumn wore on into October, we could hear heavy gun fire muttering, growling and murmuring through the fog to the north of us away beyond grim old Ypres and up near where we had the blood bath in April 1915. The staff for some reason was hammering hard at the ridge of Passchendaele and by the end of October they had fed almost every unit in the imperial forces through the mud, rain, and cold in futile attacks on the ridge. It was a repetition of the tactics used at Mouquiet Farm and Thiepeval on the Somme in 1916 only the conditions at Passchendaele were many times worse owing to the condition of the ground and the constant cold rains. The Australians were fed into the mill up north and very nearly started a mutiny by kicking in their whole-hearted way against such suicidal methods. They did not mind putting up a hard fight under hard conditions just the same as any other good troops but they felt in their hearts that it was another stupid piece of pig-headed blundering and voiced their thoughts on the spot. We saw cages full of them later, cooped up in compounds in barbed wire the same as enemy prisoners. I do not know how the fuss started but it was during their attack on the ridge following that of the imperials. The Marine Corps, naval brigade and also the crown colony forces were fed through the mill up there in addition to the other units previously mentioned. The Canadian corps had by now come to have a great reputation as shock troops and up to now never failed in an assault no matter how strong the place attacked. We had a great record behind us, St. Julien, Festuburt, Givenchy, Hill 60, Mt.

Sorel, Mouquiet Farm, Zollern Trench, Hessien Trench, Courcelette, Regina Trench, Vimy, and Hill 70 etc. Any one of these was a greater battle than Waterloo, whether you counted troops engaged, or counted casualties, or just reckoned the nature of the fighting. Each and every one was a fierce fight. Now they were looking our way after all others had failed to go over the crest of Passchendaele. We knew it would be a tough one and it was.

Passchendaele

While here I took a shot one day at an enemy plane high overhead and I must made a hit of some sort on the plane or the pilot for he quit swooping and circling instantly. He flew away east as straight as an arrow until out of sight at the horizon with out any further attempt at maneuvering his plane.

We had a lively trip across lots behind the line here one day. We were on a carrying party across. They began to move us north toward where the rumble and grumble of the guns coming dully through the fog. I was starting in on my fourth winter in the front line trenches. It seemed to me as though it might go on forever for me and I would never get relief from the soul-smashing grind except in death, dismemberment or severe sickness.

Hitch on the 80 lbs. Of equipment and pound the cobble stones again for weary after weary kilometer with mud, blood, guts, and other grisly things. At the end maybe a resting place for my rheumatic-flu-racked bones in a water filled shell-hole up on the rain swept slope of the ridge where I would have frogs, lizards and snails for company along with some ragged wire stake for a headstone. I remember there was a Cape Breton Nova Scotia Scotsman in our battalion who had a set of pipes and he played in front of us for many a weary mile on the way north. There is nothing quite as good as the pipes to march by. Up near Poperinge there was a Canadian airman in a Bristol fighter who flew low over us along the road and did the windmill-spin just to show us he was in good spirits and glad to see some real troops coming up. To do the windmill you fly at nearly full speed horizontally and turned the whole plane wings and all around and around like a windmill.

We were loaded onto the old rattle-trap French railway into the same old shrapnel riddled carriages that used to take us up nights into the salient during 1915-1916 with fritz letting fly a few more odd salvoes of shrapnel at the train on the way, just to make it seem homelike to us. We unloaded as of yore in the rain some place near the old asylum and marched on foot into Ypres City. There was a Red Cross hospital train pulling up to the city as we neared the outskirts and fritz was shelling the railway with a nine point six inch naval gun, of very high velocity. I sympathized with the engine driver on that train for he had an unenviable job of sitting in his cab, slowly creeping forward to the place where the shells were tearing things up. It was broad daylight too and fritz must have been able to get observation on the place from captive balloons and aero planes. We marched over the same route we had used on our way to St. Julien in 1915.

It was now a city of scarred pavements stretching between mounds, heaps, and ridges of broken brick and stone. There is scarcely a building left standing in the city. The German expenditure in shellfire here must have run into large figures. It costs real money to make a ruin of that extent by gunfire.

We marched past the old square at the head of the Canal Du Nord and then out into a brown sea of mud to the northwest of the city. Here we camped under small brown tarpaulins hoisted as a fly tent. These tarps made a wee shelter that you could crawl under. They were about seven feet long and wide enough for two men to lie under. The ends of the shelter were open letting in lots of rain and wind. The ground was mostly ankle deep in mud and water. If you could rustle something to lie on, alright, if not, alright too.

As soon as camp was made fritz sent over a flight of bombing planes and they circled over us dropping showers of bombs at regular intervals all through the night. In the intervals between the visits of the bombers we were shelled by long range guns. One shell just skimmed the ridge pole of our fly plunging into the mud just beyond where it burst sending up a ton or two of mud and water which came down kerplunk on top of us knocking our shelter flat as a pancake.

On the afternoon of the next day I was detailed along with two other scouts to guide a pack train of mules and horses up as near as we could get to the front line trench. A plank road had been shoved forward as far as it was possible to maintain it under the constant enemy fire, but beyond the end of that it was a wild unbroken sea of water filled with shell holes without track or landmark.

Our artillery was working here under the very extreme of hard conditions. It was impossible to move even the lighter guns very far from the plank road. The batteries that I passed that night were sunk in mud to the axles and immovable. Ever round they fired had the effect of sinking them deeper in the mire and they were without protection of any kind either visual or real. Being fixed in the one position immovably they were suffering cruelly from enemy fire day and night. The men who were staying with and operating those guns are certainly entitled to all the credit humanly possible to give any soldiers. I never witnessed greater courage anywhere. As we moved up the crowded road with our pack train we were passing the eight inch howitzer batteries massed solid, wheel to wheel just off the road on either side, I saw an odd thing happen. One of our aero planes flying low towards the front lines had just passed over the massed guns when it ran foul of a shell mid-air. It must have been a direct hit on the engine of the plane for the explosion left nothing but a few splinters and ribbons floating away in the air. The plane was destroyed so completely there did not appear to be any solid piece of any size to fall to earth.

That single track line of road across the sea of mud was a shambles, a slaughter house and a good example of Hell or Hades in full blast. I had not seen a worse looking piece of road since St. Julien in April 1915. The Baupaume Road was not a match to it in 1916. At the end of the plank road I saw a big motor truck that had been hit by an incendiary shell. There was nothing left of the vehicle except metal. There sat the cinder-black upright skeleton of its driver, bolt-upright, with both charred skeletal hands still grasping the steering wheel, with even his head still upright and straight to the front though burnt to a cinder. We steered our pack train forward into the sea of mud and were glad to get away from the road for a breathing spell from the enemy shells that were pounding it constantly. Our breathing spell was to be of short duration however for when we got forward under the slope of the hill we ran right into a barrage of shells, and I believe it was only the depth and softness of the mud that saved us from being practically wiped out. The shells would plunge deep into the mud close beside us and by leaning away from the burst as it shot skyward you got nothing worse than a mud and water bath with a bit of a shaking up from the concussion. Men from the transport lines were leading the horses and the mules and when the shell fire got real bad, there was a stampede of horses and drivers too. It fell to us three scouts to round up the strays fetching them to the unloading place to unload them as well. The loads were on saddle panniers and consisted of food rations, water, and rum as well as ammunition. We finally got them all unloaded and headed back towards home. There was a transport line sergeant along who was supposed to be in charge of the outfit but was so drunk he was unable to dismount or render any assistance at any time. There was a quarter master officer along also from the transport lines. He became so drunk we had to load him onto one of the pack horses and on arrival at the end of the plank road we loaded him into a downward bound motor lorry for he was dead to the world. By the way! That officer and that sergeant both were decorated with medals for their good work in delivering the goods with that pack train. We three poor humble scouts never received even as much as a thank you for our part in it. Jack Campbell was one of the scouts. I cannot remember the name of the third man. Such is life in the Great War. Those medal bearers had about as much chance of getting there with that train that night as a "snowball in Hell".

The following morning the Canadians attacked the ridge and by nightfall we were in possession of all objectives with the long fought fight for Passchendaele being ours. There was not really much actual resistance in the final assault. The enemy's main reliance was on scattered concrete machine gun emplacements called pill—boxes. Our men could work around these on the flanks, and by dropping bombs or stokes gun shells into the entrances make them untenable or kill all the occupants with concussion.

The tank corps ran up against a hard proposition in this sea of mud for they stalled or became slowed up so badly that they became easy victims of enemy fire. I know of a couple of tank crews that were cooked alive. The small steel doors of the tank had become bent or jammed due to enemy shell fire and the crew were unable to escape. A tank on fire is a gruesome sight especially if you are not sure if the crew is still on board it. They carry a fairly large supply of petrol or gasoline and the trail of smoke and flame can be seen a long way. There was a number of them scattered over the torn-up mounds of slippery mud on the way up to the ridge. I think the old style tank as used in 16-17 was overrated as a weapon of offence. A high velocity small bore gun of the rapid-fire type could account for them quite easily if well placed and held in reserve for the purpose. The models that came out later may stand a better chance due to their smallness, speed, mobility or ability to turn and twist crossing quickly from cover to cover on broken ground.

One of our divisions on our left was held up for a while by a strong point near the crest of the ridge to our left. On our frontage it was mostly scattered machine gun crews who put up a sort of sacrifice rear guard fight and left their corpses to mark the line of our half-swimming, half—crawling and wholly miserable advance across that morass in the cold drizzle of winter rain. The enemy that I saw appeared to be Bavarians of the tall angular and swarthy type and in death their hair, brows and mustaches etc. seemed to stiffen like bristles standing upward in the opposite angle to what a persons hair usually lies giving them a strange appearance. This trait seemed to be peculiar to them for I saw plenty of our own dead alongside them and they did not show this strange appearance above noted. In case anybody reading this tale does not become sufficiently disgusted with modern war and come to a faint understanding of its meaning, I will describe a sight I saw up there on the flat lands on top of the hill of Passchendaele. In going forward we came to a small watercourse swollen by the constant rains until it formed quite an obstacle for men on foot. This muddy stream flowed with quite a swift current and a temporary bridge had been built across it, consisting of some boards and planks supported on piers. The piers were constructed of the freshly killed bodies of Canadian boys thrown down there in the mud and swirling bloody water. When passing over it you felt it yield and give and sway with your weight. Looking down you saw the young dead faces there trampled into the slime with the filthy water flowing over and filling the bright brave eyes that a few short hours ago had borne our colors and our hopes unflinchingly across that gruesome sea of mud to victory. I had to carry stretchers across that Bridge of Hellish Memory.

It was up here that I saw Canon Scott of Quebec at his work. He had an old wool toque cap with a tin hat or service helmet perched on top of that. You could see his long spare figure moving about heedless of the sweep of bullets or shrapnel. When he found one of our boys wounded and dying in a shell hole he would read to him from his Bible and then hold his poor clammy cold wet hands trying to ease and help him in his last agony as he passed on down into the shadows. The cold grey shadows that creep on one exactly as the cold grey fog of Flanders in winter. Scott even tried to cover over the poor shattered remains of what had yesterday been youth, strength and fire endeavoring to leave a mark for the poor grave. I met him again the next day at the advance dressing station established at the end of the plank road. I was a bit puzzled by a remark he addressed to me. Four of us had just arrived with a wounded case on a stretcher that we had carried down a couple of miles from the ridge. Scott gave us a smile saying, "You are a fine lot of animals and don't know it ". I have not been able to figure that out yet. I suppose it was just a passing fancy to which he gave voice and may not have had any particular meaning.

We had a couple of strenuous days at that work of bearing stretchers before we brought all the wounded down from the desolate waste. The footing was horrible. The level stretch on the top of the ridge and beyond was swept by enfilade fire from the left where some imperial unit had failed to make good their advance or had not consolidated their gains. The enemy had crept forward to harass us by long range rifle and machine gun fire from a flank. A cement pill box up there in one place had been brought into use as a shelter in which to bandage and give first aid to the wounded. My carrying party was waiting with the rest to take our turn as the stretchers were made ready. Some of the bearers in the party ahead of us were temporally absent, so we took the stretcher up and passed on out with it. I noticed a shell hit quite close to the pill box as we passed on out. It must have been a ranging shot for the one that came over a moment later was a direct hit on the back entrance or doorway and all the men inside were killed by concussion. Had we hesitated to await our proper turn in the line up we would have been among those victims. Our fates often hung on such slender threads of chance in those days. I could tell of a number of such flukes but might not be credited by folks who never had to go through the game of life and death at such a helter skelter gait as we traveled. I forgot to mention that Jack Harron and I on the first day caught a young German officer who was quite talkative and on taking him into a shelter where they were gone over and examined by some of our intelligence staff, they decided that he might let loose some information that would prove useful if he were interviewed by the right parties. Harron and I were detailed off to take him down the line for a number of miles to the rear delivering him at a specific address for further questioning. It took us the best part of the day to make that trip and some of it was by motor truck. Some of it was quite lively due to enemy shell fire on the road going and coming. It was on the way back to the line, while circling away from one of our field batteries that was being pounded to death by shellfire. We had a close look at a couple of the tanks that had been knocked out in the attack. I never had a particular desire to be on a tank crew after that day.

On foot in the open one feels as though he had some fighting chance. After three days of the stretcher bearing job combined with a lot of other running to and fro on top of our rather strenuous trip into the salient and the battle itself we were pretty well spent. We had been without sleep or rest and had taken very little food for a week now plus working at top notch pressure all the time. Our transport lines were supposed to be at one of the old rattle trap rest camps out on the flat country south of Ypres. It seems to run in my mind that it was known as Camp B. It lay to the east of the main road north with the endless line of leaning poplars and elms looking down on the endless line of motor trucks. Ambulances, ammunition limbers, g. s. wagons and other vehicles pouring in a double stream night and day, up and down to feed the troops in the north. Back to the old rest camp, we made our own way as best we could in twos and threes in small groups with sore and blistered feet that had been in water soaked and dirty socks since we started north for the battle. We were not a very prepossessing looking bunch probably. But we had delivered the goods. I remember we met three or four Australians in spic and span sporty uniforms on their way back to their unit after a leave or furlough in England. They grinned broadly when they sighted us in our rags limping down the road and inquired with great sarcasm if we had taken the ridge. When told that we had done just that they gave us the loud haw! haw! Known as the horse-laugh, but we could afford to grin, we were too tired to laugh just then. Ours was the last laugh. It was on the way down the road that I saw the first American soldier in the field. He was an officer riding along with one of our transport officers and on his way to get posted on transport methods in the zone behind the fighting front. Later that winter some of them were attached to us and were in charge of some new style gas projectors with which they put over a gas attack on the Germans along part of the Lens frontage.

After Passchendaele we were of course taken back for a couple of weeks to recuperate and get the units filled up to near full strength again by means of the new drafts from England or from the reserve training camps there. We later went in the line in front of Suchez Village and at Cite Collone in the coal mine district.

Leave in Swansea, Wales

Just before Xmas I succeeded in getting a 12 day leave to England accompanying a Welshman by the name of Jones to his home at Swansea in Wales where he proceeded to marry his old sweetheart and of course had no further time to spend with me. I was left on my lonesome in Swansea.

I put up at the Royal Hotel and from a lack of other past times I got in with a lot of hard drinking patrons of that place. This included some new Zealanders, hussies and some native taffies spending several days and nights demonstrating to them that a Canuck could drink them under the table and still navigate alright. I was the sole Canadian in that whole city at the time, I believe, and had a reputation to keep up. I came out with high honors in the three boozing contests and was known at the hotel as the sober wonder. I soon tired of that sort of entertainment for it did not appeal to me much at any time.

I went to the Rugby Park at the Mumbles, where all the best in rugby has been played for years. There I saw the Springboks from Rhodesia play against the New Zealand team and the Welsh Guards and the Welsh Home Team. I heard the Springboks give their Zulu War Cry as they deployed on the field with it sounding fine as well as wild when rendered with the proper cadence and spirit. It went something like this.

Zulu War Cry
Ghee Camilio–Ghee!!
Wa-ta-ne-na-Wa
Ghee Camilio–Ghee!!

Wa-ta-ne-na-Wa
Ghee Camili–Ghee!!
Wa-ta-ne-na-Wa

The New Zealand team included several Maoris or natives and fine fellows they seemed to be. I met some of the young Boers or native Dutch who were with the Springboks and they were pleasant folk to meet. They were sons of the stockmen and farmers from the Veldt. I went down to the waterfront and there saw some of the motor-boat sub-chasers lying at the docks. I noticed that the men on them were armed with Ross rifles 1910 Model MK 111 the same rifle we used at Nieuve Chapelle and St. Julien in the spring of 1915. I returned to London to have a couple days there before going back to the battalion. While in Swansea I mailed home a telescopic rifle sight that I dug out the mud near the Sugar Trench on the Somme in 1916. I looked over the bright lights of the old city and then took the plunge once more into the cauldron across the channel and my path led up again to where it boiled its fiercest.

Arras

It seemed as though I had been at it for a lifetime now. In the winter of 1917-18 the Germans with their allies were determined to make one more terrific drive against us in a final desperate bid for victory. The Russians were now out of it all together and that gave the enemy a mass of available troops, supplies, and guns to transfer over to the western front to concentrate against us. We heard rumors all winter about what was impending and the enemy tried out some weak spots. They made a smash at the Portuguese troops driving a wedge into our line that extended right back to Baileuell west of Messines. They made another smashing drive south of Arras and another in the Somme country. At one time they had the imperial troops falling back, guns and all over a wide front. We were shipped backward and forward frequently by rail, motor truck and shanks mare.

At one time we were stowed away in the great chalk caves under the city of Arras. On the trip to the caves we marched through the city at night crossing some railway yards, then straight up a long street to where there was a regular stairway of considerable depth leading to the caves below.

As we marched forward towards the above entrance I could hear heavy enemy shells falling at regularly timed intervals directly ahead of us. The troops were coming up too fast for the capacity of the entrance and became massed in the square in front of it. I was wondering if we would get down the stairway in time to escape the burst of the next heavy shell for I had been noting the interval between shell bursts while coming toward the spot. The seconds ticked off as we shuffled forward a foot at a time toward the entrance. I had a mental picture of the square head gunners on that 11 inch Spandau howitzer as they methodically craned the shell forward to the breach, closed the great breach-block. Standing clear as the battery commander repeated guttural orders to the gun layer with the ugly black muzzle moving ever so slightly to the exact elevation and traverse. A couple of Cockneys just ahead of us in the entrance started to wrangle, jostling one another, and grousing in their high-pitched whining way, delaying our forward movement. We gave them heart-felt, deepthroated curses accompanied by a not too gentle push and moved forward a couple of yards inside the portal when the expected shell arrived. It burst in the square just outside on the hard cobblestone pavement and the sweep of steel fragments mixed with splinters of rock and brick tore and mangled 18 men, some of them beyond recognition. The ones that still lived were carried below, some of them minus both legs etc. The survivors that I saw were in very mangled and desperate condition. That was our introduction to the Caves of Arras.

The Caverns themselves are quite impressive as to the size and extent. In some places they remind one of the interior of a vast cathedral with high-arched vaulted roofs away up in the shadows far above, with huge supporting pillars of chalk left there to support the weight of the city above us. Some of the drifts or passages that lead tunnel wise in many directions must be miles in length. The flickering of hundreds of candles and small lights, and the moving to and fro of hundreds of armed men along with the echoing of words of command that rolled cavernously back and forth with the rumbling murmur that came to one from other unexplored caverns, gave the whole thing a weird fairy tale touch.

I was detailed along with two other scouts to go and explore out a route that was marked on a map or chart of the caves which they handed us. Our duty was to search out all the windings and turns in a series of tunnels by their numbers posted on small sign boards at the junctions. All the area beyond the main caverns was unlit and in complete darkness. We knew there were abrupt shelves without any protecting railings where one could step off into space without any warning what so ever. Our search lights were candles and the drafts in some of those tunnels amounted to a gale of wind. We searched out the route to its end finding ourselves in some support trenches in the outer eastern fringe of the city. We may have covered a couple of miles of those inky winding passages. We were required to guide our battalion over that route a couple of days later so we did not need to make mistakes. We also explored an alternative route which included a half mile or so of city sewer main. The sewer was circular and built of brick being about 12 feet in diameter. There was a concrete raised platform or bench running along one side some two or three feet above the flow of water along its bottom. This we walked on. The city at the time we arrived was in very bad shape, being somewhat disorganized due to the fact the heavy recent bombardment had driven out most the civilian populace. Numerous stores and warehouses full of goods were left without any protection of any kind. There was also stores of wines and liquors left for all comers to help themselves if so inclined. Some of the Canadian battalions got into trouble in the city. I suppose they helped themselves to the free wines etc. until they lost their judgment and ordinary good sense of proportion, then foolishly started tampering with some of the unprotected stores. At any rate there was a big To-Do over it and it was given the ugly name of looting. I believe the goods taken were in the process of being destroyed rapidly at the time by enemy shell fire. I know some of the men took long chances from bursting shells and falling debris while trying to gratify a drunken whim of getting something for nothing.

The canny heilands Scottish troops from old Scotland be it known, between you and I, got the most of the goods while succeeding in getting the blame for it shifted on to our boys, where it stuck solid. The horrible wild colonials again. Any Scottish kiltie who was in Arras or the vicinity at the time knows that to be the truth. Also the caucus were made the goat in that case which started as a playful prank as far as our boys were concerned.

Scarpe

After leaving Arras we had a trip to the line north of the Scarpe River in an open grassy country of low rolling hills and valleys. In this area we occupied two different sections of line. At one place we were in a low valley that was overlooked by the enemy lines on higher ground along our whole frontage. Here the ground was wet with our trenches and saps drained by means of square sump holes dug in the ground some few feet to the front or to one side of the trench and connected to it by a drainage ditch. In case of sudden rains the water flowed into the sump-holes gradually soaking away into the ground leaving the trench comparatively dry in spots.

There was a sap led out to one of our advanced posts with a sump-hole at one side about half way. I was looking for a place to snipe from and there being a good field of view from this sump hole I threw a piece of plank across it above water level using it as a temporary shelter to snipe from. I was by my lonesome that day and becoming chilled after an hour or so of watching from this place, I moved back toward the sap by way of the drain ditch. I had just got as far as the trench some ten feet from the sump hole when fritz put a shell right plumb and fair into that hole sending a geyser of mud and water skyward along with the plank on which I stood a moment before. Fritz sure did love snipers.

The men on the post ahead of that looked peeved because the shell missed me. A sniper is about as welcome around an advanced post as a leper would be or a person with smallpox. I did get a few pot shots at Germans on the fly while on this front. Apparently they had some poor sections of trench as well as ourselves and they took chances across the open, to escape water probably, or to get past a section of collapsed trench. As the saying goes (that was their funeral) not mine.

In the sector to the right of this we were on higher ground and could look south east across the valley of the scrape seeing the heights of Monchy, later stormed by our troops. While on this front north west of the river the Germans made a trench raid on us and drove it home with unusual energy causing some casualties in this part of the country where we had no trenches, and fritz started to chase us with salvoes of shrapnel. I was carrying two bundles of four one gallon tins of drinking water running, ducking and dodging that shrapnel up and down several hill slopes before reaching cover. One of the cans got punctured on the way.

Telegraph Hill

We were switched over to the Telegraph Hill sector marching out into the open country where the British troops had been driven back and had left supply camps, ymca. camps, stores, and ammunition dumps behind in an unaccountable scramble to the rear before a threatened enemy drive. The enemy were very slow in taking over the abandoned country so we were sent up there to establish some sort of a line to cover all the camps and supplies left exposed by the retreat.

There were some strange tales going the rounds at this time about German officer spies riding around in Rolls Royce cars dressed as British staff giving orders for troops and batteries to pull up stakes and march to the rear. There certainly was a lot that needed explaining and the people who had to pay the cost are still in the dark as to the cause of it all. There was a large dark brownish-yellow spot some where in the British army organization at that time and the only wonder is that the Germans did not follow it up right to the coast for they only had a few more miles to go to come in sight of the coast during the drive they made south of Baileuell and south of the Scarpe on the Somme. We were sent on a flying trip south also and landed after a long ride in motor trucks at some cross-road hamlet toward the Somme. There was no line here and we posted outposts the same as in open warfare. We did not know where we were going but were on our way. The Germans were not very far in front of us for their shells from their light field guns or (whiz bangs) were dropping in our lines at intervals during the one night that we were left there. I never found out the location of that place we made the flying trip to. We were not there long enough to be issued with any maps.

Scarpe River

Nothing particular happened while we were there so we loaded into motor trucks again and rode back north to the Scarpe River. We took over a section of front line with our left flank in the marsh at the river bank and our right among some rough ground to the south. There were some railway tracks on embankments as well as a gravel pit in our lines here. Now that I think of it the demoralization must have started a bit among our officers for they established battalion headquarters a good mile and a half behind the front line in an old railway embankment. Something I had never seen them do before in all the time we had been in France. It looked all most as though they too were thinking about retreats and did not want to be left behind by any chance. While we were here there was an epidemic of flu or influenza, French fever, swamp fever or malaria that broke out among us. I took sick with it myself while we were in supports billeted in a sort of barn. I had chills and fever alternately for some days and lay in an old chicken wire bed up under the eaves of the barn. I got lots of cold air if nothing else. We did not improve under this treatment, or lack of treatment, and were finally moved into some tents at the side of the road where nature was allowed to take its course. The most of us being tough by nature did not succumb but gradually were up on our feet again. We were supposed to be well in sort of a half hearted kind of way. That flu is a bad malady and I have never been clear of it to this day. I still get a recurrences of it on occasion with chills, fever and dizziness sometimes accompanied by a form of indigestion and lassitude. While I was still convalescent in the tents at the side of the road and not feeling very husky, orders were sent to me at 1:30 a.m. one morning by a runner to report at once to battalion headquarters. I was somewhat puzzled by this and wondered if I was to be shot at sunrise or something like that.

When you get orders in the field you don't stop to wonder very long but get busy and comply with them to the extent of your ability (immediately). I felt a bit groggy and dizzy as I buckled on the old front line equipment but after marching a mile or two in the cold night air I felt better.

Headquarters informed me that Captain Stevenson was in charge of an advanced machine gun and bombing post on the lip overlooking the river and the high ground in front. He reported numerous Germans seen on the high ground in front. His post being isolated by day and without communications, except across the open at night, I would have to take rations, and water preparing to stay all day. My services were required to snipe some of the afore mentioned Germans. Another sniper named Penfold was detailed to go along as my partner. We had landed there about an hour before daylight and crawled out on the rough ground in front to see the sights. Immediately on our left as we crawled out in front, the ground sloped away to the river. To our right was a wagon road with a ditch on both sides. Immediately beyond the far ditch of the road there was a high embankment or gravel fill, the grade of a railway that followed the side of the hill eastward to the enemy lines. Then it was swinging north in a long sweep to where it crossed the river at a bridge some distance down the river to the north east. Looking to the south east the ground continued to rise to some height beyond the railway grade. The skyline here showed to be rough, and broken up, with old trenches, debris and shell holes. While lying in broken ground on the low side of the wagon road we could watch the skyline and the nearer slopes against the pale light that was starting to rise in the east. While watching we suddenly saw three Germans moving along the crest of the hill above the railway. They moved to the right a few yards then appeared to be searching the ground in front with a pair of night glasses. Penfold was all for shooting at them at once and would have opened fire on them. I protested for by their actions I was convinced they intended to come down our way and were looking over the ground first to see if all was clear. As it turned out I was right in my guess for presently they hopped over the old trench that they had been in and came sliding down the side hill. When they reached the railway fill they came climbing down it on the side toward us. I decided to lie flat in the road ditch watching to see how far they would come toward our lines. They came to the far ditch of the road and I had a job to keep Penfold from opening fire on them then. I had taken the notion of capturing them alive if possible. I had heard that a raid was planned on the enemy trench the next night to identify the troops in front of us. This seemed to be like a Godsend to have them walk right into my fist. We sat tight and let them pass us with only the width of the wagon road between us. When they were some 20 yards beyond us and toward our lines I shouted to them as sharply as I knew how telling them to drop their arms. They may not have understood my English but they did not hesitate at all in complying with the order. My challenge was answered by the rattle and clatter as they dropped everything they had, reaching with both hands skyward. We had them in a bad corner alright for the embankment was on one side and ourselves on the other. We had their retreat cut of for fair. I jumped over to their side of the road making signs telling them to go forward along the roadway back to the advance post. We herded them along like this for some distance ahead of us and were within some 30 yards of the machine gun post when the man on the gun saw the party advancing. He got his wind and fired about 50 rounds at us at that distance and never touched any of us. I guess he thought the German army was after him. The sweep of that gun made our ears ring alright. I yelled some good Canadian cuss words at the gunner succeeding in getting his attention before he took another burst at us with the machine gun. In that fuss I nearly lost the smallest, slimmest of my three hinnies for he stooped and started to bolt toward an old trench that was near, I yelled at him and very nearly shot him for he had only about 25 feet to go to get under cover. It was still not daylight with poor lighting for shooting. He heard me and jumped back to the other two pronto. I asked the gunners where the entrance to the dugout was and then sent Penhold to the entrance to steer the prisoners in and down below to Stevenson's quarters. That is where I lost a fine set of glasses for the largest of the Germans had them slung on his neck and Penfold grabbed them as he arrived at the doorway. There was an amusing incident in connection with the bringing in of the fritzes. A lieutenant by the name of Cox had been detailed to stay at the advance post with Stevenson as second in command for that day and was just coming up the road to the rear of the dugout as we were herding the prisoners up the forward part of the same road just before the machine gun opened fire on us. Cox suddenly saw the Germans and I guess he thought he was took. He let out a yell whipping out his pistol and he made a running high dive for the dugout stairs and very nearly knocked down the sergeant on sentry there. He never stopped till he got well down in the bottom. Taking it all around, the advent of our fritzes caused quite a stir.

After the prisoners were safe and sound down in the dugout, Stevenson began to figure out a way to claim credit for their capture. He was going to send one of his machine gun commanders to take the prisoners down to headquarters together with a note stating that they had been captured by his machine gun post. I tumbled to the drift of it and made a strenuous objection insisting on taking down my own prisoners. He was for ordering me out in front again but I guess he thought better of it, and figured he might not get away with it in the long run. I reminded him that it was near broad daylight and if the prisoners were not started immediately they would have to stay there all day.

There was some 200 yards of open road to cover before reaching any shelter to the rear. That road was in full view of the enemy lines at daylight. By the time I was on my way with them it was quite daylight but we were not fired on before reaching cover for some reason. On the way down the road the prisoners began to talk among themselves, then starting to drop trench daggers or stilettos on the road. These I picked up as I came along behind them. I guess they did not want to be found down the line with concealed weapons on them. All three of them wore the decoration of the Iron Cross. The big sergeant wore a First Class Cross. The two privates wore Crosses of the Third Class. They were Bavarian members of a signalers corps. When captured they had been stretching a wire forward to connect to some screw stakes previously set out. They were installing a ground circuit for what is known as an amplifier or apparatus for listening in on our phones. and telegraphs etc. I believe it had a radius of some 1,100 feet from where the amplifier is installed. On arrival at headquarters we were paraded before the battalion commander who must preface the inspection of the prisoners. The first thing he did was walk up to the big Bavarian soldier and yank off his Iron Cross in a very rude and disgusting manner that jarred the sense of decency in all of us. The big Bavarian soldier eyed him straight and stood firm though you could see red rage climb up his neck right to his hair. All the rank and file had left the prisoner his medal out of common respect for the feelings of a capable looking soldier who appeared as though he might have really earned the medal. It was really no good to anybody except the bearer anyway. We who had brought in the prisoners never received as much as a thank you for our trouble or ever heard a word about it later. I was immediately stuck on a job as sentry for the balance of the day on a dugout of ammunition, never hearing any more of the incident. I believe it saved a raiding party going out that night with its attendant losses in good men's lives. I didn't hear any more about the proposed raid for identification purposes. Stevenson sent a note down with us informing the o. c. that Stevenson's post captured the prisoners but the o. c. never got that note. Why should we be party to such dirty works as that eh? What?

The following night I went up on a carrying party to the right flank of the battalion and ran into a gas barrage. I have since wondered if many previous doses of gas poison had made me immune to a certain extent from this poison for I saw lots of men with masks on that night and they complained of being troubled badly with the gas. I did not seem to be suffering any inconvenience and did not put on a mask until it occurred to me I might be getting poisoned just the same even if I did not feel it. The shell fire was quite heavy for awhile that night and I had a jolt of concussion while crossing a railway track with a shell hitting beside me breaking about five feet out of both rails as well as sending a switch stand on a flying trip to the top of the nearest embankment.

The next morning I was detailed with two others to man an observation post that was equipped with an instrument of the prism glass variety with pointer and sliding scale as you looked through the lens. It magnified some eight diameters and the scale referred to minutes and degrees to the right or left of a known reference point. It interested me as an example of how our old wood and brass director-boards that Young invented in 1915-16 (while with me in the old 8th scouts) had been elaborated and improved in the meantime to serve the needs of artillery observation work. I will never forget how majors Bertram and Newton of the 2nd army workshops worked together to do that poor lad out of any credit for bring forward his inventions at a time when they were needed so badly and came in so useful.

I was on the o. p. job for a couple of days and then tried to do some sniping from a high bluff near the railway embankment but was subjected to such a steady strafe from enemy trench—mortars that I could not get a chance to do any shooting. In fact I was very lucky to get away at all from that place alive. I had planned to make a trip forward along the fringe of the river in the thick bush and tall swamp grass and cattails or reeds that edged it making a dense cover right on into the enemy lines. Before I started on that trip we were pulled back out of the front being relieved by some old country Scottish kilties. They relieved us at night and I felt quite flattered by something I overheard from the two veteran kilties who passed me in the dark. They were discussing us and I heard the one remark to his pal, (Aye mon, but they are bonnie "fighters").

The Scarpe River along here must have been a very beautiful stream before the war. Its waters were crystal clear and stocked with speckled brook-trout. That in itself will prove to anyone that it was no polluted ditch. It wound through what must have been beautiful valleys. Further upstream we saw small mills operated by old fashioned water wheels, with shaded mill ponds over hung with a mass of tall shade trees. The river below us must have been navigable with small craft for I saw a motor boat that had been used in the days before the war. Further to the rear we saw some of our heavy guns on railway mounts. Both the long barreled naval type and also howitzers up to15 inches in caliber. We had a trip out to the Telegraph Hill country for a couple of days and it would have been good country for sniping but we were not out there long enough to get acquainted much up forward for part of our time was spent in support lines. After the big enemy drive of the spring of 1918 had been slowed up and brought to a stop on all fronts, things settled down for a few weeks.

During this time I had my first trip back to a sniping school behind the fighting area. Nearly all my snipers had been back for instructions at one time or another in the past three years but I had never even seen a sniping school yet. The only schooling I had was from fritz and he was no mean teacher of the art of sharp shooting as I can testify. I was lined up to shoot in a contest where the entrants came from the whole Canadian corps. We shot at fixed and at moving targets with telescope sights and with open sights. I took along my old Ross MK 3 with a Winchester A 5 telescope. I had used the same rifle for over a year in the line. I put on the test score of the day on the ranges that I shot from one to three hundred yards. It was for fixed and moving targets as well, as dummy figures representing the head and sometimes the head and shoulders of a man in neutral colored tints to blend with the background and our approximate service conditions. I would have liked to have had some more shooting there to see if I could hold my own with their cracker-jack school trained men but was sent back and did not get another chance at it. That was the one and only time I ever visited a sniping school and I had been in the line since February 1915 at scout and observation work.

In the warm sunny weather of late spring when the birds were nesting and nature seemed at peace the old trenches with their stench of rotting corpses, their fumes of gases from shell explosions, the spiteful rattle of machine guns and the nerve racking burst of high explosives seemed very irksome after about three and a half years of it for a steady diet. All nature seemed to be busy with the things of peace and growth and only "Man Was Vile". We were in a section of the line south west of Lens in the area east of Angre and north east of Suchez Village. All about us was ruin and desolation with the fragments of buildings, mines, mills and men's homes.

I watched fritz searching with eight inch howitzer shells for one of our six inch howitzer batteries that was concealed in a street of dwelling houses on the fringe of Lens. As each German shell struck in the middle of a house there would be a terrific burst with a great cloud of smoke and debris, tinged red with brick dust rising skyward. A slight breeze wafted the great cloud of dust and smoke aside. There would be a mound of bricks along with a few splintered sticks to mark where a moment before had been a good sized well built brick dwelling. From house to house in rotation it went the length of the street. By a freak of fortune they did not get the six inch battery. They were in the next row of houses with only a lane between and slightly to the left of where fritz spread his shells. It was great to see how the gun crews on that battery worked to fool fritz. They would wait for the arrival of a German shell and then fire their gun simultaneous so that the burst of the enemy shell hid the flash and the report of the six inch as they returned shell for shell. Fritz quit after awhile. Whether he gave it up in disgust or whether our return fire was finding his battery, I don't know. At any rate his battery was silenced with the six inch continuing to merrily hammer away for some time afterward.

I had a half day in an observation post on the shoulder of the Lorette Spur, the high bald ridge that overlooked the Lens area. You can see a fairly wide sweep of country from that vantage point and its position must have been worth much to our forces for observation purposes during the battles in that area. There were no outstanding events in the weeks we spent along this frontage at that time. We were soon taken out and put into training in open warfare in co-operation with tanks and aero planes. This kind of preparation denoted only one thing (more dirty work ahead). Though we did not know it they were getting us in shape for the great Amiens drive. The entering wedge of the great allied offensive that was to end the war in November of that year. We were to be the spear head on the bow end of that drive though we did not know it then. I believe that nearly the whole of the Canadian corps was put through that course in preparation for the work ahead. We were in the vicinity of a camp or rendezvous called "Tanks".

Toward the latter part of our training we had a sports day with a quite respectable program of games, contests and competitions for all branches of the service. Some American troops from New York City were not far from us and they sent up a baseball team to play our battalion team. I think they had the surprise of their lives for our boys trimmed them to a peak. They tried hard to rally but found a quite unexpected brand of baseball on tap in the Little Black Devils team, and hard trying of all their old tricks did not suffice to win. A couple of my old scouts put on a good exhibition in the horseback wrestling. Jack Harron and Bob McLean. Both of them had been horse wranglers in the west in pre-war days. Jack Harron was an Alberta Ranger. He was on wages during his time overseas but never got back to get the good of them for he was killed at Cambrai while heading an attacking party through a gap in the enemy wire. The period of training behind the lines came to a close with the usual inspections and march past. We felt in our bones that there were big events just ahead and knew that we would be sure to be in it.

Amiens

We moved away from the training area in long marches southward. Day after day in full equipment under the hot sun with the billowing clouds of dust from the miles of transport and troops. We pounded the cobblestones and clay from daylight on into the night. Twenty—six kilometers was an average march on that trip and woe betide the man whose shoes didn't fit. The trip was broken by rides on rail and motor buses and then foot-slogging again. The weaklings found their place alright on that trip. Some of them even found their grave, for a couple of our boys collapsed one night dying from burst blood-vessels or hearts burst due to the long continues over strain. Our guides had lost their way that night and we were kept going nearly all night on a roundabout that finally landed us at our billets at near dawn. Away again in the early morning by motor buses that took us to Amiens City.

I had a glimpse, as we passed through, at the famous cathedral that the Germans had destroyed by shellfire and bomb. A real case of wanton and senseless destruction. There were plenty of such cases, an abundance of them in fact, in spite of what the silly propagandist now tries at this time to tell us. The German people have a queer streak in them. One who has seen many samples of their dirty work cannot erase the impressions thus driven home and riveted. Their pretense at civilization is only a very thin veneer indeed and it only needs opportune circumstances to rub that veneer off at any time showing the true son of Attila The Hun. Hitler is proving it today in 1933.

We passed through Amiens before dawn finding all the roads beyond that jam-packed with tanks, artillery, transport etc. for miles. The long lines of great tanks creeping-creeping forward in the grey light with their subdued hissing exhausts. "Hush—hush—hush" they seemed to murmur as they sunk and flattened the roads under them leaving tracks like great reptiles crawling out of a distorted dream. Along with them and cheek by jowl one could see the great stuffy muzzles of howitzers. Their black noses slightly lifted as though they could already smell blood and guts and slaughter. We of necessity took to the grassland and the fields to get forward, for road space was too valuable to be cumbered by mere infantry and such. We marched through what had been a village but it was torn by tempests of shell-fire until it looked like a piece of Hades.

In turning the corner in the square of that village I was very nearly finished off by a heavy shell that fanned my lungs with its hot breath bursting on the cobblestone pavement a few feet from me and gave me one more shaking up by concussion. The shell-fire thickened with our commander wisely putting us in some old battered cellars and basements along the road side for awhile until the worst of the storm was spent. We finally worked forward into a rolling country broken by wood lots, bluffs and clumps of trees. There were some old trenches here and we were distributed among these spending the balance of that day there.

While there I was handed a couple of brand new Ross rifles marked R R Co. Quebec 1917. I had been under the impression that the factory quit work at an earlier date. They were fine looking weapons and I spent the balance of the day trimming them up for sniping purposes. The bayonet standard and the fore-stock down to the middle band had to be removed so that they could be used through sniping plates where necessary. The bayonet standard would not come off over the fore-sight and hood so I had cut it lengthwise then spreading it for removal. I had a large clasp-knife that I had found in an enemy artillery dugout in Lens during 1917. It was a great piece of steel made by the Solingen & Steeples Works. This knife I made into a hack saw to cut both bands but later on I foolishly used this blade as a pry or lever breaking it in the middle.

A radical change was made about this time about the distribution of the scouts, snipers and observers. Previous to this time they were kept together as a unit with their own billets, rations and work etc. Now they were split up in twos and threes and assigned to different companies and scattered throughout the battalion. The members were available for whatever service the company commander might require such as map work, patrols, observations, sniping, guides, runners etc. I was assigned together with another man by the name of B. Dundas to No. three Company under the command of Major Braefield. In light of past experience I did not look very favorably on this change. It could only have one result. That would be the very rapid deterioration of the unit in training, and efficiency and its certain extinction as a highly useful organization. Col. Raddell who was in command of the battalion at this time was a barrack-square type of soldier and I have no doubt that the breaking up of the unit was under his orders. Their line of work was too deep for his type and uniformity on parade stacked higher with him than real ability in map work, observation, sketching, patrols, sniping, guiding etc.. Polished boots, buttons, and buckles and general smartness of drill and turnout on parades were more in line with his ideas of efficiency. I spent a couple of years of very hard work in a sort of pioneering way to bring that unit up to a standard of efficiency that won the commendation of both the British and French general staffs in 1916.

The Canadian corps was used as the spearhead in the great drive against the enemy at Amiens on August 8th 1918. Our battalion was in the vanguard or supports to the actual front waves of attack the first day of the drive. On that day we advanced 15 kilometers with the action turning into a sort of open warfare from that date until the Armistice. I was scouting out ahead of the half-battalion about mid-day and came to a river that it was necessary for us to cross. There was a ford some two miles upstream where the cavalry was wading and swimming across. At the point where I reached the river it was widened out to a width of one—quarter mile being covered with a mat of floating bog some two or three feet in thickness. I noticed a rough pathway of boards and planks laid across this stretch of floating bog. I surmised that it might reach to the other shore so I went across to the enemy side of the river on these boards, and decided it would be better to cross here with the two companies than to wade and swim them across farther up stream. Wet clothing and wet boots are not the best equipment for men to march far in or lie out in at night after perspiring through the heat of the day. I hurried back and told the c. o. of the board walk across the bog. He asked me if I thought they could get across on it and I told him they could. No doubt the last men would have slippery footing but it would be better than getting soaked in the river to the neck at the ford. They would not run into any trip bombs or booby traps for I had tried out the trail before them for such things. Some of the enemy machine gunners who had been left behind as sacrifices were gruesome in their gore and still warm. Some of their wounded were still lingering about unattended. I remember one big Bavarian in particular who had a foot shot off standing on the good one glowering at us as we passed. We sent for a stretcher for him.

During mid-afternoon of that day I began to feel the effects of exhaustion brought on by poor physical condition arising out of a long siege of dysentery followed by an attack of trench fever that I had in April 1918. As a matter fact I was a case of attrition and the culmination of all the effects of three years and seven months of continual front line duty. Chlorine gas, mustard gas, tear gases, shell fumes of all kinds, shell-shock many times repeated, along with a generous share of exposure to wet and cold through four rainy winters in the line. Ague chills and malaria-like fevers and rheumatics were racking my bones.

About 4:30 p.m. I called a halt and we built a wee fire under an embankment making a bit of tea and ate some hard tack biscuits. I think that was the first taste of food since the previous day. That night we found a sort of hole in the side of a high cutting through a sort of reddish sandyloam embankment. The hole had been burrowed out by some enemy soldiers and floored with straw. It looked warm and inviting to us. We had visions of a bit of sleep there. We were just dozing off to sleep when fritz opened a bombardment dropping some five point nine inch shells close to our hole in the wall. We had to dig out in a hurry or be buried where we lay under tons of loose overhanging earth. I climbed to the top of the bank looking out on a wide level stubble field stretching away into the dark which was apparently free of shell fire. We walked out into this field to where it was quiet and lay ourselves down to shiver ourselves to sleep on the cold stubble.

At daylight we followed our company some distance to the right of where they were forming up under cover of a heavy wood of oak, beech, elm, chestnut etc. We had passed through the troops who had led the attack yesterday and we in turn were the first wave today. It was something like the time of the Vimy Ridge attack. Somebody circulated rumors that we were getting all kinds of support in artillery and tanks etc. In the Vimy case there was an unbroken trail of poor starved frozen dead horses from Thielus to Vimy Village to mark their passage. Those horses had been clipped in the winter weather and had their food ration cut so low that they staggered and leaned against one another for support. I believe the officer responsible for that had been serving in India and his book said they had to be clipped on a certain date and rationed accordingly. The fact of winter conditions was a mere trifle and could not change his book. The equator was in the wrong place that's all (not him).

His men were in a like condition too. Literally starving on their feet in the midst of plenty. I remember them whining around the ration dumps on our sector at Vimy, begging for food and weak mentally and physically for want of proper nourishment. No wonder we had to send badly needed platoons to the right of our own sector to stiffen them up. Those imperial troops in that sector at that time were literally starved down to a state of near collapse by incompetent officers.

But to return to the Amiens front there was many a hard march and wet night between April 1917 and August 1918, Ypres, Hill 70, Lens, Passchendaele, Scarpe River, Arras etc. On our way to the place of concentration for the attack we saw a bit of "The Charge of The Canadian Calvary Brigade" and it was a sort of murderous affair for the Calvary but not so bad for the enemy. Wire and machine guns are rather bad medicine to put horses against. The screams and cries of the wounded horses seemed to effect man more than the cries or groans of mangled men.

I saw one man trailing by one foot that was twisted in his stirrup while his head and body were being whanged, slammed and thumped along the ground as his wounded horse galloped wildly across country. Some of the horses ran with their guts trailing out to the ground. I think people should know a bit of what war is really like and perhaps some of them would not talk so freely about it while feeling so very little about it. There appeared to be a remarkable scarcity of artillery in the vicinity and as for the tanks, there were none at all. Dundas and I worked our way into the wood. I was looking for our company commander in case he needed us for any special work. The enemy were tuning up their machine guns for the attack that they well knew what was to come soon. Their bullets were glancing in all directions off the limbs and trunks of the huge hardwood trees. I stood for a moment talking with a corporal of our company. We were facing one another at some three foot distance when he received a sharp blow to his left hip. He felt around there to see what had hit him and lifted his bayonet in its scabbard. The blade had been hit by an enemy bullet and was cut off close up to the hilt.

I found Major Braefield and he certainly found a job for us pronto. He spread his map on the ground showing me the line of the proposed advance for that day. This was a totally new front to us and we had not, or I had not, at least seen a map of that part of the country before. The proposed line of advance was not in an approximately straight line by any means. It went at an angle of so many degrees to one landmark ahead, then angled off to the right or to the left to a second landmark and so on through a rolling country of wood lots and farm lands etc. The final mark or objective was a farm in a valley some eight miles ahead. He explained to me how he wanted to keep the left flank of his company as near as possible on the line marked out. This company was the left one of the battalion in this case. Now the rank and file and the n. c. o.'s do not as a rule get any chance to see maps or study the lay of the country over which they are to fight.

It naturally follows that the advancing skirmish lines have a tendency to swing too much to right or left, as a gate swings, and if this swing is not checked and guided back occasionally they are quite apt to overlap and crowd other troops on a flank. They may unknowingly swing away from other troops on a flank leaving a wide gap or even get moving at right angles to the advance or worse. My job was to fix in my mind and memorize the route along with the landmarks and see to it that the left flank of the battalion held to that line right through to the final objective. I was also to go out in advance of the attack for some few minutes and try to snipe off the enemy machine gunners in order to slow up or retard the volume of their fire as much as possible during the critical minutes when we were advancing across the four or five hundred yards of open ground immediately in front of the thick wood from which the attack was to start.

The enemy was in a thick wood on the far side of an open and very level and smooth field that dipped very slightly or concave like a saucer. My time for studying the map was very limited as the major was busy with other things as the attack was due in about five minutes. I fixed the line and the landmarks as well as possible in my mind, then crawled out to the extreme fringe of the scrub at the edge of the open field and sized up the lay of the land. It certainly looked like guts to clean and a short life and a merry one for us two scouts. The enemy gunners were tuning up all along the line with short sharp bursts of fire and were starting to cut grass out in the front right as well as the left. That grass was very short and very level looking as though it might have been cropped by horses or sheep. There was not a sign of shelter or cover for a man or a mouse out there. In the light of three years and seven months experience I did not think much of our chances of survival when we went out there in advance of the zero hour.

I heard later that there was a nest of 50 enemy machine guns sweeping that bit of ground. I looked at my mate and said "Here goes nothing" and out we trotted for some 30 or 40 yards and there I saw the flattened remains of what had once been a small haystack. The highest part of it now would not be more than a foot high. I remember an old piece of ladder under it. I had a small haversack slung across the back of my shoulders, by small webbing straps under each arm and, lying there, it seemed to me that it must be sticking up in the air to a great height. It seemed to cramp my lungs so I squirmed out of it and left it there. I had a feeling that things were about to happen and I did not want to feel cramped or encumbered too much. It had already been diagonally ripped nearly in two by a bullet I noted. I remember thinking that a small landmark like that wee swath of old hay in an open field was more likely to draw fire than offer shelter.

I moved forward again at a dogtrot noting that the bullets were cracking so close to my head that they jarred me by the concussion of their passing. The crackling of them in my ears was deafening. It gave the impression that ones head spun around and snapped back again with each ear splitting snap of a bullet. I next came to a track or farm road across the field at right angles to my line of advance and its surface being a smooth clayish soil. Machine guns were enfilading this road with their bullets, tearing its surface, bouncing a continuous shower of earth and dust some four feet high as hailstones throw up water on the surface of a lake.

A machine gunner sits on a seat like a small bicycle seat fixed on the back arm of the tripod on which the gun is mounted, with both hands holding grips similar to the grip on the end of a fork or shovel handle. His two thumbs press on two buttons conveniently placed for the grips. There is a high tangent-sight above the breech and he endeavors to hold this sight on the target.. There is a severe vibration as well as a steady backward push to the gun and ones thumbs soon tire from applying the constant pressure to the buttons.

I waited for the inevitable pause between bursts of fire then ducked across the road and was several yards beyond it. I had seen a shallow ditch or furrow some 30 yards ahead of me where I intended to stop again for another breather while trying to locate my route as well as the enemy on my front. The main volume of the enemy fire seemed to be coming from the right front or what we would call half-right or roughly a 45 degree angle. The volume of fire had increased to a heavy roar that now developed a growling undertone that goes only with real heavy fire. This sudden savage roar was boiling and surging up apparently from the bowels of the earth, mounting, mounting, up, up, up to a mad crescendo. It was the voice of the grim old war scared Hun brought at last to bay. One great drive after another had been checked, dragged down, slowed up and rolled back from the autumn of 1914 till the autumn of 1918. Now the old war dog could see the hand-writing on the wall at Amiens. Like a bright bladed-spear with a sharp cutting thrust the Canadian corps had pierced his side once more. Well he knew those slashing blows of St. Julien, Festubert, Givenchy, Ypres, Somme, Vimy, Passchendaele, Hill 70, Arras, Scarpe River, Monchy along many other deadly encounters gave him to know the deadly significance of the oncoming thrust.

Now he had dragged up anti-aircraft machine guns, and long range machine guns, ordinarily used against support lines and communication lines. He was concentrating them in his front lines to make a savage tigerlike sweep of his claws and a grinding slash of his iron jaws to try breaking or blunting or to dull the sharp edge of that bright thrusting and thrashing blade. Like a tiny atom of dust fluttering on the point of that spear we felt that day. Like an atom I momentarily expected to be swept to nothingness and oblivion. The hot snapping scorching breath of sudden and violent death dinned in my ears, screeched and howled past my skull, fanning my arms and legs. I felt light and wobbly as though nearly lifted from the ground by the sweep of the onrushing winds as if blowing in outer space between the worlds. My eyes were blinded by showers of up thrown earth, and sod with my vision cut off by clouds of dust and smoke from the crashing bursts of shrapnel shells. I seemed to lean forward against a gale.

Not since the fight at Zollern and Hessian trenches on the Somme 26-27 of September 1916 had I been caught in such a concentration of the hate of man. Here was the focal point where the fighting rage of great contending nations bore down on the face of poor old mother earth, and rent and tore in a bloody tumult. I remember thinking about that line of advance, thinking how frail an atom was my poor body or brain, and wondering what chance I had to survive long enough to be of any possible service in following up that line of advance on major Braefield's map.

The attack was in full blast now and ahead of me. I could get occasional glimpses of gradually rising ground and what appeared to be the enemy's front line of pot holes along with hastily thrown up earth works and the pasty grey faces under the pot-like helmets hugging their scanty shelters and working like demons. I looked for some place to stop and plan out my further advance or perhaps do some shooting at enemy machine gunners close on my front as per instructions. I could see what looked like an old grass growth ditch. It turned out to be an old zigzag trench that had been used by the French in the fall of 1914 in some of the see-saw fighting that rolled backward and forward across the country at that time.

I made toward it and had arrived within 20 yards when I felt a heavy shock like a blow from a sledge hammer that spun me around making me feel sort of numb. I looked at my left arm as it seemed to be where the shock came from. There was a ragged string of meat and tendons hanging from my wrist and another from my elbow. The bone of the left forearm was laid bare from wrist to elbow. The main artery was shot away with the blood pumping and gushing from it in rhythmic spurts. I had felt the burst of machine gun fire from the right front and remember thinking the top of my head was going to be lifted off surely, for it had fanned me deadly close. That flying burst of machine gun bullets must have traversed from high to low vertically for the first bullets passed close in front of my face and when my arm was hit it could not have been more than six inches in front of my body. I often wonder that I did not get some in my right leg for that would be the leg that was forward at the time I was hit. I kept going with what headway I had made it to the old trench flattening myself in the bottom of it. It must have been some sort of an explosive bullet or dumdum slug that hit me for the ragged edges of the meat that hung down at wrist and elbow seemed to be blackened and scorched as though some sort of explosion had rent it.

As I mentioned before the enemy had brought up anti-aircraft machine guns to the front lines to stem our advance. This class of gun has a sort of incendiary or explosive bullet about every tenth round in the belts for the purpose of cutting struts and stays of aero planes and igniting their gas tanks when hit. I always figured it was some bullet of this sort that hit me. I have a good idea now how it feels to a moose or a deer when they are hit by a high power expanding bullet at close range. This is the shocking power that is advertised by the arms and ammunition companies in pushing the sale of their products. It was some little time after I made that forced landing in that ditch before I could move my legs or feet. That part of me seemed to have gone numb. I could not even wiggle my toes for some minutes. When the feeling started to come back to my feet and legs it was a tickling prickly pins and needles sort of feeling for awhile before I was finally able to move my toes and then my legs.

That steady slush-slush of spurting blood from the main artery was urging me to get busy and do something if I wanted to save any of my blood for future use. I grabbed the pull through out of the butt stock of my rifle tying it around the wound and used a rifle cartridge for a twister winding it up tight until the spurting of blood stopped. We used to carry a small packet of bandage, absorbent cotton and a small vial of iodine sewed into the lining of our tunics. I ripped out these articles with my teeth, and after folding the loose flaps of meat down and inward at either end and another flap of skin and flesh from the top middle of my forearm, I poured what iodine I had over the works. Then bound the whole thing up with pad and bandage as well as I could. During the time my legs were numb I had an idea I might have been hit in the spine and had Dundas roll me over and look for bullet holes. I could hear plenty of noise of battle and stuck my head up to take a look at what was going on.

I was there to see one of the waves of our boys coming ahead in their attack. That was a sight that will stay with me for the rest of my time. Few men indeed have been privileged to see a sight like that, and it thrilled every bone and the very marrow of my carcass. This was the spear point of the Canadian shock troops bearing down close on the enemy. Sober, pale set faces and a deadly purposeful look, deadly looking as fate itself. Lean, hard with nearly four years of terrible bloody conflict behind them. Side by side, the old the old seasoned battle scarred shell wracked gas poisoned men of 1914-15 and the new draft men sent out to fill in some of the gaps in the sadly thinned ranks of a bunch of troops that saw more actual front line service and fighting than any troops of either the British or French armies. Not exempting any of them French blue devils, British guards or any of the crack outfits that stood at Verdun or Ypres. If you take the trouble to look into it you will find that it is true that the first division Canadians saw more casualties than any other allied troops engaged in the war. The different guard groups used to go back to the coast for periodical rests and to fill up, train new drafts for periods that lasted for months at a time. This cut down on their front line time or battle service as applied to individual battalions. Our troops never had rest periods extending over more than a few weeks at most and then, only when it was impossible to carry on as an effective unit due to losses. Fascinated at the sight I was staring at our boys bearing down on me like the Wrath of God and thinking it must be a creepy feeling for fritz when they closed in on him boring down with the cold steel and the whirling mills bombs or deadly Lewis guns They looked as though hells gates would not prevail to stop them and indeed I often used to think that if hell was any worse than what we had come through in the last three or four years then there must be no God in Heaven or any hope for any of us in this world or in the next. If the fathers and mothers at home could only be here to actually see pale set faces rushing calm and unresisting to meet their God. Would that some of the sheltered, pampered and coddled representatives of our churches and clergy could be dragged or driven to a place where they could see something like this to forever still their eternal chatter and meaningless platitudes. Here where they could stand face to face with life and death with no false veil of school creeds, sects, dogmas, petty humbugs between them and their maker. I would like to be able to make people see that those pale set faces and lean forms in ragged muddy uniforms sweeping on the foe with a God like faith and high purpose being faithful even to the uttermost agony of rent, torn flesh, broken bones, shattered nerves, with shattered souls or spirit were not merely military machines, not blood thirsty man killers in a feast of blood and slaughter but just plain lonely Canadian boys that played at their mothers knees, carried their books to school, played hockey or baseball, living there short lives at home feeling all the little joys and sorrows. Left sweet hearts and mothers behind as well as all the hopes or prospects of their youth and their ambitions. Turned their backs on it facing this hell fighting, bleeding or died because they believed it was the right thing to do. How many of our leaders, teachers and preachers who heckle and insult the orphans and widows these boys left behind could rise to their spiritual height and claim courage. There is one man in a position to show our people a fairly true picture of these boys as they lived, laughed, hoped, endured, fought and died in their belief that they were doing the right thing. That man is Canon Scott of Quebec. A true heart fit to speak of the true hearts that are gone before their God and perhaps intercede a good word for the few pitiful wrecks that still exist as fragments spiritually, mentally and physically. At this time 15 years after the war they are still dropping off one by one lingering half sick, and wholly sick both in body and spirit. Occasionally we hear of one of them taking his own life and immediately we hear some wise-cracker suggesting that these returned men are sort of nutty anyway. What did they want to go off to the war for anyway. Serves them right in a way. They got what they were looking for. I wouldn't want any of them working for me. They won't be so anxious to go fight for the rich moneyed guys next time. There is a strange and terrible contrast between the peoples attitude toward the dead soldier and the living one. It seems at times as though it was a serious mistake for any of them to come back to their home land, for their welcome seems to be very hard mixed and questionable and continues to be so to this day. A Lewis gunner of the first wave of the attack had seen my head over the edge of the ditch as I watched our boys advance and I guess he mistook me for one of the enemy for he would have no knowledge of scouts or snipers of ours out ahead of the attack. He gave a burst of the Lewis gun at close range and very nearly mowed my head off. My wound started to bother me a bit so I rigged a sort of sling to drape the shattered arm across my breast and lay flat on my back in the ditch to avoid as much shrapnel, machine gun and rifle fire as possible. Each attacking wave as it came forward in a sort of section-rush aforementioned used this old ditch as a temporary resting point for the next rush forward. Fritz soon got wise that this old ditch would make a fruitful target and began to hammer it with shellfire. I remember a bunch of Canadian kilties pausing there. I think they belonged to the 3rd division, and were a fine looking bunch of boys too. Prisoners soon began to filter back and the shellfire, machine gun fire, rifle fire began to thin out a bit. During the time the kilties were in the old trench fritz put over a whizzbang shell that lit in the mud just over the front edge of the old trench or what we would call its parapet and nearly buried me in the earth. When the dust, smoke and flying clods of earth had settled I shook the sand and mud off my face, looking around there was a blue-black chunk of iron, hot and smoking about two inches in diameter or so lying on top of my stomach.

To The Coast

I figured that the old trench was beginning to be no pleasure resort for invalids and thought my chances would be as good out in the open now that the first waves had overrun the enemy front lines. The old 8th battalion had made another roman holiday out of it. We started that attack about 600 strong. There was a nest of some 50 enemy machine guns in the wood on our right front. The old 8th made it alright over-running the enemy but lost 417 men out of the 600 in doing it. Colonel Raddel our o. c. at the time was killed along with several other officers. Major Braefield was wounded.

I didn't see where I could do much good by lingering where I was and started back towards the rear. I took a look at the big wood from which we had started in the attack. It looked like a combination of a volcano and a bush fire. Smoke rolled high above it pierced by frequent flaming shell bursts and I could see large chunks of beech and oak trees etc. soaring skyward from its midst. I figured the wood would not be so good as a line of retreat and bore off to my right to pass around the end of it in the open fields.

I began to pass the killed and wounded that had been caught in that hail of machine gun fire. I remember one lad in particular that gave me a queer turn. He was a fine big strapping fellow about 23 years of age and had come to us in the last draft of refills from the base. He was lying on his face and I could see he had been badly sawed across the hips by a machine gun. I spoke to him and he turned his face up to me and grinned as cheery as could be with a bright face of good color and his eyes ditto. I looked beyond and glimpsed his legs. They were literally shot to ribbons and twisted around and around inside his trousers and putties like two piece of rope. As he was flat on his stomach and unable to turn, I suppose he did not know what condition his legs were in. He must have been paralyzed or numb from the waist downward, probably from a spinal shot and as yet felt no pain. If he was to move, or be moved starting the blood to circulate he would snuff out like a candle. It was a gruesome feeling to look at his bright face and cherry smile and then to see the condition of the rest of him. He was only one of many, many that I saw in various stages of mutilation and various stages of pain and agony in the mile of ground I crossed on my way around the north end of that wood. Then I went on farther in search of some place of rest and in search of some assistance that I must soon obtain if I wanted to continue for awhile on this side of Jordan.

A lad by the name of Benjamin Dundas kindly helped me along for quite a long distance and then turned and went back to face the music up front again. I saw him in the spring of 1919 at the convalescent camp at Epsom Downs in England. I asked him how he got through that day when I got hit. He passed through without a scratch but was wounded later on.

After he turned back I kept on for awhile. I guess I was beginning to look a bit gruesome myself by now. There was a hot dry wind blowing in my face and the blood from my wounds had run down the front of my tunic to my boots caking on there in a dry shell so I was literally painted in my own blood from head to heel. After awhile I began to feel the effect of all I had gone through in the past week including forced marches, lack of sleep, food, and water. It was combined with a rundown condition from the trench fever or flu or sort of malaria, that I had in the spring of that year from which I had not yet recovered from. My loss of blood by this time was also considerable. I began to get a roaring sound in my ears so much like the roar of a big waterfall in a river. Things began to look grey like a London fog only I didn't hear any high-heels tapping on the pave and nobody shrilled Hello!! Caw-naw-da. Finally I began to hear tiny little tinkling bells in my ears with the fog becoming thicker.

By this time I had come in sight of a road and sat down beside it figuring that the navigation was not so good and perhaps a rest might clear things up a bit. I remember somebody coming along that road but cannot tell who or what they were for the fog had stayed with me. I remember requesting a stretcher from a dim figure and later remember being carried along on it by two German prisoners.

They finally slid me off that onto a small table in the basement or wine cellar of a village church that was doing duty as a surgery. That table was something to conjure with too. One stretcher followed the next one on and off that table continuously day and night without a pause. This kept up as long as the battle lasted. Just that long did these surgeons stay right there and saw, carve, patch, mend, cut and sew the fragments that poured across that table in a steady stream. There were some great men among the surgeons. You found the great ones up in little holes like that where the shells were slamming down all day over the roof of some frail shelter where the blood and guts ran in a steady stream under their flying fingers as they patched to the best of their ability. They slashed off all the soiled and dirty ragged ends of flesh from my wound tied up anything they could get hold of in the way of cords, leaders, tendons etc., snubbed up the artery that was shot away and laid me on a stretcher outside in the sun. There I lay till dark that night. There was quite a few shells landing around close too sprinkling me with bits of broken brick and wooden splinters.

It is a mean feeling to lie helpless on your back in the open and have shells plunking around just when you figured on some respite. The roads in the vicinity were being shelled and they had to wait for darkness to get any ambulances up there to take the wounded back. That is a simple sounding statement and does not signify much to the reader I guess but it meant life or death to a lot of poor fellows who had been shot to pieces and hoped to get out and live to see their folks. They had to linger while hope slowly faded and vanished away from them hour by hour, minute by minute and bit by bit. I was in comparatively good shape and lucky (to no end) in contrast to some of them.

Dusk and the coming of the ambulances at long last. I was lifted into the top rack on the right hand side of a small ford truck that had racks or hooks to take the poles of a stretcher and held three stretchers on each side. The whole thing was covered over (prairie schooner style) by a brown tarpaulin. The drivers were not allowed lights on account of shell fire and bombing planes and had to feel their way around and through numerous shell holes in the dark. It was pretty rough. The man next below me on my side seemed to be in much pain as the weary miles jolted, jiggled, bumped, and jarred along he did a lot of moaning, groaning and crying out in his agony. Soon after we started we experienced a hard jolt and the ligature or snub where they had tied up the artery of my arm broke away and I started to bleed again. We rode several hours and my old arm became, pretty painful swelling up till it shone like a piece of stove pipe and just about as black. My stretcher filled full of blood and I lay in a bath of my own blood for the rest of the ride. The loss of blood began to make me very cold and I remember there was a square open hole in the back of the truck cab behind the driver just level with my head. In my condition the stream of cold air that came through that hole felt like ice water and I felt cold as though I might freeze. The constant screams and groans of the man below finally got on my nerves and when we were near the end of our journey I can remember I was moaning and taking-on in a doleful sort of way myself. Just as the eastern sky began to show a streak of grey light along the horizon we arrived at some advance hospital and they lifted our stretchers out onto the ground. I was certainly feeling pretty cold by now and my teeth were rattling in my head in grand style. I was probably moaning a bit for I remember a surgeon and a nurse (probably matron of the hospital) stooping over me. The surgeon asked "What is the matter old fellow"? I told him I was terribly cold. They took a second look at me then and clapped a sort of chloroform cup over my mouth and nose right there and then.

When I woke again I was on a railway train loaded with wounded and pretty sick people. There was a case across the aisle in my coach who had been burned by the bursting of a mustard gas shell and he was in a terrible condition. He was one mass of blisters, big raw wet looking ones from head to heel, all the scalp of his head, even his privates in fact every inch of his anatomy. Talk about the old time savages and their cruel ways, and their tortures. I have also seen men burned by the flammenwerfer or flame thrower and it is no toy for a Sunday school picnic. Landed in a hospital at the coast where they kept us a day and night to wait our turn on the channel boat to Folkstone. This transfer hospital at the coast was run by an American staff of doctors and nurses, and they did seem a very friendly lot to me. They seemed to be rather puffed up with over officiousness and went out of their way to impress one with the importance of their particular selves. A little wee taste of war would have done them good I think. The second day we said goodbye to La Belle France.

Coalition House, Dorchester Dorset

From Folkstone I was shipped to a v. a. d. Hospital set up in Coalition House at Dorchester Dorset. In addition to the house itself there were a number of marquees or large tents set up in the grounds. These tents were set in rows or tandem-fashion with a sort of vestibule sort of connection set up between individual tents. This made the whole row rain and water proof and quite snug. These tents are really a work of art and well worth seeing. In addition to the main body of the tent itself, there is an outer or weather cover to protect it from the constant rain. On the inside again there is a softer or almost gauze-like lining to absorb any fine spray of dampness that might radiate from the main lining during heavy storms. During the time my wounds were healing I was kept in the house, but was later moved to the marquees. I believe these tents were constructed in the East Indies and appeared to have a lot of handwork in their makeup One of the v. a. d's gave me a bad hour after my arrival by ripping my bandage dressings off dry. Man-O-Man & Boy-O-Boy. I was as wet with sweat as though I had jumped in a lake after that session and the wound was jumping, jerking and quivering like a boiling pot with a column of steam rising from it near to the ceiling. I was a bit dubious about the effects that this sort of proceedings would have on the wound and made inquiry when the surgeon came around on inspection. We found that the young lady who ripped them off did not know any better being new at the game of nursing. I was spared a repetition of that. The horrors of war are not all to be seen on the battle field and some of the worst memories of the great conflict that kept coming back and coming back are memories of the sights, sounds, personal dramas, and agonies gone through by the mangled torn ones that kept pouring into the hospitals while I was a patient there.

The big drive was in full blast during that time Cambrai, Monchy, The Canal, The Hindenburg Line, Valenciennes etc. and the wounded came pouring over to blighty by the ship—load, a constant bloody stream. They taxed the capacity of all the hospitals v. a. d.'s. The surgeon who made the rounds of our hospital semi-daily was himself a sort of voluntary aid official and was contributing his knowledge and service along with a whole lot of hard work more or less gratis. He seemed to be a very fine type taking a personal interest in all his cases when it was humanly possible.

There came a couple or three big battles in France at this time and the resultant flow of wounded to blighty must have given him more than he could rightly handle. He set a date and made arrangements for a skin graft on my arm wound. I was all set, hand in splints and my arm slung from the ceiling in a sort of pulley-block arrangement. A Miss Brown, v. a. d. the identical one who ripped off my dressings dry had volunteered to donate a strip of skin from the inner side of her thigh for the grafting job. No doubt she was trying to make amends for the rough passage she gave me on my first arrival. A skin graft has to be done at a certain stage in the process of healing a wound. At first a deep wound throws off a lot of fluid and is too moist for the job. Later when new tissue has grown to some extent it is too late. The surgeon had planned to graft my wound on a certain date but due to the great rush of more serious cases from the front he never arrived there until several days later and I never received any skin graft. A graft in the centre of a large wound keeps it from drawing or pulling inward from the sides leaving it a more normal state when finally healed up. In the case of an arm it prevents the hand from being drawn down until the fingers are hook shaped.

While I was still bed ridden with wounds I took a very high fever one day going up to a temperature of 107.5. My breath whistled through my nostrils and carried with it small flecks of a sort of dry foam and I felt like a balloon that was blown up to the bursting point. The doctor kept asking me if I had malaria fever previously, saying I had all the symptoms of it. I had a sort of trench-fever while on the Scarpe River in the spring of 1918 which may have been a form of malaria. There were quite a few mosquitoes in that area and there were plenty of men lying around that country both dead and alive with malaria in their blood. Men who have served in India and Africa as well as the Near East could have been carrying it in their blood. In the spring of 1915 we were in swampy country on several occasions alongside Indian Troops and we were mosquito bitten for weeks. I have been bothered by chills and fever along with periodical dizziness ever since the end of the war. A Dr. Creighton in Winnipeg took a blood test one time but never told me what the test showed. My original medical papers did not mention malaria so that was final for them.

There were several Australians in the same hospital ward with me at Coalition House. One of them used to give us an imitation or impersonation of the great chameleon or Australian horned lizard. When disturbed this lizard climbs a tree proceeding to grimace and make faces at the passer-by. It is supposed to have the gift of changing color to suite it's surroundings. The Aussie did not change his colors but he certainly made some comical faces. Other Australians who had seen the chameleon said his mimicry was good. There was a Tasmanian who used to regale us with tales of a small wild cat they have in that country known as the Tasmanian tiger. It was here that I had a moment of weakness one day and showed an Aussie bedmate a couple of pound notes that were beautifully dyed in blood that I was keeping as a souvenir. He promptly stole these notes spending them in town and I had to steal a good Bengal razor off him as the only method in sight of getting even.

The winter weather in that part of the English country is terribly wet and I only remember three partly clear days in that whole fall season. Some mornings when you looked outside the marquee the clouds seemed so low they dragged the tree tops and every tree had a steady drip-drip from its limbs. The different small yards and fields were all enclosed by tall stone walls or fences with a peaked tile roof crowned by iron spikes or broken glass set in cement. These brick and stone walls in the winter were simply oozing water. They were covered with mould and mildew as well as a sort of wet moss. There was a small species of night owl that used to perch in the oak and chestnut trees near the marques at night repeating a cry that was squeaky and high pitched sounding like the name Willie Whitmore.. We had a patient by that name and of course he was ragged about it.

Shortly before leaving that hospital I heard about colonel Lipsett's death in France. He had asked for a reconnaissance by some of his junior officers and they had not made it. He went up front to do the job himself and was shot through the head by an enemy sniper. When he was with us in the old 8th battalion we used to fear for his safety for he was of a very fearless and venturesome nature, seeming to have a complete contempt of danger.

The country surrounding Coalition House must be very pretty in the spring and summer time. I went out for a walk around one day when it eased up on the rain for a short time. I came to a small bridge that spanned a beautiful brook or small stream. This stream reminded me of the ones I used to know in my childhood in far off Nova Scotia. Leaning over the bridge rail I instinctively started to look for speckled trout in the stream below. Sure enough there they were and I caught a glimpse of two or three darting across a shallow pool below the bridge. That was worth a whole lot to me for I had not seen a brook trout in his native element since about 1904. While watching the trout a couple of English folks came by and noting that I was a Canadian they enquired what a tuna fish was. They had been getting canned tuna lately but did not know what sort of a creature it was. I believe they started to can and export tuna somewhere in the Maritimes about the time of the war. I do not remember having seen it in cans previous to that time. There was an Australian girl nurse working for awhile at Coalition House. I believe that was the only Australian girl I saw during the period of the war. In the evenings in our ward we used to each donate a few pennies, and pooling it together we would collect enough to send out to the village for a feed of fish and chips. We came to be quite fond of that dish during our stay in the old country.

Epsom Downs, London England

The day before the armistice we were on our way to be transferred to a convalescent camp near Epson Downs to make room for more cases coming along from the front. There were three or four cases in our party who were on crutches so were not very mobile. I was supposed to keep an eye on these crutch cases at all transfer points where trains were changed. We landed in the big smoke just when the news of the armistice got there. We were caught in the crush where it was massed for miles. Traffic was completely stalled and the streets were a seething mass of humanity from wall to wall. The crush was such that one was often jammed so tight that ones feet left the ground at times and was carried along suspended like a pulp-wood stick in a log jam. That night the Aussies, and Canucks and others, do not forget, there were plenty of others who collected furniture, barrels along with any thing that would burn and heaped it at the base of The Nelson Column in Trafalgar Square. They soon had a roaring bonfire going there, around which they whooped it up celebrating in torrid style. Their enthusiasm was tempered with more booze than good judgment for they succeeded in putting a bad heat blister on the granite at the base of the column disfiguring it considerably. I think this was remedied to some extent later and there was no serious permanent defacing of the memorial. It was a wild day and a wild night in the big smoke. The blimey bloke seems to be very sedate normally but believe me when I say he can cut loose when he feels like it. I naturally lost track of the crutch cases in that wild sea of humanity. I believe each man had some paper to identify him and give his proper destination and no doubt they all finally arrived after the great melee.

In those convalescent days they used to sew a large blue cloth band around the left sleeve of your tunic and great coat to show to all and sundry that you were disabled or invalid.

Proprietors of pubs, estaminets, etc. were not supposed to serve beers or liquors to men with the blue tag. In order to obtain even a few beers we had to borrow someone else's great coat before parading to a pub. We managed a few during the short stay in London on our way to Epsom. We were also taken on a conducted tour of the Parliament Buildings where we were shown all the places and spots of historical interest in that famous pile. Stood on the brass plate in the floor that marked the place where Oliver Cromwell stood when he broke up the house. Sat on the famous stone that is supposed to have come from the Holy Land, Stone of Scone, via Spain, Ireland, Scotland etc. and now rests at Westminster. There were relics of Nelson, Rodney, Raleigh and many other old timers. We were also shown where the ancients used to dock or land and tie up their gondolas or barges when they used to come to Westminister via the Thames. We had a few hours in the British museum and it is certainly a marvelous place.

One would need months to even begin to ferret out it's wonders We had a trip to the Zoo-Gardens and were lucky to arrive about the time the larger carnivores were being given their rations of meat, fish etc. I had a close up view of a black manned African lion when he was roaring. He humped up his back, working his ribs in and out like an accordion or a bellows, with short coughing grunts ending this performance with a real deep-throated roar. I enjoyed watching this performance very much. There was also a good—sized hippo who stood patiently with open mouth while children threw peanuts down his foot-wide gullet. I could look down that tunnel about four feet. He seemed to know when the peanuts landed however and crunched his big square molars in evident enjoyment of these tiny tidbits. The giraffes had a very strong musty sort of smell that I did not enjoy at all. The elephants did some trumpeting too at their feeding time and I noticed a sort of weird tone in their call that reminded me of the bugle note in the call of a cow moose. Both the elephant and the moose are said to be survivors from the pre-glacial era. There is certainly the same unearthly quality in their calls that makes the hair prickle up on the back of ones neck.

There was a considerable encampment at Epsom and we stayed there for the balance of the winter. During my stay here I met corporal Young the inventive guy who used to be in my scout section in France. You will remember he is the one who was done out of his patents by the 2nd army workshop staff. Newton of Newton Pippin fame and Bertram late of the black watch and later of the black devils and later of something else black maybe. Young was not looking too bad though somewhat peaked and aged a bit. I also met Ben Dundas who was with me at Amiens when Major Braefield sent us out on that nice job just before zero hour of the attack on August 9th, 1918.

Our stay here was rather uneventful mostly. I got pinched one day for not jumping up quick enough when the inspecting hoffiser was making his daily round. I had met a lad who had canoed through a considerable part of northern Ontario and had walked on a survey party right through to James Bay. I was always very fond of canoeing and we were so busy talking about canoes and canoe trips that we did not notice his majestic entrance in time. I did two days confinement, the first and last in my military career. This surveyor chap and I tried out a sort of pocket range-finder while here, a tiny thing of prisms and about three and one half inches long and perhaps one and one half inches wide. It was called the Hyman's pocket rangefinder and it worked first rate too. I bought one and fetched it home but a servant girl who was cleaning my room one day let it fall breaking the prism glasses in its innards. This put it out of business. I often thought a combined rifle scope and range-finder could be made up thus. The tube of the A 5 Winchester sight is about 18 inches long and about three quarters of an inch in diameter. Set two tubes together as the barrels of a shotgun are set side-by-side. Make them of thin hard dent-proof steel and as light as practical. Let the left-hand tube contain the scope sight, having the right tube made up in a miniature of the barr and stroude range finder. You would have a foot and a half base line which should do for ranges over which a rifle can shoot. The centre eye piece of the miniature range-finder could be on the top of the right hand tube and the lens at either end could face to the right. The double barreled tube could be made to slide end wise in the yoke above the front mounting to avoid damage to the mechanism from recoil when firing. The tube to be held in alignment by spring tension in the same way as the ordinary Winchester A 5 scope. Put a scale of yards on the on the elevating mechanism and you should have a fairly complete outfit. Stick a Hagler .280 mauser under it to shoot through. With an eight and one half pound rifle the whole works would go to the neighborhood of ten pounds weight but you should be able to pull more weight than that in a long range rifle duel.

We walked over from the camp one day and had a look at the track where they run the famous derby races. It looked pretty sloppy and soggy the day we saw it but that was in the middle of the rainy season. We began to have ambitions to get back to Canada and towards spring there was a terrible epidemic of false rumors about moving etc. In some camps in other parts of the country, notably in Wales, the men became restive and discontent to the point where there were disturbances that in one or two cases attained the dimensions of a riot.

In April we were shipped to Liverpool and housed in an old people's home or poor house until they were ready to ship us home to Canada. The Liverpool folk used us first class. We had free transportation on street cars and on ferry boats across the Mersey to Birkenhead and another adjoining town of which I forget the name now. On one of my trips across the river I went into a miniature rifle range or shooting gallery where they shot indoors with 22 calibers. We tried out the ordinary targets, still and moving. Then I took a shot at a ball that they had bouncing at the top of a water jet. I burst the ball with it being replaced a couple of times, but the proprietor refused to put up any more balls. I noticed after shooting that there was no backstop behind where the ball bounced on the water jet. I don't believe it had been shot at previously. We went to see a show in the city. I believe it was the Maid of The Mountain. We also visited the Liverpool Museum. Here I saw the complete skeleton of a beast that used to be known as the Bog Elk. This animal is now extinct but it must have been a moose, nothing more or less. The specimen I saw sported a set of horns about seven feet wide and real moose horns too as to shape and general layout but I never saw a spread of horns to come near it in size. His front quarters did not seem to be quite so high in proportion to the hind-quarters as in our moose but outside of that he was apparently all Moose. They had the skeleton of a man along side some species of ape or gorilla, standing side by each, in a large glass case where you could walk completely around them having a good look see. After studying them for awhile it gave one seriously to think about the origin and relation of the two species.

Set Sail For North America

We set sail for home about the first of May on the hospital ship Essequibo. This vessel had been purchased by the Canadian government and fitted up for hospital service. She had been previously been in the coast-wise trade down around Venezuela and got her name from the Essequibo River down in those parts. She was a nice little boat and in mid-ocean we weathered quite a storm in her. We sailed by the southern route or down where the gulf stream warms things up a bit. We were in very nice weather for several days.

We passed around the south end of Ireland having no Para vanes on either side to guard against floating mines in these hostile waters. I had heard that Ireland was a rich green to look at from the sea. This was a dirty sooty-looking expanse of bare rounded hills, quite treeless all together desolate to look at. The morning was dead calm and you could see an occasional tall finger of blue peat smoke rising from the odd gully or ravine in the hills. We passed a lone fishing sloop and beyond this and the few smokes in the hills there was no sign of life. There must have been some life there in 17-18 when the subs had their supply bases in the deep fiords along that shore. About the time Ireland was getting hull-down on the horizon we saw a couple of whales spouting off to star board. We did not get close enough to have a very good view of them. We soon began to get into warmer waters and during the voyage we saw a lot of odd things floating or drifting along apparently in the gulf stream current. We passed what looked like a lot of rail road ties completely coated with barnacles. We passed through big patches of something that resembled large raisins or plums with a rich purple color. Schools of porpoise played along with us racing the boat in the same way that playful dogs will race a train or automobile. They always ended up diving down into the bow wave. One calm morning we looked over-side and saw a big school of bright coral-red starfish or jelly fish. The body part was perhaps six or eight inches across with a lot of radiating feelers. This part seemed to be just awash, but above that seemed to be a semi-circular affair that looked like the half of a glass fruit dish set on edge. This part was clear or transparent being tinted from pink through lavender to purple. It's upper edge or circumference was scalloped or ridged in corrugations. This upright portion was evidently used as a sail to catch the breeze. There were several good-sized fleets of them sailing along that morning.

In mid-ocean we met a real gale and we weathered a rip-roaring storm for a couple of days or more. At one time the waves broke right over the captain's bridge and the promenade deck was washed with tons of solid water from end to end. The ships nose would plunge right out of sight and all the drums and winches on the bow deck forward of the bow hatch and waist would go completely under water. The galley where they cooked for the crew was just aft of the winches and forward of the bow hatch, and in order to reach it from below the bridge crew had to follow lines strung fore and aft across the waist. If you lost your grip of that line you reported to Davy Jones. This was about the time that the three American seaplanes were to cross to the Azores and thence on to Europe. During the height of the storm, we passed two American destroyers stationed out there in mid-ocean at a certain latitude and longitude sent there to watch for the seaplanes. When we passed them they were certainly having a rough ride, and were pitching pretty badly in that giant sea. They were apparently using just enough steam to keep their head into the wind and not lose ground from their appointed post. First their bows would plunge into a wave submerging the bow gun and everything else right up to the bridge.

When their bows went under their sterns came all out of water and you could see all of their propellers and rudders in the air at once with their engines racing. It must have been a severe test of their sea worthiness and the strength of their engines and propeller gear. Quarters for the crew on this class of ship are pretty cramped too and they must of had an unpleasant time of it for about three days. There was not much danger of the seaplanes passing by in that storm.

284

I was never subject to sea sickness but on the last day of this storm we were dished a lot of stale sausage for breakfast. In the hot confined space below decks with everything batted down tight on account of the storm and the surrounding quarters chock full of seasick cases going strong on all eight cylinders the smells of that place got pretty powerful. In addition to the stale sausage there was a large batch of oatmeal porridge. I did not feel equal to facing the hot dogs, so filled right up on porridge and started out to try to go on deck for a bit of air. On my way and doing fine so far. But I had to pass right by where they were cooking that sausage and a torrid wave of steaming hot air hit me in the face as I passed. That porridge shot out of me just like the charge from a minen werfer hitting the wall about ten feet away. I got on deck ok but empty. My sleeping quarters were up in the bow of the boat so I was getting the full benefit of the plunge and heave in stormy weather. The midship section was reserved for the more serious cases for they had lots of pretty sick men on board too.

There was one burial at sea. He was a native of Halifax N. S. and had a long siege in hospitals in the old country but hoped to make it home. Sea regulations are iron clad re the keeping of dead bodies aboard and though he was at long last quite close to his home in N. S. they had to bury him at sea. They sew him in a trap with iron placed along his legs to carry the body down below the sharks. A tilting plank is fixed at the ship's rail and the body placed thereon. A burial service is read by the Padre backed by the ship's officers. Then the plank is tripped and the weighted corpse shoots out and down to sea.

The sea, The blue lone sea holds one
He lies where pearls lie deep
Perhaps the Loved of all, Yet none
Over his low bed may weep.

I had often heard and read about sharks following a ship but had never happened to see it until this trip. A couple of days before this sea burial while on the promenade deck we noted back fin of a large shark cross-cutting a zigzag in the wash behind us. In a couple of minutes it disappeared and we were leaning idly over the rail on the port side looking into the water when suddenly a form took shape in the clear

285

greenish water directly below, about 20 odd feet long with a dirty muddy brown color.

It was Mr. shark. He would swim up forward of us and lie on his side with his nose toward the boat and his tail out to sea and float thus, just below the surface with the cold staring eye looking directly up at us. We had a good look at that eye and it was something to remember. I don't know why he should lie on his side unless it was to keep his high back-fin concealed. This fellow was old, big, and ugly and may have been shot at some time previous from some boat. That may be why he drifted thus quietly by, submerged and still until he reached the wash astern of the ship, when up came the big back fin and the zigzag course in search of anything fallen over, or thrown overboard. We certainly wished for a rifle when that fellow did that drifting-by act a couple of times or more. Sailors (old salts) tell you sharks know if there is a corpse aboard ship. I am not claiming that this fellow knew about the death aboard our ship, but the fact remains indisputably that he pulled off the stunt above described just previous to the sea burial of the Halifax man. Truth is often stranger than fiction.

On nearing the American shore we ran into fog and proceeded at reduced speed for some time. We were heading for Portland, Maine among its rocky islands. We must have made our landfall and picked up the pilot on the evening of May 16th an entry of five dollars in the old pay book was dated May 17th.

Returned To Canada

We took the train from here and made the overland journey right around to Halifax, Nova Scotia, where we were put into Camp Hill Hospital where we remained until our final discharge from service in September 1919.

On our arrival in Halifax people were still talking about the great explosion that had taken place in some stores of munitions on board ship and on shore up near the bottle neck of the Bedford Basin. I believe it was a pretty heavy explosion causing quite a bit of damage in the vicinity.

We visited the north west arm having a look at the big Swedish squarerigged ship riding there. She was a beauty. She had been captured with contraband and towed in there until such time she obtained release. Some natives invited us to a picnic out in the country north and west of the town of Dartmouth one day. Here we saw the remains of what had been one of the earliest British settlements in Nova Scotia. You could still trace the old cellars and bits of foundation walls where those first settlers built their cottages. There were trees a foot in diameter growing in some of the old depressions that had been the house cellars of the first village. In the vicinity of the ancient settlement there are the remains of an old barge canal that used to extend right across the peninsula where it connected with the upper reaches of the Bay of Fundy waters. The old granite gates and locks were still intact. The granite had been brought by ship all the way from Scotland. I guess they figured that the rock on this side of the water was bound to be inferior. (aye-mon!).

I obtained a few days leave and went to visit my old home village in the south end of the province in Yarmouth County. It was my first glimpse of home since 1905. In the latter part of May and on into the first part of June the old province is a regular fairyland of breath-taking beauty. The miles and miles of fruit orchards are in full bloom and you can ride for hours between miles of endless bloom. At this season the trees too are of a fresh and vivid green, also the grass land. The Annapolis Basin reflects its surrounding hills and a perfect sky. You would have to see in order to believe. Just take a trip through from Yarmouth to Halifax about that season and be convinced. I found the home folk pretty much the same, perhaps a bit older. On the whole things had not changed very much since 1905. The rural districts had apparently gone to seed to a certain extent. The lumber industry had apparently petered out and the farmers in that country where you can grow almost anything always seemed to lack any worthwhile market for their produce. The local market was very soon glutted and after that you could not give away the produce. The country roads were falling into disrepair, showing unmistakable signs of neglect and lack of upkeep. Alders and scrub grew across the one time ditches right up to the wheel tracks of the roads. The crown of the roads themselves were worn down to a concave that held water causing many small wash-outs and bumps. Many of the farms had a similar look of neglect and decay. Due to this lack of markets the young generation does not stay on the old home lands but hie themselves across to Boston and New York as soon as they are old enough to rustle a job. The New England States have bled old Nova Scotia pretty badly since about 1900. Nova Scotia folk and their children form a remarkable percentage of the present population of the New England States and further south as well. I had a trip out to some of the old brooks and streams where I used to catch speckled trout in my kid days. The treatment of my wounds continued until my discharge in September when I had a few more days of a visit at home.

Return To The Lake Of The Woods

Then I then took the train for The Lake of The Woods and my old stamping grounds of the pre-war days. Shortly after my arrival I took a motor-boat and canoe trip to the English River via Minaki, Sand Lake, and Fiord Bay. I enjoyed this trip very much after five pretty strenuous years absence. I found that I did not altogether fit into the old associations and could not enthuse about things that seemed to interest, and make up the daily life of former side kicks. That is one of the penalties one pays I suppose for seeing a little too much of life and death and the woes of man.

The End

Name and Place Index

Note: The index not only gives the page numbers for "8th. Battalion" but references to that Battalion as it was my Fathers Battalion.

Bully Grenay   177-8

About the Author

Glenn R. Iriam was born in Kenora, Ontario, Canada spending a short period in school. While in school he had good grades excelling in math, physics and shop. Glenn was having a large number of bouts of migraine headaches putting him in bed for days at times.

While watching out the school window one spring day and observing the arrival of the float planes in Kenora Bay once more, he decided to approach the major bush airline for a job. He landed the job and on a sunny day in May he went to work much to his Father's disappointment.

After three years with the airline work he took some time out one fall and spent the winter wandering the Lake of the Woods between Kenora and Sioux Narrows.

Once again work interfered with the fun times and he hired on with the city Hydro and Telephone Company where he worked as a lineman for 24 years. Physical problems prompted him to take an inside job at this point and he retired in 1994.

Now Linda his wife and companion for 50 years live in a comfortable apartment in Kenora enjoying visits from their three children or visiting them. Linda loves to fish both summer and winter and that is a blessing.

Contact the author:
gandl@kmts.ca

Lightning Source UK Ltd.
Milton Keynes UK
UKOW05f2151120617
303198UK00001B/140/P